HEGEL ON THE SOUL
A SPECULATIVE ANTHROPOLOGY

HEGEL ON THE SOUL

A SPECULATIVE ANTHROPOLOGY

by

MURRAY GREENE

MARTINUS NIJHOFF/THE HAGUE/1972

Truth, aware of what it is, is Spirit.
(PhM 178)

PREFACE

The present study seeks to treat in depth a relatively restricted portion of Hegel's thought but one that has not yet received intensive treatment by Hegel scholars in English. In the Hegelian system of philosophical sciences, the Anthropology directly follows the Philosophy of Nature and forms the first of the three sciences of Subjective Spirit: [1] Anthropology, Phenomenology, and Psychology. The section on Subjective Spirit is then followed by sections on Objective Spirit and Absolute Spirit. The three sections together comprise the Philosophy of Spirit (*Philosophie des Geistes* [2]), which constitutes the third and concluding main division of Hegel's total system as presented in the *Encyclopedia of Philosophic Sciences in Outline*.[3] Hegel intended to write a separate full-scale work on the philosophy of Subjective Spirit as he had done on Objective Spirit (the *Philosophy of Right*), but died before he could do so.[4]

Thus the focus of our study is quite concentrated. Its relatively narrow scope within the vast compass of the Hegelian system may be justified,

---

[1] Iring Fetscher (*Hegels Lehre vom Menschen*, Stuttgart, 1970, p. 11) notes the lack of a modern commentary to Hegel's *Encyclopedia*, and in particular to the section on Subjective Spirit. Brief accounts of this section in English may be found in: Hugh A. Reyburn, *The Ethical Theory of Hegel* (Oxford, 1921), Chapter V; and G. R. G. Mure, *A Study of Hegel's Logic* (Oxford, 1950), pp. 2-22.

[2] Translated as Hegel's *Philosophy of Mind*, hereafter referred to as *PhM* (see list of abbreviations, below, p. XVII).

[3] See Table of Contents in *Enzyklopädie der philosophischen Wissenschaften im Grundrisse* (1830), ed. Friedhelm Nicolin and Otto Pöggeler (Felix Meiner, Hamburg, 1959).

[4] For an account of Hegel's plans, see F. Nicolin, "Ein Hegelsches Fragment zur Philosophie des Geistes," *Hegel-Studien*, bd. 1, 1961, pp. 9-15; also F. Nicolin, "Hegels Arbeiten zur Theorie des subjektiven Geistes," in J. Derbolav and F. Nicolin, eds., *Erkenntnis und Verantwortung. Festschrift für Theodor Litt* (Düsseldorf, 1960), pp. 356-374.

I believe, by the proverbial complexity of Hegel's thought in general
and the difficulty of the task to which the philosopher addresses himself
in the Anthropology. This task is to show speculatively a necessary
development of Spirit as pre-objective subjectivity or soul (*Seele*) to the
ego of objective consciousness. The present study first of all seeks to
elucidate the nature of this task within the wider Hegelian problematic,
and secondly to follow step by step the course of the philosopher's
demonstration in the Anthropology. In a concluding chapter that has
the nature of an appendix, an effort is made to show the connection
between the doctrine of the soul and that of consciousness, and to provide
a transition from the science of Anthropology to the science of Phenomenology.

The Anthropology is important to Hegel's general position for several
reasons. The human spirit, says Hegel, "stands between the natural and
the eternal world" and connects them both as extremes; its "origin" lies
in the former, its "destination" in the latter.[5] As shown by its place
among the philosophical sciences, the Anthropology deals with a transition
stage of Spirit. In the Anthropology we see Spirit's recovery from its
self-externality in nature and its rise through successive phases as "natural
soul" to its actualization as the ego of consciousness. The Anthropology
contains Hegel's main treatment of such questions as the mind-body
problem and the nature of sentience. But these topics of perennial
philosophic interest are discussed within the particular notion of the
selfhood as totality, which Hegel calls the "feeling soul." The treatment,
unlike that of most philosophers up to his time, includes aspects of
normal and abnormal psychical life, the phenomena of "animal magnetism" and trance states, and the nature and forms of mental illness.
Hegel's discussions of these topics in the context of his speculative notion
of Spirit are of interest in themselves and are also presupposed in his
later treatments of cognition and volition in the sciences of Phenomenology and Psychology. But in addition, Hegel's Anthropology forms an
important part of his doctrine of Subjective Spirit, which is one avenue
on which Hegel claimed to go beyond what he called the subjective
idealism of Kant.

Though Hegel's notion of the soul in some ways surprisingly anticipates
later depth psychology, he was not entirely an innovator among modern
thinkers in dealing with this realm. Kant, for example, had dealt with
aspects of the psychical life in his Anthropology. But Kant hardly treats

---

[5] *FPhG* 17, 48.

of the psyche as a selfhood, much less as Spirit.[6] Hegel's speculative treatment of the soul differs in content and method from that of Kant, and part of our study is to see the why and wherefore of this difference.

The Kantian Anthropology "from the pragmatic point of view" seeks to know man in regard to "what can be made out of him." [7] The work is expressly termed by its author as outside the science of the a priori principles of knowledge.[8] In Hegel the Anthropology presents the first moment of the notion of Subjective Spirit and is thereby one of the necessary sciences of cognition. The Kantian work brings together a number of connected topics discussed on the order of empirical generalizations. There is no claim of necessary sequence, let alone deduction. For Kant, as we shall see, there can be no such claim in this area. Though not rigorously systematic, the Kantian Anthropology is rich in aperçus into human nature. But Hegel seeks something more. The Hegelian speculative Anthropology puts itself forward as a demonstration according to the "logical Idea," and without this character of necessity the Anthropology loses its meaning as a science of Subjective Spirit. If the Kantian Anthropology had been lost or never written, the Kantian metaphysic of knowledge would remain essentially unimpaired.[9] If Hegel's Anthropology had been lost, the foundation would be missing in the logical structure of Subjective Spirit, which is an important part of Hegel's metaphysic of knowledge.

The difference in treatment of the two works derives from an important difference in principle. Unlike Kant, Hegel attempts to demonstrate an "emergence" of consciousness. What is the nature and meaning of this attempt, and what are its implications for the Hegelian position generally and the problem of knowledge in particular? What

---

[6] "For were I to enquire whether the soul in itself is of spiritual nature, the question would have no meaning." (*CPR* A684 = B712) The notion of the soul as spirit, according to Kant, can only be employed "regulatively," not "constitutively" (see below, p. 10 n. 35). This applies to our theoretical knowledge, not to our knowledge of the soul under the moral law.

[7] *APH* 246.

[8] *APH* 119, 134 n., 141-143. See also *The Methaphysical Principles of Virtue* (Part II of *The Metaphysic of Morals*), trans. James Ellington (Bobbs-Merrill, New York, 1964), pp. 16, 43, 65.

[9] Feeling, for example, an important topic of Anthropology for each thinker, is for Kant "not a faculty whereby we represent things, but lies outside our whole faculty of knowledge." (*CPR* A801 = B829 fn.) But for Hegel, as we shall see, in order to understand how we are able to "represent things" we must follow the development of the "feeling soul" to the ego of consciousness.

role does this demonstration play in Hegel's purported overcoming of the Critical Philosophy? This relation to Kant, as well as the need to view Hegel's treatment as part of his overall "speculative method," has required a somewhat long introductory section where we have had to draw upon the *Phenomenology* of 1807, the science of logic, and other works.

The discussion of the problem of self-knowledge in our introductory section turns largely on Kant's formulation of this problem as one of "access," and to Hegel's transformation of the Kantian formulation. For Kant, we cannot in an anthropology or psychology go beyond empirical generalization. In these sciences we cannot proceed from first principles for we can have no knowledge of the soul or ego or self as it is "in itself." The Critical Philosophy's limiting of self-knowledge to an empirical study of "appearances" is part of that philosophy's endeavor to establish a certain knowledge of physical nature generally as a knowledge of appearances. This outcome of the Critical Philosophy, both as regards self-knowledge and knowledge generally, is seen by Hegel as tantamount to a surrender of the philosophic quest.

The problem of knowledge of first principles is resolved by Hegel partly in the manner of the ancients, namely, by a dialectical critique of opinions.[10] But the "opinions" for Hegel are prescientific stages of consciousness which, by its own self-criticism, raises its unverified "certainty" to philosophic science. In this way, consciousness's internal movement, demonstrated phenomenologically, provides the initial access to first principles.

But in what, we may ask, lies the nature and possibility of consciousness to be such a successful self-critic? Any alleged demonstration of consciousness's movement must presuppose a certain concept of consciousness as such. For this reason the phenomenological "pathway" to knowledge remains in an important sense ungrounded. The demonstration in the *Phenomenology* of 1807 begins with the "natural consciousness," whose notion, we may therefore say, is presupposed in the conception of the enterprise itself.[11] By the nature of the enterprise, the presupposition cannot be overcome until after consciousness itself has become philosophic.

As Fichte demanded that each particular science be demonstrated

---

[10] See, for example, Aristotle's *Topics* 101a39ff., and Socrates' *deuteros plous* in *Phaedo* 99D.

[11] See below, p. 29.

from a first principle which cannot be demonstrated within the science itself,[12] so the first principle of the Hegelian science of Phenomenology, namely, that of consciousness, needs to be demonstrated in a science other than that of Phenomenology. In the Hegelian encyclopedic system of philosophical sciences, consciousness derives its "logical Idea" from the science of logic's doctrine of essence.[13] But consciousness in its "concrete notion" derives from the science of Anthropology, which demonstrates the nature of consciousness as arising from a development of the soul. We thus see briefly the place of the Anthropology as providing the first principle of the science of Phenomenology, whereby Hegel means to overcome the Kantian limitation of knowledge to appearances. But what about the first principle of the Anthropology, namely, soul? Here too, as we shall see in our introductory chapters and thereafter, the logical Idea derives from the science of logic and the concrete notion of the soul from the preceding sciences of nature.

Another consideration that has required our going outside the compass of the Anthropology itself is the nature of demonstration in that science and the meaning of demonstration for Hegel generally. This necessitates a discussion of Hegel's "speculative method," whose importance for any understanding of Hegel cannot be overstated. One may or may not accept Hegel's demonstration of the soul's development to the ego of consciousness. But unless one knows beforehand what Hegel is about in showing a movement "according to the logical Idea," the sequence of stages in the Anthropology, like all "unfolding" in Hegel, cannot but strike the reader as arbitrary if not utterly incomprehensible

With certain exceptions, which Hegel explicitly notes, the demonstration of the soul's development to ego does not show a process in time.[14] In the Hegelian sciences of nature and Spirit, "development" is all-important, but its meaning is essentially logical. For Hegel, genuine demonstration is a movement of the subject matter itself (*Sache selbst*) that is at the same time an unfolding of its "notion" (*Begriff*). This is possible, Hegel contends, because the Notion as logical Idea is itself a self-moving life, the heart and soul of every *Sache selbst*. Here perhaps lies a main source of difficulty for the student of Hegel. Everything

---

[12] See Fichte's essay *Über den Begriff der Wissenschaftslehre* (1794), inspired by the Kantian transcendental philosophy.

[13] See below, p. 162.

[14] When Hegel deals with habit, for example, the three moments of habit are the moments of its notion, not phases in habit formation. (See below, p. 136)

in Hegel is "proven," everything "demonstrated"—but the whole meaning of demonstration in Hegel is *sui generis*. It can only be understood in terms of the speculative method, which Hegel claims to be the only method wherein the *ordo rerum atque idearum idem est*.

For this reason I cannot agree with some writers, often friendly to Hegel, who would separate "what is living" in Hegel from the omnipresent form of demonstration according to the Notion. To be sure, hardly anyone will maintain that Hegel's demonstrations are in all cases felicitous. It remains a question in my own mind whether the purported demonstration of the emergence of consciousness is to be regarded as "successful." Yet I have sought to show this aspect of the Anthropology in its strongest possible light, for without it the Anthropology would be quite bereft of its meaning in the doctrine of Subjective Spirit.

Hegel's claim to demonstration brings in a number of problems that we shall only touch on peripherally in the course of our study. In the sciences of nature and Spirit, as Hegel tells us, we are no longer dealing with pure logical categories but a concrete content that must arise for the philosopher empirically.[15] In the philosophical treatment, however, the succession of shapes cannot remain "externally juxtaposed," but must be known as "the corresponding expression of a necessary series of specific notions." But how can we be sure that we grasp the particular empirical shape according to its proper notion? And how far into the empirical material does the philosopher mean to push his claims for demonstration? In his treatment of the concrete sciences, Hegel sometimes tells us at certain points that we are now entering a realm where contingency prevails over the Notion. Are we to say at these times then that the discussion is mainly illustrative and possesses philosophic interest marginally? But we shall find that the text is not always clear as to whether a particular discussion intends to carry demonstrative force. Perhaps Hegel means here to suggest guidelines for a philosophic overview of the empirical material? In the *Naturphilosophie* Hegel says, we cannot demonstrate everything but must have faith in the Notion.[16] But if this is the case, ought we not also to regard some of the demonstrations "proper" as tentative and subject to revision in the light of further empirical knowledge? [17]

---

[15] *PhM* 26.

[16] *PhN* 359.

[17] With regard to questions similar to those raised in the preceding paragraph, see Mure, *op. cit.*, chapters xx-xxii.

While I have entered little into direct criticism in the present work, I believe it would not be contrary to Hegel's intentions to view the demonstration in the Anthropology as within limits subject to revision. Even with regard to his *Science of Logic*, where there can hardly be a question of empirical material, the philosopher tells us near the end of his life that he wished "leisure had been afforded to revise it seven and seventy times." [18] Many scholars have called attention to revisions, often serious, in the development of Hegel's thought, [19] and I believe it is a misunderstanding of Hegel's meaning of "absolute knowledge" to regard the possibility of revision as a threat to his system as demonstrative science. Demonstration for Hegel is not *more geometrico*, where it may perhaps be said that a miss is as good as a mile. I do not see why Hume's meaning need be accepted—that demonstration is "either irresistible" or has "no manner of force." Perhaps the reader of Hegel's Anthropology will come away with the thought that, while the demonstration is rather less than irresistible and absolutely and at all points clear, it is nevertheless in the highest sense suggestive as a program. But this very suggestiveness can only emerge where the demonstration is studied on its own terms and for what it purports to be.[20]

While the above methodological considerations are paramount for a study of Hegel's Anthropology, they do not come before—and should not be allowed to obscure—other essential aspects of the Hegelian endeavor in this work. Anthropology, the science of man, is for Hegel a science of Spirit, albeit in its finitude. The finitude of Spirit, says Hegel, is a contradiction, and means that Spirit is here struggling to rid itself of its untruth.

This struggling with the finite, the overcoming of limitation, constitutes the stamp of the divine in the human spirit and forms a necessary stage of the eternal Spirit.[21]

Hegel's demand that we view man scientifically as Spirit means to say that man in his essential being is never to be taken—as by certain approaches in Hegel's time that have become all too familiar in our

---

[18] *SL* 42; see also *SL* 54.

[19] For a discussion of such revisions in the area of Subjective Spirit, see Walter Kaufman, *Hegel: Interpretation, Texts, and Commentary* (Doubleday, New York, 1965), pp. 246 ff.

[20] Kant, in dealing with another problem of extreme difficulty, asks the reader's indulgence "for some hardly avoidable obscurity in its solution, if only it be clearly established that the principle is correctly stated." (*CJ* 6)

[21] *PhM* 182.

own—as a bundle of impulses or matters, a concatenation of neural patterns or behavioral responses. On this score the Hegelian effort is to be seen as continuous with the Socratic-Platonic tradition at the beginning of Western philosophy: through *episteme,* which is divine, to comprehend man in his kinship with the divine.

The *episteme* of Spirit, Hegel maintains, is loftier than that of the Greeks in affording a notion of freedom not attained by Greek thought. To be sure, one cannot miss the similarities between the Hegelian notion of soul as Spirit and the Aristotelian *psyche* as *entelecheia.* Nevertheless a great religious tradition of the soul separates the two conceptions. According to Hegel, this religious tradition came to be expressed philosophically in the modern principle of the subjective consciousness. Hence we shall see that for Hegel the soul actualizes itself in the body not only in the way of the Aristotelian *ousia* but essentially in the manner of a subjectivity, whose destiny is to make itself "for itself" what it is implicitly in its substantial being.[22] Thus while Hegel expressly tells us that his sciences of Subjective Spirit will seek to rekindle the Aristotelian speculative tradition in psychology, he tells us also that he is indebted to the Kantian original synthetic unity of apperception for his notion of subjectivity, and to the Critical Philosophy generally for the posing of the problem that led to his own speculative method.

With regard to the discussion of Kant in the present study, a word of explanation is in order. Our work is one on Hegel, and because of the closeness of the two positions we have utilized aspects of the Kantian the better to set off the Hegelian. Though perhaps onesided in this respect, our study is not intended to come to any conclusion about the merits of the two thinkers. There is no doubt that in order to establish his own position, Hegel in some sense had to overcome the Kantian, and our study must reflect the Hegelian claim in this regard. Nevertheless we hope that it will contribute to a better understanding of the two thinkers in their relationship by focusing upon certain areas and topics where the two positions join issue.

Having for the most part laid aside the role of critic for that of interpreter and expositor, I have also not sought to link aspects of the

---

[22] Idealism, says Hegel, "asserts that nothing whatever can have a positive relation to the living being if this latter is not in its own self the possibility of this relation, i.e. if the relation is not determined by the Notion and hence not directly immanent in the subject." (*PhN* 385) Even in this statement about organism we see Hegel's debt to the transcendental approach of Kant and Fichte.

Hegelian treatment of the psychical life with present day studies in psychology and philosophy of mind.[23] Even now just past the bicentennial of Hegel's birth, a main task for English-speaking Hegel scholarship, I believe, is to understand the philosopher through a detailed knowledge of his texts, on his own terms, and within the Kantian framework that provided the main starting point for his own thinking. If the present work, within its modest compass, aspires to open new ground in intensive studies of Hegel in English, it is also meant as a beginning toward further intensive work in the Hegelian doctrine of Subjective Spirit, where Hegel places his main effort to supplant the Kantian doctrine of cognition.

In the present study I have not sought to trace the evolution of Hegel's own thinking whereby he came to hold the notion of Subjective Spirit that appears in his middle and late periods.[24] I have based my discussion mainly on the philosopher's mature thought as contained in the third and last edition of the *Enzyklopädie* (1830) published during Hegel's lifetime, and on the lecture notes of Hegel and his students presented by the editor, L. Boumann, as additions (*Zusätze*) to the 1845 edition of the *Philosophie des Geistes* and recently made available for the first time in English.[25]

Present editors of the forthcoming *Gesammelte Werke* have made us aware of how much is still in store for Hegel scholarship in the way of hitherto unpublished material. Since the long awaited critical edition of the collected works under the direction of the *Deutschen Forschungsgemeinschaft* hopefully will be completed within the next few decades, Hegel scholarship must look forward to further work in the area of Subjective Spirit and elsewhere in the Hegelian system of philosophical sciences.

Murray Greene

Graduate Faculty, New School for Social Research
New York, August 1971

---

[23] For a brief account of Hegel's Anthropology which connects points of Hegel's discussion with depth psychology, the work of Sartre, Merleau-Ponty, Plessner, and others, see: Jan van der Meulen, "Hegels Lehre von Leib, Seele, und Geist," *Hegel-Studien*, bd. 2, 1963, pp. 251-274.

[24] See F. Nicolin, "Hegels Arbeiten zur Theorie des subjektiven Geistes," in Derbolav and Nicolin, eds., *op. cit.*

[25] See "Foreword," by J. N. Findlay to *PhM* vi.

ABBREVIATIONS USED IN THE PRESENT WORK [1]

HEGEL'S WORKS

L   *The Logic of Hegel* (Part I of the *Enzyklopädie*), trans. William Wallace, 2nd ed. (Oxford, 1892)

PhN   *Hegel's Philosophy of Nature* (Part II of the *Enzyklopädie*), trans. A. V. Miller (Oxford, 1970)

PhM   *Hegel's Philosophy of Mind* (Part III of the *Enzyklopädie*), trans. W. Wallace and A. V. Miller (Oxford, 1971)

Phen.   *The Phenomenology of Mind* (Spirit), trans. J. B. Baillie, 2nd ed. (Macmillan, 1949)

SL   *Hegel's Science of Logic*, trans. A. V. Miller (Humanities Press, 1969)

PhR   *Hegel's Philosophy of Right*, trans. T. M. Knox (Oxford, 1949)

PhH   *The Philosophy of History*, trans. J. Sibree (Colonial Press, 1899)

HPh   *Hegel's Lectures on the History of Philosophy*, trans. E. S. Haldane and Frances H. Simon, 3 vols. (Humanities Press, 1955)

JR   *Jenaer Realphilosophie: Vorlesungsmanuscripte zur Philosophie der Natur und des Geistes von 1805-1806*, ed. Johannes Hoffmeister (Felix Meiner, Hamburg, 1967)

FPhG   "Ein Hegelsches Fragment zur Philosophie des Geistes," ed. Friedhelm Nicolin, *Hegel-Studien*, bd. 1, 1961, pp. 9-48.

KANT'S WORKS

CPR   *Critique of Pure Reason*, trans. Norman Kemp Smith (Macmillan, 1956)

CPrR   *Critique of Practical Reason*, trans. Lewis White Beck (Liberal Arts Press, New York, 1956)

CJ   *Critique of Judgment*, trans. J. H. Bernard (Hafner, New York, 1951)

Prol.   *Prolegomena to Any Future Metaphysics*, trans. Peter G. Lucas (Manchester University Press, 1953)

APH   *Anthropologie in pragmatischer Hinsicht*, in *Kants Werke*, bd. vii (Walter de Gruyter, Berlin, 1968)

[1] In any particular reference the number following the abbreviated title indicates the page. In *FPhG* the page number is that of the particular volume of the *Hegel-Studien*. In *CPR* the references are in the standard pagination.

NOTE ON TRANSLATION

In the case of *FPhG, JR, APH,* and other untranslated works referred to, the translations are my own. In certain instances of the translated works, I have at times altered the translator's renditions.

CONTENTS

PART I

INTRODUCTORY:
KNOWLEDGE AND SELF-KNOWLEDGE

Spirit essentially is what it knows itself to be.
(PhM 21)

CHAPTER ONE

KNOW THYSELF AS SPIRIT

Hegel begins his Philosophy of Mind (Spirit) by citing the Delphic inscription *Know Thyself*.[1] As oracles are wont to do, however, this terse injunction raises questions about its own meaning. To whom is it addressed, and by whom? It is of course directed to the ancient Greeks by their god, the Delphic Apollo. Does it tell the Greek to know himself as simply the particular individual that he is? Is he to know himself as a Greek? as a mortal and not a god? as a man in general?

Hegel sees the meaning of the inscription as one with his notion of the self-knowing Spirit. The self-knowledge enjoined by the god, Hegel says, did not come as the word of an alien power. The command to man was self-given, arising out of a particular people's genius at a particular moment in world history. But at the same time, says Hegel, it was a universal or absolute command for man. It gave notice of the historical destiny of the human spirit [2] and also embodied the timeless law of Spirit as such. For all of Spirit's doing is but a grasping of its own self, and "the aim of all genuine science is just this, that Spirit shall recognize itself in everything in heaven and on earth." [3]

But how, we may wonder, can there be such a uniting of the historical and eternal, particular and universal, human and divine? If, as Hegel says, the two are united as *Geist* in the command, then man's knowing himself must also be Spirit's knowing itself. But if Spirit, the divine, issued the command, it must have known it could be fulfilled, hence knew and knows eternally of man in his fulfilled knowledge of self. Then in what sense can there be a movement toward self-knowledge by the human spirit that also belongs to Spirit in its eternal Idea? In

---

[1] *PhM* 1.
[2] *PhH* 220.
[3] *PhM* 2.

what sense is the ancient Greek injunction a universal command for man? Hegel's viewing the oracle in terms of his notion of Spirit seems to magnify the difficulties of the original utterance, and Hegel warns us to this effect. The Philosophy of Spirit—at once a doctrine of man's knowing himself in his spirituality and Spirit's knowing itself in its eternal Idea—is the "highest" knowledge but also, says Hegel, the "most difficult" because the "most concrete." What does Hegel mean by the "most concrete" knowledge, and why, if most concrete, should it be the most difficult?

Whatever else man's concrete knowledge of himself as Spirit might be, it will not be, Hegel tells us, what in his time went under the name of *Menschenkenntnis* and in our own time shows up in the rather uncertain realm of study called psychology. Neither in its initial utterance nor in its timeless significance, says Hegel, did the command Know Thyself mean that each individual should preoccupy himself with the peculiarities of his own makeup.[4] The command did not call for the kind of knowledge that supposedly fathoms the secrets of the human heart, or purportedly reveals how great men are after all motivated by petty passions, or exhibits the foibles to which human kind is prone and how men may be calculated to react under different circumstances. This knowledge of man, according to Hegel, is not genuine knowledge and is without philosophical interest. Dealing with the contingent and trivial in men, its effect is to reduce man to the contingent and insignificant.[5] Not only must it be said to be spiritless (*geistlos*). It is *geistlos* because *begrifflos*. It lacks the form of the Notion, which is the soul of science and alone gives knowledge its rational necessity.[6] For this reason, says Hegel, this *Menschenkenntnis* can never attain to the essential, the universal, the substantial in man.

To claim that man can know himself as Spirit scientifically—nay, more: that he can know himself as Spirit only when he knows himself scientifically, and conversely—not only has for us today the ring of deepest paradox. It was a claim that hardly any great thinker since the

---

[4] Such *"subjective Menschenkennerey,"* says Hegel, was alien to the Greek mind and is a modern phenomenon. (*FPhG* 18)

[5] See also Schelling's *On University Studies,* trans. E. S. Morgan, ed. Norbert Guterman (Ohio University Press, Athens, 1966), p. 65.

[6] The Notion, aptly termed by G. R. G. Mure as Hegel's *minimum rationale,* is universality "that is *determinate* and possesses its determinations in this true way, namely, that it differentiates itself within itself and is the unity of these fixed and determinate differences." (*SL* 665)

scientific revolution of the sixteenth century, with the possible exception of Leibniz, would any longer dare press. Put forward by Hegel in the teeth of Newtonian science, it was the same claim that the Socrates of the *Phaedo* had put forward against the fifth century B.C. *phusikoi*: that man's knowledge of himself is only possible as an *episteme* insofar as it takes man in his kinship with divinity.

No doubt Descartes, Malebranche, Spinoza, and Leibniz could be said to have striven valiantly in the face of the new physics to conceive man as intellect and will in some sense as spirituality.[7] But to these efforts, insofar as they purported to carry the stamp of theoretical science, Kant firmly closed the door. Hence in establishing his claim of a science of man as Spirit, Hegel had to take up the cudgels especially against Kant. But to enter a contest with the great Critical thinker means to engage him on his own ground. This he forces one to do, inasmuch as he formulates the issue in terms of the very nature and possibility of knowledge. Hegel had to meet the challenge of the Critical Philosophy's canon of knowledge that swept from the domain of strict theoretical science everything but physics and mathematics.[8] In pressing his claim to a science of Spirit, Hegel willingly joins issue on the epistemological ground, since for him Spirit "essentially is only what it knows itself to be."

Since the Hegelian critique of Kant proceeds to the foundations of knowledge in general, let us follow Hegel's skirmishes with other modern approaches to the problem of man's self-knowledge. This will lead us to the Critical Philosophy's denial of the possibility of a strict theoretical science of man, and to Hegel's reformulation of the Critical Philosophy's approach to the problem of knowledge in general.

Hegel singles out for discussion two opposed approaches to a science of psychology: the old pneumatology or metaphysical psychology, as preserved mainly in the pre-Kantian "dogmatic" philosophy of Wolff, and the still flourishing empirical psychology. The selection itself would seem to reflect the Kantian critique, which demolished the former and permitted only the latter.[9] According to Hegel, the science of psychology had least profited from the advance of thought in modern times,[10] in spite of—or more truly, in Hegel's view, because of—the efforts of some

[7] See below, p. 59.

[8] *CPR* B x.

[9] In Kant's critique, Hegel tells us, Kant "had generally in mind only the state of the metaphysics of his time...; the genuinely *speculative* ideas of older philosophers on the notion of Spirit he neither heeded nor examined." (*SL* 777)

[10] *PhM* 186.

thinkers to bring the "science of human nature" into step with the successes of the physical sciences.[11] The ancient treatises of Aristotle on the soul, Hegel tells us, are still the foremost, if not sole works of merit on the subject, and Hegel hopes that his own Philosophy of Mind will rekindle the Aristotelian speculative tradition in psychology by reintroducing the Notion into the knowledge of Spirit.[12]

The old pneumatology or rational psychology had asked whether the soul is "simple," "selfsame," a "substance."[13] When Hegel wrote, this metaphysic of the soul was already a dead dog—justly laid to rest, says Hegel, by the Kantian critique. But Kant was right for the wrong reasons, Hegel tells us. No doubt Kant was correct in pointing out that the method of this psychology consisted in illegitimately substituting "metaphysical terms" for "statements of experience."[14] According to Hegel, however, this psychology was not deficient because it argued paralogistically from empirical phenomena to pure thought categories. Rather, says Hegel, its categories themselves were of a stamp that "neither can nor do contain truth."[15] Essentially the old psychology approached the soul as a fixed and static "thing," to which it sought to apply the abstract categories of the understanding.[16]

The soul, for Hegel, cannot be comprehended in the categories of thingness because it is essentially process. Far from a static *ens,* the soul is "absolutely restless being, pure activity, the negating or ideality of every fixed category of the abstractive intellect."[17] The soul is not "abstractly" simple but a simpleness that is at the same time a self-distinguishing. It is not a selfsame essence lurking behind its manifestations; it is only actual in its manifestations. To ask whether the soul is simple or composite, immaterial or material, selfsame or not selfsame, according to Hegel, is to employ barren dichotomies that can never grasp Spirit as at once sheer restlessness and absolute selfsameness, at once simple and differentiated, the concrete unity of opposed determinations.

---

[11] Cf. Hume's Introduction to his *A Treatise of Human Nature* (1738-1740).

[12] *PhM* 3. *FPhG* 24. See also Hegel's discussion of Aristotle's doctrine of the soul in *HPh* II, 180-202; and Frederick G. Weiss, *Hegel's Critique of Aristotle's Philosophy of Mind* (Martinus Nijhoff, the Hague, 1969).

[13] See *L* 68 ff.; *SL* 776.

[14] *L* 95. In Kant's words, rational psychology is founded on "a transcendental illusion in our psychological concepts." (*CPR* A 384)

[15] *L* 96; see also *SL* 776.

[16] *L* 68, 69; *FPhG* 21.

[17] *PhM* 3.

Kant did well to rid philosophy of pneumatology's lifeless notion of the soul-thing, says Hegel. But in arguing that this psychology exceeded the legitimate bounds of human reason, Kant missed the true ground why its metaphysic of the soul was inadmissible. The thought categories of the old psychology were not barren because they soared beyond the limits of human reason but because they never attained to its speculative use. It is only the speculative reason that is capable of grasping Spirit, whose essence is the "absolute unity of opposites in the Notion." [18] In its phenomenal aspects and relation to externality—as in the phases of the soul that Hegel will show in the Anthropology—Spirit "displays contradiction in its extreme form." [19] Spirit, however, "is all the greater the greater the opposition out of which it returns into itself." [20] Hence a knowledge of Spirit demands a *begreifendes Denken,* a grasping together of the highest oppositions as contained in the nature of Spirit itself. It is this that makes the Philosophy of Spirit the "most concrete" and at the same time the "most difficult" knowledge.

The conceptual thinking required for a knowledge of Spirit, however, is no more to be found in empirical psychology than in the old rational psychology, according to Hegel. The empirical psychology that emerged with the rise of the sciences, says Hegel, sought the "solid footing" lacking in the old metaphysic of the soul. "From empiricism came the cry: 'Stop roaming in empty abstractions.' " [21] Taking as its principle that in perception "consciousness is directly present and certain of itself," empiricism claimed to bring forward a concrete content for the study of human nature based on observation and experience. But the failure of this approach, Hegel claims, lies in the inadequacy of the principle itself. In its stance of relating itself passively to a content "merely found," empiricism bars itself from a genuine knowledge of Spirit, whose essence is such that it does not let itself be thus "found." [22]

Empiricism, according to Hegel, proceeds by breaking down the concrete content of experience and reconstructing the concretum from

---

[18] *SL* 776.
[19] *Ibid.*
[20] *Phen.* 366; see also *PhN* 399.
[21] *L* 78.
[22] "What merely *is* (*das Seiende*), without spiritual activity, is a thing for consciousness, and so little is it the essence of mind that it is rather the very opposite of it, and consciousness is only actual for itself by the negation and abolition of such a being." (*Phen.* 364-365)

its elements.[23] In its analysis of the "given," empiricism supposes that it introduces nothing but its act of separating. But in this separating, the elements of concrete experience acquire the form of universals. Empiricism therefore deceives itself in supposing it leaves the objects as they were. In fact it transforms the living object of experience into abstract attributes, that is to say, thoughts. And thus, says Hegel, "once more we see the axiom of bygone metaphysics reappear, that the truth of things lies in thought." But empiricism is all the while unaware that it contains metaphysics and wields its thought categories in an "utterly thoughtless and uncritical" manner.[24] In its separation of the given into "parts," for example, and the mind itself into "faculties," "operations," and "forces," empiricism leaves the living totality a mere "aggregate" and the "parts" a collection of members that possess neither inherent connection with one another nor with the mind as such.[25] Spirit's own self-feeling in its totality, says Hegel, protests against this splintering.[26]

In reconstructing the concretum of experience and establishing the higher connections of mind, empiricism proceeds essentially by narration. It presents the "natural evolution" of what "happens" in "pictorial and phenomenal thinking." [27] But philosophy is not meant to be a narration of what happens, says Hegel, but a cognition of what is true in happenings. A historical account may be correct enough for some purposes, but when regarded "as the truth and the first in the Notion," it necessarily results in limiting knowledge to sensuous experience. For when it is a question not of truth but merely history, says Hegel, then the "substrate" of feelings and intuitions from which understanding abstracts its universals is not negated and transmuted in the ideality of thought, but remains left over "as if it were the true and essential foundation." [28]

---

[23] See the description given of his method by Hume, who refers to himself as an "anatomist" of human nature: *An Enquiry Concerning Human Understanding* and *An Enquiry Concerning the Principles of Morals*, ed. L. A. Selby-Bigge (Oxford, 1902), pp. 13, 173 ff.

[24] *L* 78, 80; see also *Phen.* 177, 338 ff.; *HPh* III, 181-182.

[25] *FPhG* 20; on the so-called forces or faculties of the soul, see *SL* 498. Discussing the logical categories "parts" and "whole," Hegel says, the "external and mechanical relation" expressed in these categories is even more unsuited to the spiritual realm than to the organic. "Psychologists may not expressly speak of parts of the soul or mind, but the mode in which this subject is treated by the analytic understanding is largely founded on the analogy of this finite relation." (*L* 246; see also *L* 365)

[26] *PhM* 4; see also *SL* 498.

[27] *SL* 588.

[28] Hegel would seem to have in mind mainly Locke (the "historical, plain

Hegel's critique of empirical psychology, however, is not to be construed as a rejection of determinateness and concreteness.[29] Without analysis, says Hegel, there can be no knowledge of Spirit, for Spirit itself is "division within self" (*Scheidung in sich*).[30] But the question is how does a science of Spirit come to know this division? Hegel's answer, as we shall see in Chapter Two, is that only a "speculative logic" can comprehend the inner self-differentiation of Spirit in its living unity. If analytic thinking is not to remain caught in the artificial abstractions of its own analysis, it must learn to separate in accordance with Spirit's inner self-determination.

Hegel's critique of empiricism thus poses the question of how we find the true *arthra* [31] which at once separate and unite so that our "concrete" comprehension arises out of the *Sache selbst* rather than analysis as an act of "external reflection." [32] Empirical psychology is wrong not because it seeks determinateness but because its way of seeking bars a finding of the true *arthra*. Whether empiricism deals with external reality or with consciousness itself, it approaches its object as a "prefound existent confronting it," [33] to which it need only hold itself passively in order to "take it truly." [34] But such an approach inevitably discovers that it cannot reconcile its object as a "one" and also a "container" of

method"), Hume, Condillac (see *PhM* 183), or in general any approach to knowledge in terms of "origin of ideas." Kant, in describing his transcendental approach, says, "we are not talking about the origin of experience but about what lies in it." (*Prol.* 63) For Kant a "merely historical" knowledge is one that has not arisen "out of reason." (*CPR* A836 = B864) Hegel, nevertheless, charges that the a priori in Kant is presented in an order "solely based upon psychological and historical grounds." (*L* 84) Kant, says Hegel, "hunts through the soul's sack to see what faculties are still to be found there." (*HPh* III, 443, 432-433)

[29] "All knowledge begins subjectively with perception and observation, and the knowledge of appearances is of highest importance, indeed a thoroughly indispensible knowledge." (*FPhG* 20) See also *L* 21-22; *HPh* III, 176-177; and George Schrader, "Hegel's Contribution to Phenomenology," *The Monist*, vol. 18, no. 1, Jan. 1964, pp. 18-33.

[30] *L* 80. Criticizing Bacon's organization of the sciences, Hegel says: "The true method of division is found in the self-division of the Notion, its separating itself from itself." (*HPh* III, 178)

[31] See Plato's *Phaedrus* 265E ff.; *Sophist* 253C ff. See also *SL* 830.

[32] See Mure, *Introduction to Hegel, op. cit.*, p. 145.

[33] "*Ein vorgefundenes ihm gegenüberstehendes Seiendes*" (see *L* 365).

[34] Hegel sees the approach of empiricism as essentially that of the attitude of perception (*Wahr-nehmen*), which takes its object as a ready-made "in itself." (See *Phen.* 166, 176 ff.; *PhM* 160 ff.)

many properties; or consciousness itself as a manifold of "faculties" that are somehow to be brought into a "harmony." [35] Thus neither the abstract categories of rational psychology nor empirical psychology's spurious concreteness can provide a knowledge of Spirit as a self-differentiating unity, according to Hegel.

At this point in his preliminary discussion of the problems of methodology, Hegel offers an apparently odd observation but one that concerns an important aspect of his treatment in the Anthropology. Empiricism boasts of its solid footing in experience. Yet, says Hegel, a whole dimension of mental life has recently been opened to us which empirical psychology is simply unable to handle. In the face of empiricism's clinging to the fixed identities of the abstractive intellect, the "phenomena of animal magnetism" now offer undeniable evidence of the "underlying unity of soul, and of the power of its ideality." [36] These phenomena, Hegel contends, have thrown into confusion all the rigid distinctions of the understanding, and show the direct necessity of a "speculative" approach to Spirit.

Though we today usually think of the "unconscious" as having gained prominence in psychology only towards the end of the nineteenth century, Hegel sees in the mind's "unconscious pit" (*bewusstlose Schacht*) a hitherto neglected and ill-understood realm of mental life tat possesses essential philosophic interest. Advancing daringly where he perhaps should have treaded more cautiously, Hegel claims to demonstrate a kind of rational and purposeful life of Spirit even on the pre-objective level that he calls "soul." The new findings, arising in part out of the work of Anton Mesmer in the late eighteenth century, are regarded by Hegel with great interest and excitement. The phenomena of animal magnetism, Hegel claims, remain incredible to the empirical understanding and refute its restriction of knowledge to the spatial and temporal conditions of sense experience and the finite categories of cause and effect.[37] Hegel regards the psychical life revealed in the "magnetic" phenomena as important to his notion of Subjective Spirit, and his treatment of the psyche as a moment of Spirit "prior" to objective consciousness plays a role in

---

[35] *PhM* 4; *FPhG* 20. Hegel's reference to the "harmony" (of faculties) that "ought to be" but never "is" may have been meant also against Kant's notion of the "regulative" use of the transcendental idea of the soul to "detect the hidden identity" of the various mental powers. (*CPR* A649 = B677)

[36] *PhM* 4. See also *FPhG* 22.

[37] *PhM* 6; *FPhG* 22.

his reformulation of the Kantian notion of consciousness and the transcendental philosophy's doctrine of cognition.

Kant was well aware of a level of mental activity prior to the reflective intelligence. Those representations of which we are not "conscious to ourselves," says Kant, may be termed "obscure" (*dunkel*), and he notes that the area of the obscure representations comprises the "greatest" in the mind.[38] Kant distinguishes "obscure," "clear," and "distinct" representations in a manner that takes the problem beyond the treatment by such predecessors as Leibniz. Kant points out that the possibility of "distinct" representations rests on nothing else but an "order" imposed on a given manifold by the spontaneous rule-giving activity of consciousness.[39] Thus the problem of clear and distinct representations becomes more than merely psychological: it becomes the transcendental problem of accounting for the nature of consciousness in its giving of rules for objective thinking. But Kant sees no possibility—or, for his purposes of demonstration, necessity—of accounting for the "emergence" of such an objective rule-giving consciousness from a possible pre-objective subjectivity of the "obscure" representations. This latter subjectivity is sometimes termed by Kant the ego of "inner sense" or "ego of apprehension," as distinguished from the ego of apperception, which gives objective rules. The treatment of the former is a matter for psychology and not logic.[40] Such a psychology of inner sense is of necessity empirical, according to Kant, and has no place "in that metaphysic which has to do with the possibility of a priori knowledge." [41]

In Hegel's recasting of the Kantian doctrine of cognition, the demonstration in the Anthropology of the soul's development to objective consciousness will make possible Hegel's discarding of the Kantian *Ding an sich*. To do this, however, Hegel will have to show the reality of a pre-objective psychical subjectivity. Hegel therefore seizes upon the new findings concerning the psychical life as revealing a veritable life of the mind that will develop to objective consciousness. Kant apparently believed that we have no access to such a knowledge of the mind.[42] For Hegel, the soul is to be seen as a self-determining subjectivity with a life

---

[38] *APH* 136.
[39] *APH* 138.
[40] *APH* 134n.
[41] *APH* 143. See also below, p. 15.
[42] "But human insight is at an end as soon as we arrive at fundamental powers or faculties, for their possibility can in no way be understood and should not be just arbitrarily imagined or assumed."(*CPrR* 48)

of its own. Its activity of making itself the identity of its pre-objective manifold, which Hegel will claim to show in the Anthropology, is quite different from the Kantian pre-objective "synthesis of apprehension." Kant's rule-giving "synthesis of apperception," which makes knowledge possible but limits it to phenomena, will be shown to "awaken" in the soul in the course of development of subjectivity as Spirit. This notion of a genesis of the subject-object relation of consciousness will have important implications for the doctrine of knowledge.

If Hegel succeeds in demonstrating an "emergence" of consciousness, he would seem to have advanced on at least one important front in his endeavor to overcome the Critical Philosophy. The limitation of the Kantian position, declares Hegel, can be seen most particularly in its having conceived Spirit in the form of consciousness.[43] The Critical Philosophy's point of view remains confined "within consciousness and its opposition" with a thing-in-itself as "something else left over." [44] In thereby perpetuating the antithesis between "thought and thing," says Hegel, the Critical Philosophy bade men go feed on "husks and chaff." [45] In viewing consciousness ever as "relating to a something out in the beyond," the Critical Philosophy restricts itself to a phenomenology. But "pure science," according to Hegel, presupposes the liberation from the subject-object antithesis of consciousness.[46] Hegel will claim to show that the subject-object opposition first comes about as an "original dividing" (*Ur-teil*), a "judgment" of Spirit itself in the course of its actualization as soul. Hereby we obtain a more universal principle of subjectivity than that of consciousness as such. If we can therefore display a genuine Being-for-self (*Fürsichsein*) of subjectivity that is not yet that of the Kantian "I think," then we shall have shown that the Kantian principle of the transcendental unity of apperception is contained within a more concrete and deeper principle of Spirit.

For Kant, the transcendental apperception, or pure identity of self-consciousness, establishes the "function of synthesis" and is thus the highest principle of all our knowledge.[47] While Kant's stress on the

---

[43] *PhM* 156.

[44] *SL* 62.

[45] *L* 62. With regard to Kant's refutation of pneumatology, Hegel says that at least the old metaphysic "had for its end the cognition of the truth," whereas the victory of the Kantian critique consists rather in "doing away with the investigation." (*SL* 780)

[46] *SL* 60.

[47] *CPR* B 134.

identity of self-consciousness is all-important for a doctrine of knowledge,[48] this identity, Kant makes clear, is in no way to be conceived as a spiritual life but as a "formal" condition of our knowledge. It can itself have no applicability whatsoever "to any assignable object." The transcendental apperception has to do with "the logical exposition of thought in general" and is not to be mistaken "for a metaphysical determination of the object." [49] This means that we cannot know ourselves as pure ego but only as we appear to ourselves in the flux of empirical consciousness.[50]

As Hegel points out, the Kantian position with regard to the possibility of self-knowledge is in effect a going back to Hume.[51] For Kant, as for Hume, the command Know Thyself can only be fulfilled by an empirical psychology,[52] whose approach in principle, as we have seen Hegel charge, violates the living truth of Spirit. The Critical Philosophy, to be sure, is by no means equated generally by Hegel with Hume's empiricism. Kant's transcendental unity of apperception, says Hegel, is "one of the profoundest and truest insights" of the Kantian critique of reason.[53] But in Hegel's view, Kant was unable to develop this insight as a "genuinely synthetic progress—the self-producing Notion." [54] Let us try to see more clearly why this was so.

For Kant himself the principle of the original identity of self-consciousness made possible all universal and necessary knowledge of external nature within the unity of experience. But if such a knowledge of externality is now established, what about the internality of the self? Here lies a certain irony in the Kantian position. Fulfillment of the god's command to man to know himself is barred by the very possibility of his knowledge of the nonself. In the Critical Philosophy the conditions for the possibility of a knowledge of the external world of nature are at the same time the conditions for the impossibility of a knowledge of the inner world of Spirit. In order to understand the thrust of Hegel's endeavor in the Anthropology, we need to see why this was so for Kant.

---

[48] See Hegel's comment, below.

[49] *CPR* B 409. The analysis "of the consciousness of myself in thought in general, yields nothing whatsoever towards the knowledge of myself as object." (*Ibid.*)

[50] *CPR* B 156, B 158, A 278 = B 334; *APH* 142.

[51] *SL* 777.

[52] *CPR* A 382.

[53] *SL* 584.

[54] *SL* 789.

Kant's barring of the possibility of self-knowledge derives from his position with regard to the possibility of theoretical knowledge as such. In the Preface to his first great Critique, Kant distinguishes his approach to knowledge from that of the "dogmatic procedure of pure reason." The latter, says Kant, advances to its subject matter "without previous criticism of its own powers." [55] A "critical" philosophy, on the other hand, must first undertake a critique of the "organ" of cognition to determine the possible limits of its use.[56]

Thus the Kantian formulation of the problem of knowledge, as Hegel often points out, distinguishes at the outset between the faculty of cognition as an "organ" or instrument, and the object about which this instrument can or cannot obtain knowledge. As applied to the problem of self-knowledge, this formulation would mean that, for the knowing consciousness to know itself as it is "in itself," it would have to be at once instrument and object known through the instrument. This, for the Kantian philosophical position, is in principle impossible for all purposes of theoretical knowledge.

We can have no knowledge of the self as it is "in itself" for at least two main reasons, according to Kant. In the first place, we have no sensible intuition of the pure self—and intellectual intuition is lacking to us—which therefore must remain for us an "empty concept" as regards all theoretical knowledge. Secondly, we can have no knowledge whatsoever of the self as transcendental ego, since we cannot have a knowledge of the transcendental source of knowledge. All our knowledge is knowledge of an "object," but the categories of the understanding, which make objective knowledge possible, cannot be applied to knowing as an "object" the very source of these categories themselves. Such a knowing, says Kant, would entail a circularity.

We can thus say of the thinking 'I' (the soul)...that it does *not* know *itself through the categories,* but knows the categories, and through them all objects, in the absolute unity of apperception, and so *through itself.* Now it is, indeed, very evident that I cannot know as an object that which I must presuppose in order to know any object...[57]
The subject of the categories cannot by thinking the categories acquire a concept of itself as an object of the categories. For in order to think them, its pure self-consciousness, which is what was to be explained, must itself be presupposed.[58]

---

[55] *CPR* B xxxv, B xxxvi.
[56] See also the discussion of "dogmatic" and "critical" philosophy in *CJ* 243 ff.
[57] *CPR* A 402 (Kant's italics).
[58] *CPR* B 422; see also B 406 ff.

If we may be permitted a crude analogy: the telescope can be trained upon any star in the heavens but cannot be turned to look upon itself.

But apart from the question of a knowledge of the "pure" self, we cannot even know the "phenomenal" self with the same kind of knowledge that we can know the phenomenal world of nature. Although we have sensible intuitions of ourselves in our inner affections, such intuitions cannot yield the kind of synthetic a priori judgments that constitute an apodictic science of nature. Kant compares a "*doctrine of the soul* as the physiology of inner sense" with a "*doctrine of the body* as a physiology of the object of the outer senses.[59] In both, says Kant, there is "much to be learnt empirically." But where we are dealing with the body, "much that is *a priori* can be synthetically known from the mere concept of an extended impenetrable being"; whereas when we are dealing with the object of inner sense, "nothing whatsoever that is *a priori* can be known synthetically from the concept of a thinking being." [60]

For these reasons, Kant holds, "the hope of succeeding by *a priori* methods" in a knowledge of the soul must be "abandoned" and psychology "banished from the domain of metaphysics." [61] Kant adds, however, when psychology is in "a position to set up an establishment of its own in a complete anthropology," then it can assume its place as "the pendant to the empirical doctrine of nature." [62] Such a psychology would deal, for example, with the empirical laws of association of ideas in the reproductive imagination.[63] In his own lectures and writings on anthropology, applied ethics, and education, Kant deals with what could be called "psychological" material. By the Critical Philosophy's canons, however, these treatments do not rank as theoretical science in the sense of apodictically certain knowledge.

---

[59] *CPR* A 381.

[60] An appearence to outer sense "has something fixed or abiding which supplies a substratum as the basis of its transitory determinations and therefore a synthetic concept, namely, that of space and of an appearance in space." On the other hand, "in what we entitle 'soul,' everything is in continual flux and there is nothing abiding except...the 'I,' which is simple solely because its representation has no content, and therefore no manifold." (*CPR* A 381) "...In inner sense no permanent intuition is to be met with." (*CPR* B 292) See also *CPR* B 406 ff., and *APH* 134.

[61] *CPR* A 849=B 877.

[62] *Ibid.* See also *CJ* 13; and *Metaphysical Foundations of Natural Science*, trans. James Ellington (Bobbs-Merrill, New York, 1970), p. 8.

[63] *CPR* B 152.

Thus for the Kantian critical position there can be no philosophical doctrine of the soul beyond a negative critique of metaphysical psychology's transcendental illusions. Fulfillment of the command Know Thyself, for theoretical purposes, can only be through "a kind of *physiology* of inner sense" [64] whose empirical generalizations can pretend to no knowledge from necessary concepts, or from any intuition of the "identity of the subject" whereby it is "given as object" signifying the "identity of the person." [65]

This outcome of the Critical Philosophy for the problem of man's self-knowledge was repudiated by Hegel. With regard to Kant's claim that the pure ego must remain an "empty concept," Hegel grants that it is surely impossible to have the "slightest notion" of ego as the abstract "I think." But this is no less true of any other notion which we empty of content and where we "stop short at the simple, fixed general idea (*Vorstellung*) and name." [66] Hegel rejects Kant's argument that the ego's knowledge of ego would entail a vitiating circularity. The ego which supposedly "makes use" of self-consciousness as a means in order to judge "is indeed an *x*" of which, "taken in its isolation, we can never have the least conception." [67] It is therefore ridiculous to stigmatize as circular—as though it contained a fallacy—"this nature of self-consciousness, namely, that the 'I' thinks itself, that the 'I' cannot be thought without its being the 'I' that thinks." Hegel's point is, that the ego does not "make use" of something—even itself—in judging; rather ego *is* the subject-object relation, *is* judgment. And its judgings are precisely what render it concrete and determinate, rather than "an *x*."

It is in this very self-relation, says Hegel, that ego manifests itself as Notion, as "the absolute relation-to-self that, as a separating judgment (*Ur-teil*), makes itself its own object and is solely this process whereby it makes itself a circle." [68] Hence Hegel calls it "barbarous" to set down

[64] *CPR* A 347.

[65] *CPR* B 408. To be sure, this negative outcome is said by Kant to have the positive aspect of making "room for faith" (*CPR* B xxx), and in our "moral destination" we can know ourselves as free spiritual beings. But such knowledge through practical reason does not extend our theoretical knowledge beyond appearances. We need not go into the problem of the two kinds of knowledge, or of how on the one hand we can know ourselves only as physical beings subject to natural necessity, and on the other hand as noumena freely subject to the moral law.

[66] *SL* 777.

[67] *SL* 776. See *CPR* A 346=B 404; also *Prol.* 80.

[68] *SL* 777-78. In "judgment," as we shall see later, the ego divides itself like the *Scheidung in sich* of Spirit. Discussing "judgment" in its logical sense, Hegel

as a "defect" the truth that, in the ego's thinking of itself, the ego itself as subject cannot be omitted.[69] To say with Kant that the ego can only use itself as subject of a judgment, while the "intuition" is missing by which it could be given as object, is, according to Hegel, to decide beforehand that the notion of a thing which can exist only as subject can in principle have no objective status for knowledge.[70] The empirical and the "pure" self-consciousness are not in principle severed as regards the possibility of self-knowledge, as Kant would have it. Rather in both cases the "inseparability of the two forms in which it [ego] opposes itself to itself belongs to the innermost nature of its notion and of the notion itself." In this criticism of Kant, Hegel indicates a central tenet of his own notion of Subjective Spirit: the ego, both empirical and as abstract "I am I," which essentially relates itself to itself by positing itself opposite itself,[71] is identical with the *Scheidung in sich* of Notion. The way Hegel demonstrates this as an actualization of the soul, will constitute the culminating point of the Anthropology and of our study.

Hegel claims that the Kantian denial of the possibility of self-knowledge derives from a fundamental error in the Critical Philosophy's approach to the problem of knowledge. Through the very conception of its enterprise, the Critical approach condemns itself to an inability to break out of its own starting point.[72] By first undertaking an examination of the faculty of cognition as "instrument" or "medium" through which the "light of truth reaches us," says Hegel, the Critical Philosophy already

says: Ordinarily in judgment we regard subject and object as independent extremes that we connect in some way by the copula "is." But "the etymological meaning of the judgment (*Urteil*) in German goes deeper, as it were declaring the unity of the Notion to be primary, and its distinction to be the original partition." And, Hegel adds, "that is what the judgment really is." (*L* 297) In our present study we shall have several occasions to note Hegel's use of *Urteil* as meaning "original partition."

[69] "A stone does not have this *inconvenience*; when it is to be thought or judged, it does not stand in its own way. It is relieved from the burden of making use of *itself* for this task; it is something else outside it that must give itself this trouble." (*SL* 778)

[70] "If external intuition, determined in space and time, is required for objectivity, and it is this that is missing here, then it is quite clear that by objectivity is meant merely sensuous reality; and to have risen above *that* is a condition of thinking and of truth." (*SL* 778)

[71] See below, p. 148.

[72] See Jean Hyppolite, *Genèse et structure de la Phénoménologie de l'esprit de Hegel*, 2 vols. (Paris, 1946), vol. 1, p. 11.

"presupposes a distinction of ourselves from this knowledge." [73] The very notion of an instrument or means for securing us possession of the essential truth, inevitably brings in the consideration that the "application" of an instrument does not leave this essence "as it is in itself."

Hegel, however, calls for no return to a precritical position but for a genuine notion of critique. The Critical Philosophy's demand that thought investigate its own capacity for knowledge is a fair enough demand, says Hegel, provided it be properly conceived. In the case of ordinary instruments, we can test them before putting them to use. But how else can we criticize cognition except by another cognition? "To examine this so-called instrument is perforce the same as to know it," but to seek to know before we know is like resolving not to enter the water until we have learned to swim. In the investigation of thought by thought, says Hegel, the action of the forms of thought must be combined with a criticism of them. In this way the forms of thought "examine themselves," and the critical activity of thought, "instead of being brought to bear upon the categories from without," is "immanent in their own action." [74]

But in what consists such a method of "immanence" and how can it be attained? Hegel contended that the notion of a genuine critique of thought was present in germ in the modern principle of subjectivity as such. It is implicit, for example, in the Cartesian concept of the *ego cogitans,* which draws its thought forms from within itself as a thinking self-consciousness, and thereby has its own inherent activity as its object. At the same time, however, Descartes took what is to be known by these thought forms as an external reality independent of the activity of thought as such. Only in transcendental philosophy's notion of the "category," says Hegel, does the truth first come to be apprehended in its native element as subjectivity. For the true significance of the category, according to Hegel, is that "self-consciousness and Being are the same essence," and the "essentiality (*Wesenheit*) of 'what is' (*des Seienden*)" is grasped as "thinking actuality" (*denkende Wirklichkeit*).[75] But this conception provides only a prerequisite of the genuine philosophic method and not the method itself.

---

[73] *Phen.* 133. See also *SL* 36, 841; *L* 17; and the early work *Glauben und Wissen* (Hamburg 1962), pp. 14-15, where Hegel criticizes Locke and Kant for their conception of first examining the understanding as to its capacity for knowledge.

[74] *L* 17, 84.

[75] *Phen.* 276. The category is "the unity of ego and Being." (*Phen.* 369)

The principle of subjectivity—that nothing is to be taken as true that does not posses inward evidence for consciousness—is not of itself the pathway to truth, according to Hegel. Hegel cites the endeavor of Descartes, whose "new beginning" is born in the abstract resolve by the subjective consciousness to accept no other authority for the truth but to "produce everything itself and hold only its own act for true." [76] But in fact, says Hegel, this approach had not yet "equipped itself" for the task it desired to undertake. In proceeding "straightway to criticize and test," it employed canons of evidence that were uncritical and untested.[77] Whether one calls opinions one's own or belonging to others, says Hegel, the content is not necessarily altered and truth "has not thereby taken the place of error." Thus Descartes' rule of the "inner" certainty of the thinking consciousness can also be but a form of "external" reflection.

The methods of analysis and synthesis, or resolution and composition, as developed by post-Cartesian thinkers, were no less methods of external reflection, Hegel maintains. Again, it is a question of finding the true *arthra*.[78] Where analysis, as we saw, separates the concretum of experience into abstract universals, synthesis starts with the universal and proceeds to the individual. But the synthetic method presents the universal in the form of definitions that possess no "constraining necessity" for the content defined, and hence this method likewise constitutes a "purely subjective cognition which is external to the object." [79]

The inadequacies of analysis and synthesis are purportedly overcome in the method of "construction" that takes its clue from geometry. In construction in geometry, says Hegel, we proceed arbitrarily by making assumptions that obtain *ex post facto* justification in the proof.[80] But in this way, Hegel charges, "an external purpose controls the process," and the movement of thought in demonstration is dictated by no necessity inherent in the notion of the demonstrandum. These inadequacies for

---

[76] *Phen.* 136.

[77] For example, its criterion of "clear and distinct," Hegel says, is a "psychological" rather than a "logical" criterion. (*L* 296; *SL* 613) Kant, as we saw (above p. 11, had made the transition to the logical.

[78] On external reflection as contrasted with speculative thinking, see below, p. 35 n. 60.

[79] *L* 366. Spinoza's demonstration, says Hegel, is the "fundamental defect in the whole position." (*Hph* III, 283 ff.)

[80] *Phen.* 102. For Hegel's contention that the methods of mathematics are unsuitable for philosophy, see *Phen.* 105-106.

philosophic thought in geometry, says Hegel, are evident in the "method of construction" that Kant supposedly "brought into vogue" in his phrase that "mathematics 'construes' its notions." But all that Kant meant here, says Hegel, is that mathematics does not have to do with notions but with abstract qualities of sense perceptions.[81] The method that "construes its notions," Hegel grants, has in the background a "dim consciousness of the Idea, of the unity of the Notion and objectivity" insofar as, in demonstration, subjectivity "shows itself a modifying and determining principle." [82] But the demonstration is after all "ruled by an external end." The proof is not "a *genesis* of the relationship that constitutes the content of the theorem"; and for this reason it is altogether "an *external* reflection" that goes "from without inwards," i.e. "infers from external circumstances the inner constitution of the relationship." [83]

Therefore, the various post-Cartesian claims of "new methods" notwithstanding, the Kantian challenge to philosophic thinking remained yet to be met. For Hegel, the Critical Philosophy's requirement that the forms of thought be justified in a deduction from the principle of the thinking consciousness marked the first emergence of the "absolute method." [84] But in Kant himself this method was left "lifeless and uncomprehended" and in the post-Kantian transcendental thinkers it remained a mere "schema" where scientific organization became a "synoptic table" and the method as yet had "no right to the name of science." [85]

The profound discovery of Kant, which Hegel regards as the basis for his own method, was that:

The unity which constitutes the nature of the *Notion* is recognized as the *original synthetic* unity of apperception as unity of the *I think* or of self-consciousness.[86]

Kant, in Hegel's view, had hereby enunciated the supremely important principle of the identity of ego and Notion: the pure forms of thought, i.e., the forms of the Notion, are forms of the unifying activity of the thinking consciousness.

***

[81] *L* 369; see also the useful notes of the translator, pp. 430-31. On Kant's distinction between philosophical and mathematical knowledge, see *CPR* A 713= B 741 ff.

[82] *L* 371.

[83] *SL* 812.

[84] *Phen.* 107.

[85] *Phen.* 108.

[86] *SL* 584; see also *SL* 589. For a comparison of Kant's transcendental ego with Hegel's Spirit, see R. C. Solomon, "Hegel's Concept of 'Geist'", *Review of Metaphysics*, vol. xxiii, no. 4, June 1970, pp. 642-661.

But Kant himself, Hegel claims, provided no genuine demonstration of his great principle; he had no inkling of the original apperception as "the self-producing Notion." [87] It was Fichte who was the first to set about the task of a genuine deduction of the pure forms of thought. By deriving the categories in terms of the moments of thesis, antithesis, and synthesis, Fichte took the first great step in transforming the Kantian "triplicity" of the categories into the universal form of the Notion. But Fichte himself, Hegel maintains, never moved beyond an "abstract empty idealism." [88] Fichte begins with the ego's certainty "that in all being there is this bare consciousness of a 'mine' ". But for all further distinction and development of this abstract "mine," Fichte needed the "impact (*Anstoss*) from without," and this is supplied by the philosopher's introduction of the non-ego. But in this way, says Hegel, the approach fails "to link up its contradictory statements": on the one hand, that pure consciousness is all reality, while all the time the alien *Anstoss*, an indifferent externality, remains equally reality. For this reason, Hegel declares, a "filling" can only be brought into such an idealism in external fashion, no differently in principle from empiricism.[89] There remains no inherent connection between the abstract categories of the ego and the concrete content of philosophic science.

Thus even in transcendental philosophy, Hegel contends, the movement of thought in demonstration came from the reflecting philosopher rather than the *Sache selbst*. Even in this approach whose *arche* and highest principle is self-consciousness, the procedure of "external reflection" could not attain to the Notion and to Spirit as it is in and for itself but only as it is "in reference to something else." [90]

But what sort of methodological principle can overcome "external reflection" and render the movement of philosophic demonstration immanently one with the *Sache selbst*? The *Sache selbst* for our particular study is man himself, who is commanded to know himself by the law of his own being as Spirit. But the command of self-knowledge, as we

---

[87] The deduction of the categories, says Hegel, "should have been by the exposition of the transition of that simple unity of self-consciousness into these its determinations and distinctions." (*SL* 789; see also *Phen.* 227; *L* 87) By making possible a genuine notion of consciousness, the science of Anthropology will also make possible a deduction of the objective categories as a "genuinely synthetic progress." (See below, pp. 167 ff.)

[88] *Phen.* 279. See also *SL* 75 ff., *L* 120, *PhM* 156.

[89] *Phen.* 279.

[90] *PhM* 156.

have seen, raises the most difficult and basic of methodological problems. In following Hegel's critique of rational and empirical psychology in the introductory pages of his *Philosophy of Mind,* we have needed to go rather far afield to understand Hegel's specific criticisms of forms of external reflection, whose very stance, Hegel contends, makes impossible an identity of the order of things and ideas. We were led to Kant, whose solution of the problem of knowledge generally contained the built-in prohibition against the possibility of self-knowledge. But this situation, in Hegel's view, derived from but another form of external reflection: the Critical Philosophy's proceeding by way of a prior examination of the faculty of cognition as an "instrument" of knowledge. In place of this and all other forms of external reflection, Hegel puts forward his own philosophical method, which will purportedly carry through the "fair demand" of the Critical Philosophy by a genuine critique of thought by the forms of thought themselves.

Hegel's method initially takes the form of a "pathway" to philosophical thinking.[91] But if we are not merely to substitute "pathway" for "instrument," the pathway must be shown in some way to be contained in the goal itself. The pathway must be an ascent as it were to the kingly realm which, once attained, enables the traveller to see that his route was after all within the realm itself. The pathway is termed by Hegel "phenomenology." The kingly realm is the encyclopedic system of philosophic sciences, which includes the science of Anthropology. Hence in order to understand Hegel's procedure in his doctrine of the soul, we need to view briefly the pathway to the kingly realm, as well as how we are to proceed once within the realm itself.

[91] *Phen.* 135.

CHAPTER TWO

THE SPECULATIVE METHOD

Presenting the first full statement of his system of philosophy in the *Encyclopedia,* Hegel says in the Preface to the first edition (1817) that he is offering a "new treatment of philosophy on a method which will, as I hope, yet be recognized as the only genuine method identical with the content." [1] This is the "speculative method," which comprehends the development "of all natural and spiritual life" as resting "solely on the nature of the pure essentialities which constitute the content of logic." [2] These logical essentialities are "pure thoughts," the "immanent development of the Notion." Their "self-movement" is "their spiritual life" and that through which "philosophy constitutes itself and of which it is the exposition." But although philosophy constitutes itself through the pure essentialities of logic, it goes on to apply the method of the logic to the concrete sciences of nature and mind. Since the essentialities of logic comprise the moments of the Notion, however, demonstration in the concrete sciences "does not behave like external reflection" but "takes the determinate element from its own subject matter, since it is itself that subject matter's immanent principle and soul." [3] The method, therefore, is both "soul and substance, and anything whatever is comprehended and known in its truth only when it is completely subjugated to the method; it is the method proper to every subject matter (*jeder Sache selbst*) because its activity is the Notion." [4]

---

[1] Even before the first full presentation of his system, Hegel tells us in 1812 (Preface to *SL*): "The essential point of view is, that we have to do, altogether, with a new concept of philosophical method." (*SL* 28) Indeed the entire Preface to the *Phenomenology* of 1807 is an announcement of the method, and the work itself the first application.

[2] *SL* 28.

[3] *SL* 830.

[4] *SL* 826.

Thus Hegel put forward the speculative method as possessing revolutionary significance for philosophical thinking, and from his first to last major published work [5] he was concerned to show that philosophy could not establish its claim as demonstrative science except on the basis of the speculative method. The exposition of the speculative method, says Hegel, properly belongs to the province of logic.[6] Its first employment, however, is in the *Phenomenology* of 1807, which is an example of the method "as applied to a more concrete object, namely, to consciousness." That the first employment of the speculative method is in a treatment of consciousness bespeaks in part Hegel's endeavor to conceive an "immanent" critique of cognition, as contrasted with the Kantian. It also bespeaks the fact that, while the possibility of Hegel's method arises out of transcendental philosophy's principle of consciousness, the Hegelian endeavor is to sublate that principle, since "pure science presupposes liberation from the opposition of consciousness." [7] In one of Fichte's formulations of the transcendental principle in his *Wissenschaftslehre* of 1794, he says: In the assertion of any proposition, the predicate "designates what the self, reflecting upon itself, discovers to be present in itself, because it has first set this within itself." [8] Out of Fichte's conception of the ego as self-positing, Hegel will go on to demonstrate the ego as *ur-teilend* or self-dividing, so that in its relation to its object, ego is at once "the content of the relation and itself the process of relating." [9] But this is precisely the inner self-distinguishing and return-to-self of Notion. Ego is identical with Notion.[10] The initial demonstration of this supremely important principle is through the speculative method as applied to consciousness. At the same time the demonstration affords —and is designed to afford—a "liberation" from consciousness's opposition of subject and object, thereby providing the "pathway" to the kingly realm of philosophic science.

In the *Phenomenology* of 1807, transcendental philosophy's fundamental insight that ego is Notion is demonstrated by a speculatively conceived

---

[5] See the Preface to *PhR*.

[6] *SL* 53.

[7] *SL* 49; see also *SL* 51.

[8] Fichte, *Science of Knowledge,* ed. and trans. Peter Heath and John Lachs (Appleton-Century-Crofts, New York, 1970), p. 97n.

[9] *Phen.* 209.

[10] *SL* 583.

movement of "experience." The subject's claims to a knowledge of the object take form also as succeeding shapes (*Gestalten*) of consciousness, "each of which in realizing itself at the same time resolves itself, has for its result its own negation—and so passes into a higher form." [11] The "immanence" or speculative nature of the procedure consists in that the method is "not something distinct from its object and content;—for it is the inwardness of the content, the dialectic which it possesses in itself, which is the mainspring of its advance." [12] In this way the *Phenomenology* is a critique of cognition that is not preliminary to its exercise, for the forms of thought are at once the "object" of critique and the "action" of that object.

Phenomenology in general, for Hegel, is the science of Spirit as consciousness. [13] Insofar as it is presented in terms of "experience" as a movement of consciousness to the philosophic standpoint, it is to be distinguished from "pure science," which presupposes "liberation from the opposition of consciousness" in the subject-object antithesis. [14] The *Phenomenology* of 1807, conceived within the problematic of "experience," is an "introduction" to philosophic science proper, and in the first instance to logic as the science of the pure "essentialities" of thought. [15] The 1807 work purports to show knowledge in its "appearing," science's "coming on the scene" (*auftreten*). [16] The movement of Spirit as consciousness is

[11] *SL* 54.

[12] *Ibid.*

[13] *SL* 781. The *Phenomenology* of 1807 was termed by Hegel at its original publication the "first part" of the system of science, later the "introduction" to the system. In its original intention of showing how the "immediate consciousness" developed to the "standpoint of philosophic science," Hegel tells us years later in his *Encyclopedia*, it was not possible to remain with "the form of mere consciousness," and much that belonged to the system's "concrete branches" was "already in part included" in the "introduction." (*L* 58-59) But how the 1807 treatment of those concrete branches is to be understood in relation to their later treatment in the system proper is not entirely clear. Since the concrete branches dealt with in the 1807 work do not include the area of the Anthropology, the problem in this respect does not directly concern our study. For discussions of the problems of the relation of the 1807 work to the system, see Otto Pöggeler, "Zur Deutung der Phänomenologie des Geistes," *Hegel-Studien*, 1, 1961, pp. 255-294, and "Die Komposition der Phänomenologie des Geistes," *Hegel-Studien*, Beiheft 3, 1964, pp. 27-74; Hans F. Fulda, *Das Problem einer Einleitung in Hegels Wissenschaft der Logik* (Vittorio Klostermann, Frankfort am Main, 1965).

[14] *SL* 49.

[15] *SL* 29, 48-49.

[16] *Phen.* 134.

the "pathway appointed for it by its own nature" that proceeds through necessary stages from the phenomenal knowing of the "natural consciousness" to the absolute knowing of the philosopher. But if science's "coming on the scene" is not to be but a barren assurance that it is better than the phenomenal forms of knowing, the latter must be criticized. Yet how can any standard for criticism justify itself, when science has not yet come on the scene ? By these questions, Hegel defines his enterprise of the critique of the forms of thought by the actions of thought itself, which will overcome the Kantian critique of cognition as an "instrument" of knowledge.

The standard for criticism, says Hegel, need not be brought in through an external reflection by the philosopher. It is implicit in the very nature of consciousness itself. For consciousness "distinguishes from itself something, to which at the same time it relates itself" ; or "there is something *for* consciousness." [17] This aspect of there being something "for" it, consciousness calls its "knowledge." But as against this "Being-for-other" of the object, consciousness distinguishes "Being-in-itself." In this way what is "related" to consciousness is "distinguished" from its knowledge and posited by consciousness as "outside" the relation.[18] In contrast to what it calls its "knowledge," consciousness calls the "in-itself" the "truth." But the distinction just made falls inside consciousness itself : both moments, the "in-itself" and the "for-other," are at once contained in the knowledge we are examining. Hence in what consciousness itself terms "the in-itself or truth," we have the standard it itself sets up, and by which it "tests and examines itself."

In this self-examination of consciousness, should its "knowledge" not correspond with its "object," consciousness must evidently alter its knowledge. But in consciousness's altering of its knowledge, the object also is altered, for the knowledge "was essentially a knowledge of the object." Consciousness hereby comes to find out that "what formerly to it was the in-itself is not in itself, or that it was in itself only *for consciousness.*" In this way the standard for examining is itself altered, for that whose criterion this standard was to be, "does not hold its ground in

---

[17] *Phen.* 139. See Kenley R. Dove, "Hegel's Phenomenological Method," *Review of Metaphysics*, vol. xxiii, no. 4, June 1970, pp. 617 ff.

[18] Why consciousness claims its knowledge refers to an "in itself" is here not explained; *that* it does so is simply presupposed. The presupposition will only be overcome in the sciences of Subjective Spirit. (See above, Preface, p. X; and below, pp. 159 ff.)

the course of the examination." The examination becomes not only an examination of knowledge "but also of the criterion used in the examining."

In this brief survey of Hegel's method in the *Phenomenology* of 1807, we see how the Socratic principle of self-examination has been converted by Hegel into a dialectic of the subject-object relation under the inspiration of the Kantian enterprise of critique. The slogan of consciousness in the course of its movement through the succession of phenomenological shapes may be taken as the characteristic Socratic remark: Come let us examine this word of ours.[19] Consciousness by its nature pronounces upon its object, and then by its nature pronounces upon its pronouncement. It is Hegel's claim that in this self-examination alone lies the ascent to the philosophic standpoint in a necessary and demonstrable sequence.

The impetus of consciousness's movement, Hegel purports to show, derives from the nature of consciousness itself as, on the one hand, "consciousness of the object," and on the other, "consciousness of itself": consciousness of what "to it is true" and consciousness of "its knowing of that truth." [20] Because of this "twofoldness" (*Zweideutigkeit*) in identity that lies at the heart of its own nature, says Hegel, consciousness is ever driven to transcend itself, ever destined to suffer violence at its own hands and destroy its limited satisfaction, until it has

traversed the series of its own forms, like stages appointed for it by its own nature, that it may possess the clearness of spiritual life, when, through complete experience of its own self, it arrives at the knowledge of what it is in itself.[21]

The "clearness of its spiritual life" unfolds as the sciences proper of Spirit, the encyclopedic system of philosophic sciences, including the sciences of Subjective Spirit.

Our brief glimpse into the *Phenomenology* of 1807 is not meant as a discussion of the work in its own right, but rather to see how Hegel purports to gain access to the realm of Subjective Spirit so as to be able to write a speculative doctrine of the soul. Hegel's "immanent" procedure may be illustrated by way of contrast with the empirical approach already criticized.[22] In the phenomenological exposition of the "perceiving consciousness," Hegel does not ask about how things come to be regarded as subsisting independently of us in the first place, as Hume had asked: "What causes induce us to believe in the existence

[19] *Euthyphro* 7A.
[20] *Phen.* 141.
[21] *Phen.* 135.
[22] See above, pp. 7 ff.

of body? [23] Since the phenomenological demonstration starts out with
the "natural consciousness," the "independence" of the object is accepted
as given in consciousness's own claim to a knowledge of the object.
Though bracketed as it were in the very notion of the phenomenological
enterprise, the claim is not criticized from an external vantage point.
Rather the claim is taken on its face and shown to lead through contradiction to a higher kind of claim and a higher shape (*Gestalt*) of consciousness until—with the attainment of the scientific consciousness—the claim
turns out to understand itself and thereby to resolve itself.[24] Only at this
point has there emerged the possibility for a genuine science of human
nature that Hume and others attempted by asking about the "origin of
ideas" and thereby presupposing the relation of externality to the mind
as a "prefound existent confronting it." [25]

The philosophic consciousness that has emerged in the phenomenological demonstration has been "liberated" from the subject-object antithesis,
and in the first instance sets about in a science of logic to demonstrate
the pure forms of the "logical Idea" that are at once determinations
of subject and object. Then, in the concrete sciences of nature (*Naturphilosophie*), the movement of nature "according to its Idea" is shown
to lead to Spirit proper as nature's "truth." [26] Finally in the realm of
Subjective Spirit, philosophic science shows how the object as an independently subsisting "in itself" first "emerges" through the subject's own act
of "self-dividing." [27] Since the scientific standpoint has been achieved
precisely through a critique of consciousness's notion of the "in itself"
as an absolute "other," the sciences of Subjective Spirit need no longer
speak, like empirical psychology, in terms of "impressions" on the mind,
or view consciousness's content as an "effect" of external causation.

[23] *A Treatise of Human Nature*, ed. L. A. Selby-Bigge (Oxford, 1965), p. 187.

[24] If we may borrow a phrase from Kant, consciousness's movement is shown by
Hegel "as step by step it comes to apprehend its own requirements." (*CPR* B 618)

[25] See above, p. 9. Josiah Royce notes that in any psychological explanation in
terms of a "natural history of cognition," one "presupposes an environment whose
facts already have a recognized form of existence" as well as "a conscious process
as an existent fact, whose development is to be described." The basis of one's
description "is then the principle that the external facts, which are supposed directly
or indirectly to determine the conscious process, arouse responses in the organism
of the being whose consciousness is in question." (*The World and the Individual*,
2 vols., Dover, New York, 1959, vol. 2, pp. 30-31) It is such presuppositions that
Hegel's approach is designed to overcome.

[26] See below, pp. 41 ff.

[27] See below, pp. 142 ff.

Here we must note that Hegel's speculative claim to overcome external reflection and resolve the problem of "access" is, and in principle must be, "circular." The sequence and necessity of the demonstration in the *Phenomenology* is of course the doing of the philosopher, who organizes "the series of experiences through which consciousness passes" into "a scientifically constituted sequence." [28] While the necessity of the advance lies in the nature of consciousness, this necessity is not known to consciousness itself while it is "in the grip of experience." [29] Its becoming known to consciousness occurs only at the end of the movement,[30] the course of which has been to bring forth the philosopher who has organized consciousness's experience into "the science of the experience of consciousness." [31]

It is evident that in this claim of demonstration lies the presupposition that the demonstrator has come on the scene who can perform it.[32] In the concept itself of the demonstration lies the necessary circularity that the philosophic consciousness selects, presents, and arranges the *Gestalten* of consciousness so that they constitute the necessary advance toward the emergence of the philosophic consciousness. As we have already seen, Hegel indirectly justifies his method by his critique of those thinkers from Descartes to Fichte, whose philosophizing begins with a principle of consciousness. To these thinkers Hegel says : Unless such a looking into consciousness is already an "educated" looking, its "findings" will be merely subjective and contingent.[33] But whence arises the "education" ?

[28] *Phen.* 143; see also *Phen.* 790-791.

[29] *Phen.* 144.

[30] *Phen.* 145.

[31] For a discussion of problems concerning the relation of the philosopher to the experiencing consciousness, see Dove, *op. cit.*, pp. 627 ff.

[32] In the first edition of the *Enzyklopädie* (1817), Hegel notes the main obstacles to the attainment of the scientific standpoint as consisting in the presupposition of the fixed opposition of subject and object in consciousness (par. 35). Referring to his earlier work of 1807, he goes on to say: "I have dealt earlier with the Phenomenology of Spirit, the scientific history of consciousness, as having the import of the first part of philosophy, since it would precede pure science as yielding its notion. At the same time, however, consciousness and its history, like every other philosophic science, is not an absolute beginning but rather a link in the circle of philosophy." (*Sämtliche Werke, Jubiläumsausgabe in zwanzig Bänden,* ed. Hermann Glockner, bd. vi., Stuttgart 1956, p. 48) I understand Hegel to mean here that the 1807 work is to be viewed in part within a historical context; but the necessity —within the nature of Spirit—for the subject-object problematic of the 1807 work can only be demonstrated within the sciences proper of Spirit.

[33] *L* 134.

Hegel's answer lies in the whole course of the *Phenomenology*. That a necessary movement of consciousness will produce the philosopher, who will then turn around and demonstrate the necessity of his own emergence, cannot be proven beforehand but only in the process itself.[34] The demonstration is admittedly and in principle circular, for it cannot be otherwise. Circularity is as essential to the speculative method as Spirit's "closing together" with itself is essential to the nature of Spirit.[35]

The enterprise of the *Phenomenology,* however, involves a circularity in another sense. For the circle of the speculative sciences to be complete, it must encompass the whole system of science, to which the *Phenomenology* is but the introduction. But what about the introduction itself ? In the first place, if the Phenomenology is to be a demonstration through "experience" of transcendental philosophy's supreme insight that ego is Notion, such a demonstration stands on one leg until there is a demonstration of the Notion in logic, the science of "the pure Notion that relates itself only to itself." [36] But the task must even yet await completion until the philosopher's role in presenting the *Gestalten* of consciousness is justified within the accomplished system. Here we find that the science of Phenomenology takes its place in the sequence of the philosophic sciences of nature and Spirit. Now the problem is no longer one of access to the kingly realm, for the thinker is in the kingly realm. In the system proper the science of Phenomenology plays its assigned role as one of the sciences of Subjective Spirit: the science of consciousness.[37] But the concrete nature of consciousness in its *Zweideutigkeit* [38] is no longer presupposed (as in the *Phenomenology* of 1807) but demonstrated in the preceding science of Anthropology.[39]

---

[34] *L* 58.

[35] *Phen.* 81; *L* 28; *SL* 842.

[36] *SL* 842.

[37] We may note here that within Subjective Spirit, Phenomenology is not said to be a science of experience like the 1807 work. The term "experience" occurs in the Phenomenology of the *Enzyklopädie* only in a polemical context (see *PhM* 161-162).

[38] See above, p. 27.

[39] The above account does not seek to solve all the problems of the relation of the *Phenomenology* of 1807 to the system but to understand the characterization of the 1807 work as the "deduction" of "the notion of pure science" (*SL* 49); and of the science of Phenomenology as "a science which stands midway between the sciences of natural Spirit and Spirit as such." (*SL* 781) See Fulda, *op. cit.,* pp. 105 ff. for a fuller discussion of the problem of the relation of the 1807 work to the encyclopedic system.

An important outcome of the *Phenomenology* of 1807 for the problem of self-knowledge is the rejection of the Critical philosophy's denial of a knowledge of the ego as inaccessible to experience. Here we must note a difference between the Kantian concept of experience and experience conceived phenomenologically by Hegel. Since, for Kant, experience means "a knowledge which determines an object through perceptions," [40] the result for a knowledge of the self cannot be other than what Hume reports in "tracing the impression" : "I never can catch *myself*" as a pure self. But the immanent critique of consciousness, Hegel claims, shows not that knowledge is limited to sense experience, but rather that consciousness's claim to the knowledge of sensuous reality proves to have its truth and ground in a knowledge of the nonsensuous, including consciousness of self. Hereby "experience" acquires the meaning of the universal relation of consciousness and its object, a relation of which sense experience of an external object is but a particular case.[41]

In the sections in the *Phenomenology* on consciousness, the sense consciousness's certainty of the singular "this" is shown to pass over into the conditioned universal of the perceiving consciousness's "thing of many properties," and the unconditioned universal of the understanding's "law of force." At this point Hegel has purportedly passed beyond the Critical Philosophy's concept of experience as sense experience, as well as the Kantian concept of knowledge as limited to possible sense experience. But the very course of the movement has constituted at the same time a new demonstration of self-consciousness, in which the ego need no longer be a "transcendental x" of which it is impossible to obtain any knowledge.

At the point in consciousness's comparison of its knowledge and its object where the object is no longer a sensuous "other" but the "law of force," the object is revealed to be the understanding's own work of "explanation." [42] Consciousness's knowing of its object as an "other"

---

[40] *CPR* B 218. Experience is "knowledge of the objects of the senses interconnected by universal laws." (*Foundations of the Metaphysics of Morals*, trans. L. White Beck, Chicago, 1950, p. 110)

[41] Experience "is called this very process by which the immediate, the unexperienced, i.e. the abstract—whether it be in the form of sense or of a bare thought—externalizes itself, and then comes back to itself from this state of estrangement, and by so doing is at length set forth in its concrete nature and real truth, and becomes too a possession of consciousness." (*Phen.* 96)

[42] *Phen.* 200 ff.

has turned out to be in truth its knowing of itself, and consciousness has become self-consciousness.

Consciousness is for itself (*für sich selbst*), it is a distinguishing of what is undinstinguished, it is self-consciousness. I distinguish myself from myself; and therein I am immediately aware that this that is distinguished from me is not distinguished. I, the selfsame being, thrust myself away from myself; but this which is distinguished, which is set up as unlike me, is immediately on its being distinguished no distinction for me.[43]

Hereby the principle of self-consciousness, which in Kant was enunciated by the philosopher in the form of an analytic proposition,[44] and which in Fichte formed a beginning in the mere abstract self-certainty of the ego, has been demonstrated in the movement of "experience" to be the necessary ground and truth of consciousness itself.[45]

In knowing the realm of appearance as a "play of forces" in its "absolutely universal moments and in the process of those moments," consciousness has grasped the truth of the supersensible world as that "inner region" lying beyond the curtain of appearances. The supersensible world has shown itself to be "infinitude, this absolute unrest of pure self-movement" which "is itself and its opposite in a single unity" ; it is distinction as "inner distinction." [46] But in this way the object of consciousness is experienced as nothing other than "absolute Notion." In thus experiencing its object as its own activity and as Notion, consciousness itself has emerged as Notion. The internal self-distinguishing of the object is now implicitly one with the internal self-distinguishing of the subject, and subjectivity as "self-consciousness" now moves toward establishing this identity "for itself." This it achieves on succeeding levels of self-consciousness, reason, and Spirit, its endeavor culminating in philosophic thinking generally and absolute idealism in particular, wherein Spirit knows itself unconditionally as Spirit.

With the emergence of the philosophic consciousness, the *Phenomenology* of 1807, as the "science of the ways in which knowledge appears," has been completed. According to Hegel's claim, which we need not seek to assess, the movement comprises the "comprehended organization" [47] of the "entire world of conscious life in its necessity." [48] Having

---

[43] *Phen.* 211.
[44] *CPR* B 135.
[45] *Phen.* 211-12.
[46] *Phen.* 208.
[47] *Phen.* 808.
[48] *Phen.* 95.

laid aside its "semblance of being hampered with what is foreign to it," consciousness has reached the position where appearance has become identified with essence.[49] At this point, says Hegel, Spirit "descends into the depths of its own being" and brings forth philosophic science.

As an introduction to philosophic science, and in the first instance logic, the *Phenomenology* of 1807 demonstrates, in the form of the "experience" of consciousness, the speculative comprehension of truth as identity of "substance" and "subject." [50] The "pure essentialities" that are to be developed in logical science are at once determinations of Being and thought.[51] By way of an immanent critique of cognition designed to overcome the Critical Philosophy's approach of external reflection, the *Phenomenology* has shown that the side of ego, subjectivity, the "for itself"—and the side of Being, objectivity, the "in itself"—alike present the movement of inner self-differentiation of Notion.[52] Henceforward in the pure philosophic sciences the movement of thought in demonstration is no longer a movement of "experience," i.e., no longer in "shapes of consciousness," but rather in "notions" and as "the organic self-grounded movement of these notions." [53] The science which first develops the forms of thought in the "simpleness of knowing" is logic.

We have now briefly seen the role of the *Phenomenology* of 1807 as the pathway to science. But in fact we have been shown more than a pathway.

---

[49] *Phen.* 145. If Hegel's demonstration is to be accepted, then he has made the transition—within the medium of experience viewed phenomenologically—from what Kant called the "heteronomy of efficient causes" in the sensible realm of appearances to the "autonomy" of causality through freedom in the supersensible realm of noumena. Such a transition, Kant held, was impossible for theoretical knowledge, even of a knowledge of man. (See *CPR* A 550 = B 578)

[50] *Phen.* 80, 86.

[51] "Being is entirely mediated; it is a substantial content that is likewise directly in the possession of the ego, has the character of self, is Notion." (*Phen.* 97) In the words of Hyppolite, the *Phenomenology* of 1807 has made possible "une spiritualisation de la logique" (*op. cit.* vol. II, pp. 554 ff.)

[52] *SL* 585.

[53] "While in the Phenomenology of Spirit each moment is the distinction of knowledge and truth, and is the process in which that distinction is sublated, science does not contain this distinction and its sublation. Rather, since each moment has the form of the Notion, it unites the objective form of truth and the knowing of self in immediate unity. Each moment does not appear as the process of passing back and forth from consciousness or representation to self-consciousness and conversely: on the contrary, the moment's pure shape, liberated from its mode of appearance in consciousness—the pure Notion and its further development—depends solely on its pure determination." (*Phen.* 805-806)

Within the realm of experience, where each turn in the road came unexpected, the traveler nevertheless received a foretaste of what he would find in the kingly realm. As an example of the speculative method in the realm of consciousness, Hegel tells us, the *Phenomenology* has brought forward the simple insight necessary for "scientific progress" : the recognition of the logical principle "that the negative is just as much positive." [54] In the 1807 work we witness a succession of shapes of consciousness where each "has for its result its own negation—and so passes into a higher form." We thus have the supremely important principle that "what is self-contradictory does not resolve itself into a nullity" but is a "negation of a specific subject matter" and thus a "specific negation" and "has a content." [55] The new notion that emerges in this movement is

higher and richer than its predecessor; for it is richer by the negation or opposite of the latter, therefore contains it, but also something more, and is the unity of itself and its opposite.[56]

The movement of *Aufheben* (sublation) that Hegel here describes in the experience of consciousness is nothing other than the pure movement of Notion, on whose succession of forms "in this pure ether of its life" the science of logic itself "has broadly to be constructed." Such a logic has never been developed before and is essentially different from "formal thinking" which "lays down for its principle that contradiction is unthinkable." [57] In truth, says Hegel, "the thinking of contradiction is the essential moment of the Notion," and for this reason speculative logic alone provides the *begreifendes Denken* that can grasp the unity of opposites constituting Spirit in its notion.

In a more restricted sense, "the speculative" is one of the three moments into which "the logical" is divisible from the point of view of form.[58] The first moment is that of thought as "understanding," by which Hegel means all formalistic thinking that takes its finite determinations as fixed in their distinctions from one another. In clinging to its rigid identities, understanding severs truth from life and leaves itself with neither.[59] When carried to their extremes, the distinctions of under-

---

[54] *SL* 54.
[55] *Ibid.*
[56] *Ibid.*
[57] *SL* 835.
[58] *L* 143 ff.
[59] For this formal thinking, life must remain an "absolute contradiction" and an "incomprehensible mystery." (*SL* 763) "It is said that contradiction is unthinkable;

standing veer around into their opposites. Dialectic, the second moment of thought, is this sublation of the fixed determinations through their own opposition. The result of dialectic thus seems merely negative, the sceptical dissolution of all fixed determinations. But the third moment, the speculative, grasps their unity in opposition, and brings forth the positive truth implicit in their negative dissolution.

Dialectic reveals the formalism of the analytic understanding's external reflection but it is more than a tool of critique. Dialectic, Hegel maintains, expresses at once the essential movement of Spirit and the living process of reality.[60] In exhibiting the nature of the finite "to suppress itself and put itself aside," dialectic "constitutes the life and soul of scientific progress, the principle which alone gives immanent connection to the content of science."[61]

The ceaseless passage of the finite into its opposite is not the ultimate truth, and dialectical thinking, which expresses the moment of not-Being in all finitude, is not the highest form of thinking. The passing of every "something" into its "other" proves to be the Notion's own inner self-distinguishing and return to identity with itself, and thereby the inherent truth of both the something and its other.[62] This Being-for-self of Notion in all its determinations is the meaning of "ideality," "negation of negation," the "true infinity" that is not separated from the finite but includes it as a moment of itself. It is pure self-activity, an absolute movement

but the fact is that in the pain of a living being it is even an actual existence." (SL 770; see also PhN 274; PhR 261-262) For Kant too life as "internal purposiveness" cannot be grasped by the categories of understanding (which do not proceed beyond mechanism) but only by the aesthetic and teleological judgement. But the principle of internal self-organization, which we obtain by analogy with our own free action, can be employed only "regulatively," not "constitutively" for a knowledge of nature, and by our "reflective" and not our "determinant" judgment: i.e., purposiveness is only valid for the subjective constitution of our faculties of cognition. (See CJ 222 ff.)

[60] "Reflection," says Hegel, is initially "that movement out beyond the isolated predicate of a thing which gives it some reference, and brings out its relativity, while still in other respects leaving it its isolated validity." But "dialectic" shows "the indwelling tendency outwards by which the onesidedness and limitation of understanding is seen in its true light, and shown to be the negation of them." (L 147)

[61] L 147; see also SL 835, 56. "The Idea itself is the dialectic which for ever divides and distinguishes the self-identical from the differentiated, the subjective from the objective, the finite from the infinite, soul from body. Only on these terms is it an eternal creation, eternal vitality, and eternal Spirit." (L 356)

[62] L 176 ff.; SL 116 ff.

that is as much a state of unbroken calm. We can perhaps do no better to illustrate "the speculative" in logic than to quote Hegel's vibrant passage from the *Phenomenology* on "life" :

This simple infinity, or the absolute Notion, may be called the simple essence of life, the soul of the world, the universal blood, which courses everywhere, and whose flow is neither disturbed nor checked by any obstructing distinction, but is itself every distinction that arises, as well as that into which all distinctions are dissolved; pulsating within itself, but ever motionless, shaken to its depths, but still at rest. It is self-identical, for the distinctions are tautological; they are distinctions that are none. This self-identical essence stands, therefore, in relation solely to itself. *To itself*; which means this is an other, to which the relation points; and *relation to itself* is, more strictly, breaking asunder; in other words, that very self-identity is internal distinction.[63]

In the new speculative logic that makes possible such a comprehension of "life" scientifically, Hegel claims, man in his thought is for the first time equipped to fulfill the command Know Thyself as an even higher kind of life, that of free Spirit. Although Kant in his doctrine of the teleological judgment had made a beginning toward grasping the genuinely spiritual process of life and mind, he did not go on to develop the categories necessary for a thinking of these highest forms of spirituality. Hegel in his science of logic claims to show the emergence of Notion from Being and Essence, whose categories include those of the traditional metaphysics as well as the Kantian transcendental philosophy.[64] As the culmination of the demonstration of Essence, the "relation of substantiality" passes over into the "subjectivity" of Notion as its "foundation and truth." [65] The categories of "objectivity" and "necessity" are hereby shown to have their ground in "subjectivity" and "freedom." In this way, Hegel claims, the Kantian antithesis of appearance and thing-in-itself, which had been overcome phenomenologically,[66] is now overcome in the strictly logical realm. The logical ground has been prepared for that genuine transition from nature to free mind which Kant had sought in his third great critique.[67]

In its demonstration of the concrete sciences of Spirit, Hegel tells us, the speculative method combines analysis and synthesis—not, how-

---

[63] *Phen.* 208.

[64] *SL* 63-64.

[65] *SL* 580, 577, 581-582. For a brief discussion of the "transition to subjective Notion," with certain references to Kant, see Mure, *A Study of Hegel's Logic, op. cit.,* pp. 151-156.

[66] See above, p. 33.

[67] See *CJ* 12, 32-34.

ever, in "bare juxtaposition or mere alternating employment" [68] but as
the inner self-differentiating of Notion, a movement at once of self-exter-
nalization and inwardization.[69] Inasmuch as every "unfolding" is at the
same time a further inward concentration, the movement holds "merged
within itself" the two moments of analysis and synthesis.[70] For this
reason, in the sciences of Subjective Spirit such determinations as
sensation, imagination, memory, do not appear as "parts," "faculties",
or "forces," but as "moments" of Spirit, each of which at the same time
is a "definition" of Spirit in its wholeness, just as in the science of logic
each succeeding determination of the logical Idea "is only a closer
determination and truer definition of the Absolute." [71] Since each
determination arises out of its predecessor as a further concretization,
the movement is a progressive enrichment,[72] but not in the mere sense of
accretion. Each step in the advance from the "beginning" is at the
same time a "getting back nearer to it," so that the apparently two
processes of "retrogressive grounding of the beginning" and its "progressive further determining of it" in fact "coincide and are the same." [73]
It is in this sense of the inherent identity of *arche* and *telos* within the
self-actualization of Spirit that Hegel will seek to rekindle the Aristotelian
speculative flame in the sciences of Subjective Spirit.

---

[68] *L* 376.

[69] "Each new stage of forthgoing (*Aüssersichgehen*), that is, of further deter-
mination, is also a withdrawal inwards (*In-sich-gehen*); and the greater extension
(*Ausdehnung*) is equally higher intensity." (*SL* 840-841; see also *Phen.* 806-808;
HPh I, 28)

[70] *L* 376; *SL* 830.

[71] *L* 162.

[72] *SL* 840.

[73] *SL* 841. In the speculative movement of the Notion, "advance is a retreat into
the ground, to what is primary and true, on which depends and, in fact, from which
originates, that with which the beginning is made." (*SL* 71)

CHAPTER THREE

THE NOTION OF SUBJECTIVE SPIRIT

Having seen how Hegel poses the problem of self-knowledge and how he proposes to resolve it by a new logic and a new philosophical method, we must now focus on his notion of Subjective Spirit within the perspective of his total system of science. In introducing the Philosophy of Spirit, we recall, Hegel said that the command Know Thyself comes to man from his own inner oracle that is at the same time the voice of divinity. The problem of the "relation" of the divine Spirit's eternal self-knowing to man's coming to know himself as Spirit concerns the relation of the eternal "logical Idea" to the concrete sciences of nature and Spirit.

We have seen that the *Phenomenology* of 1807 showed the ego is Notion and the natural consciousness develops to the philosophic consciousness that knows itself as Notion. From this "absolute" standpoint, the science of logic demonstrates the forms of the Notion as "pure essentialities" that are at once determinations of Being and thought. In principle the question can no longer be asked as to how thinking attains to Being.[1] But while logic presents the categories as forms of the Notion and "thinking actuality" (*denkende Wirklichkeit*), it does not present them as concrete shapes of nature and Spirit. With regard to Spirit, for example, Hegel tells us that the logic presents Spirit in its "logical Idea," wherein ego is "immediately the free Notion... that in its judgement (*Urteil*) is itself the object, *the Notion as its Idea.*"[2] Hence the logical Idea of Spirit does not have "to watch Spirit progressing through its entanglement with nature, with immediate determinateness and material things, or with pictorial thinking." This progress of concrete Spirit is dealt with in the sciences of Anthropology, Phenomenology, and Psychology, which

---

[1] Such a question is possible only *within* the problematic of consciousness and its opposition of subject and object.

[2] *SL* 782.

comprise the doctrine of Subjective Spirit, as well as the sciences of Objective Spirit, which includes History as the development of Spirit in time. In contrast to these concrete sciences, the science of the logical Idea may be described in its content as "the exposition of God as he is in his eternal essence before the creation of nature and a finite Spirit." [3]

Logic, therefore, is the science of the "divine Notion," whereas the sciences of man's coming to know himself as Spirit comprise the sciences that show Spirit in its finite forms wherein it relates itself to its content as an "other." But the movement shown by these sciences proves to be the very process whereby Spirit "liberates itself" from its finite forms and "goes on to grasp the truth of itself, which is infinite Spirit." [4] Man's coming to know himself as infinite Spirit, however, means his attainment to philosophic knowledge, which includes the science of logic or the "divine Notion" itself. Once again then we see the total system as a circle in which the science of logic can just as well be "the last science" as the "first science, out of which the Idea first passes over into nature." [5]

While the logical Idea of Spirit does not require "to watch Spirit" in the process of overcoming its "entanglement" in nature, the notion of the logical Idea implies no total separation from nature and concrete Spirit. A mere glance at some of the highest categories of the logic—e.g., Mechanism, Chemism, Teleology, Life, Cognition—is sufficient to show this is so. In the same way, while the sciences of nature and concrete Spirit do not look to the science of logic as to a blueprint,[6] nevertheless as philosophic sciences that need to comprehend their content in notions they are indebted to logic for the pure forms of the Notion. Every philosophic comprehension of a concrete subject matter will be according to its logical Idea.[7] Such comprehension is made possible by the Notion, whose pure forms belong to the science of logic but which nevertheless are the indwelling forms of the concrete subject matter itself. To be sure, the demonstration of the logical Idea of Spirit is different from the demonstration of the shapes of Spirit in the concrete sciences. Thus the

---

[3] *SL* 50. For definitions of the logic in nonmetaphorical terms, see, for example, *SL* 825, 843.

[4] *SL* 782.

[5] *Ibid.*; see also *SL* 842 and *PhM* 313.

[6] See *SL* 592.

[7] Concerning the "eternal life of nature," Hegel says, "the Idea displays itself in each sphere so far as it can within the finitude of that sphere, just as each drop of water provides an image of the sun." (*PhN* 27)

science of logic demonstrates "the Idea of life"; the science of Organics within the Philosophy of Nature deals with life in its actual forms in nature.[8] The "Idea of cognition" is demonstrated in terms of analysis and synthesis, definition, theorem, etc., whereas the "process of cognition" in the sciences of Subjective Spirit demonstrates how finite subjectivity raises itself to thinking intelligence through the stages of sensation, intuition, imagination, and memory.

In demonstrating the forms of the Notion in the concrete sciences of nature and Spirit, the philosopher must rely heavily on the results of empirical investigation. Thus the Philosophy of Nature, says Hegel, "presupposes and is conditioned by empirical physics," [9] and in the progress of philosophical knowledge generally "we must not only give an account of the object *as determined by its notion*, but we must also name the *empirical* appearance corresponding to it, and we must show that the appearance does, in fact, correspond to its notion." But, Hegel adds, this is not an appeal to experience for the "necessity" of the content. Once again to cite an example: On every level of finite subjectivity the logical category of the "negative" or "spurious" infinity will make its appearance.[10] The presence of this category will mark a particular content as such where the sublation of a contradiction is but the beginning of a fresh one, and so on *ad infinitum*.[11] According to Hegel, however, this is neither an importing of a logical category into the subject matter by an external reflection, nor is it merely a generalization based on "experiences." Thus the "negative infinity" of "desire," where each satisfaction becomes the occasion for the awakening of another desire, is essential to the philosophic demonstration of this moment of Subjective Spirit and at the same time immanent in the *Sache selbst*.[12] It is in this sense that the speculative method "takes the determinate element from its own subject matter, since it is itself that subject matter's immanent principle and soul." [13]

---

[8] In Philosophy of Nature, life is dealt with "as projected into the *externality of existence* and having its *condition* in inorganic nature, and where the moments of the Idea are a multiplicity of actual formations." In logic the moments of the Idea of life "do not receive the shape of external actuality but remain enclosed within the form of the Notion." (*SL* 762)

[9] *PhN* 6. See also *L* 13; 16; *HPh* III, 176.

[10] See *SL* 137 ff.; *L* 174 ff.

[11] See below, p. 45, n. 41.

[12] *PhM* 169.

[13] *SL* 830.

Having attained to the standpoint of philosophic science as a result of the movement of experience of consciousness (the *Phenomenology* of 1807), and having developed the absolute method of science in the logic, the philosopher's "demonstrating" of the movement of Spirit in the concrete sciences is at the same time but a "looking on." Without introjecting his preconceptions or any material extraneous to the *Sache selbst,* the philosopher allows the object of investigation to unfold its determinations out of the necessity of its own inner process according to its notion.[14]

Our subject matter is now "concrete" Spirit, and its investigation has the sciences of nature, as well as the logic, as its "presupposition." [15] The Philosophy of Spirit has the Philosophy of Nature as its "direct" and the logic as its "mediate" predecessor in the system of philosophic sciences. The Philosophy of Nature must therefore have as its "end result" the proof of the necessity of the notion of Spirit: that Spirit is the "truth and final goal" of nature.[16]

Nature, like Spirit, Hegel holds, is rational, divine, a "temple of God" and a manifestation of the eternal Idea.[17] In nature, however, the Idea appears in the medium of the *partes extra partes* or "asunderness" (*Aussereinandersein*).[18] Nature's expressions in space and time exhibit the aspect of a "this-besides-this" (*Dieses neben Diesem*), a this after this. Not only does nature present "to us" this character of externality, says Hegel, but nature is "external to itself." [19] For this reason nature is a realm of external necessity and contingency rather than freedom.[20] The forms in which nature unfolds are existences more or less independent of one another, more or less indifferent to one another. It is this that marks

---

[14] *PhM 5;* see also above, p. 20.

[15] *PhM 8.*

[16] *PhN 24.* In terms of the three moments of the Notion, the pure logical Idea is the "immediate, simple Being-within-self" of the Idea; nature is the "Being-outside-self" of the Idea; Spirit is the sublation of this "Being-other" and the Idea's "turning back into itself from its other and its being that very return." (*PhM 9*) For Kant this would be a running "riot into the transcendent." (*CPrR 59*) Nevertheless Kant sees man "as subject of morality" as the "ultimate purpose of nature" (*CJ 279* ff.), though such a principle can play no "constitutive" role for theoretical knowledge.

[17] *PhN 13; PhM 9.*

[18] *PhN 13-14; PhM 9; FPhG 26.*

[19] For Hegel there is no distinction, equivalent to that in Kant, between nature as "appearance" for us and as it is "in itself."

[20] *PhN 17.*

nature as reality." [21] The bodies of the solar system, for example, though attracted by the sun, have the appearance of existences independent of the sun and of each other. This "contradiction," as Hegel terms it, is exhibited in their movement around the sun.[22]

Thus although contradiction, as we saw,[23] is regarded by Hegel as in the highest degree characteristic of Spirit, it is no less essential to nature. In nature, however, the media of asunderness (space and time) make for a different kind of contradiction and a different form of self-externality than we shall encounter in the realm of Spirit. Indeed one of the problems for our investigation of Spirit, Hegel warns us, is that, unlike the processes of formation in the physical realm,[24] the stages of mental development do not "remain behind as particular existences" but are sublated as "moments" in the higher stage. Hence in the earlier phases of our study of the soul, we shall sometimes have to "anticipate" a content that will appear in its full concreteness only later in the development.[25]

The emergence of Spirit, says Hegel, is to be viewed only in one aspect as a "result" of nature's development. In a deeper sense Spirit is its own bringing itself forth out of nature, which Spirit has created as "Spirit's own presupposition." [26] Thus the transition from nature to Spirit is no passing over of a "something" to an "other" but a return of Spirit to itself. Hence there can be no absolute gap between the two realms. The animal, the plant, even in some measure the forms of inanimate nature display the "self-identity in difference" of Notion. It is for this reason that nature is divine and rational. But the highest expression of Notion in which it comes to its own soul and essence, is Spirit.[27]

In life, which foreshadows the inwardness of Spirit proper, nature as the self-external "overpasses itself." The negative self-relation of Notion in life is the individual organism insofar as it is its own self-process and

---

[21] *FPhG* 26. The truth of reality (*Realität*) is ideality, which is the basic category of mind. (*L* 180; see below, p. 106)

[22] *PhM* 9. Kant, says Hegel, was willing to attribute contradiction to reason, but this "could not be allowed to mar the essence of the world"; but Kant here showed "an excess of tenderness for the things of the world." (*L* 98)

[23] See above, p. 7.

[24] *PhN* 278.

[25] *PhM* 8.

[26] *PhN* 444. See also the meaning of "beginning" and "end," above, p. 37.

[27] *PhN* 13.

end (*Selbstzweck*), and preserves itself as selfsame in its "inorganic nature" as its "other." [28] Life as Idea, says Hegel, is

the movement of itself whereby it first constitutes itself subject, converts *itself* into its other... gives itself the form of object in order to return into itself and to be the accomplished return-into-self.[29]

For this reason Hegel speaks of a "plant subjectivity" as Aristotle spoke of the vegetable soul.

In the plant we see a center flowing forth into a periphery—a differentiatedness developing outwardly from within—and hence we can ascribe to the plant an "urge" (*Trieb*).[30] The plant subjectivity, however, does not yet display the infinite form of the Being-for-self of Spirit but "only immediate, formal Being-for-self, not yet the genuine infinity." [31] In the emergence of the whole as an articulation process of its members, each member is the whole as its "repetition." The movement presents the aspect of a "coming-outside-self" and a "falling apart" into several individuals that remain in incomplete subordination to the vegetable subjectivity.[32]

The animal life presents a higher form of inwardness, a higher form of subjectivity, and hence a higher form of the Notion than the plant. The animal, says Hegel, "has freedom of *self-movement* because its subjectivity is, like light, ideality freed from gravity, a free time which, as removed from the real externality, *spontaneously determines its place*." [33] The animal possesses voice, "for its *subjectivity* as *real* ideality

---

[28] *PhN* 377; *L* 359-360; *SL* 769 ff.; *Phen.* 208, 221 ff.; see also above, p. 36.

[29] *PhN* 275. Cf. Kant's notion of an "organized being" (*CJ* 219 ff.). Since "purposiveness" in nature, according to Kant, exceeds our "legitimate" cognition of nature as mechanism, life can be grasped only by analogy with our own purposiveness, and teleology is justified only from our subjective point of view and not for nature itself.

[30] *PhM* 9.

[31] *PhN* 303.

[32] *PhN* 303 ff.; *PhM* 10. The "return-into-self" of the plant in its assimilation process "does not have for result the *self* as inner, subjective universality over against externality, does not result in self-feeling (*Selbstgefühl*). Rather it is the plant drawn out of itself by light, by its self which is external to it, and climbs toward it, ramifying into a plurality of individuals." (*PhN* 336; see also *PhN* 276)

[33] *PhN* 352-353. The whole movement in Hegel's *Naturphilosophie* from physical materiality through plant and animal organism to the "light" of consciousness can virtually be traced through the treatment of the notion of light. (See below, pp. 87, 160)

(soul), dominates the abstract ideality of time and space and displays its self-movement as a free vibration *within* itself." The asunderness of spatial existence "has no truth for the soul." [34] As sentient, the animal is the feeling-unity of itself throughout all its members, and thereby the omnipresent subjectivity in every point of its corporeality (*Leiblichkeit*).[35] The animal organism feels within itself a "lack" (*Mangel*) and the "urge" to get rid of it, which is thus "positive self-relation" in the face of "this its negative." [36] For these reasons, according to Hegel, sentient organism emerges as the highest form of the Notion within the realm of nature, and the inner truth of the Being-outside-self of the physical realm as such.

Yet in the animal this sublation of the *Aussereinandersein* of nature is one that does not proceed beyond the immediacy of sense singularity. The singular animal life is only universal in the genus (*Gattung*) and not "for itself" the universal. The animal senses the genus but does not know it. The high point in the animal life, wherein the universal comes into its own or comes forth, is the reproduction process (*Gattungsprozess*), whereby the genus is continued. Here, however, the universal is "for" the animal subjectivity only in the form of another singularity. Therefore even in the animal life, the highest form of the Notion to which nature attains, nature does not bring forth the universal as "for itself" the universal: the in-and-for-self universal individuality that is Spirit in its proper form.

---

[34] *PhN* 352; see also below, p. 116.

[35] *PhM* 10. See also the account of sensibility in its logical Idea (*SL* 768).

[36] *PhN* 384-385. We reproduce the following passages both as characteristic for Hegel's meaning of "the negation which is positive" and as crucial for understanding Hegel's theme of the development of the soul as a "liberation struggle" (*Befreiungs-kampf*):

"Only what is living feels a *lack*; for in nature it alone is the *Notion*, the unity of itself and its specific opposite. Where there is a limitation (*Schranke*), it is a negation only for a third, for an external comparison. But it is a *lack* only insofar as the lack's overcoming is equally present in the same thing, and contradiction is, as such, immanent and explicitly present in that thing. A being which is capable of containing and enduring its own contradiction is a *subject*; this constitutes it infinitude." (*PhN* 385)

"The sentient creature, in the limitation of hunger, thirst, etc., is the urge to overcome this limitation and it does overcome it. It feels *pain*, and it is the privilege of the sentient nature to feel pain; it is a negation in its *self*, and the negation is determined as a *limitation* in its feeling, just because the sentient creature has the feeling of its *self*, which is the totality that transcends this determinateness. If it were not above and beyond the determinateness, it would not feel it as its negation and would feel no pain." (*SL* 135)

It is with the emergence from nature of subjectivity as in-and-for-self universal individuality that we enter the realm of Spirit as Spirit. The animal "stands *within nature,* and its subjectivity is only *implicitly* the Notion but is not *for its own self* the Notion." [37] In the *Gattungsprozess,* life as the "immediate form of the Idea" [38] falls asunder into the living singularity, on the one hand, and the universal as genus, into whose superior power the singular life sinks. The very disparity "between its finitude and universality" is the singular life's "original disease" and "inborn germ of death." [39] As this "contradiction" of immediate singularity and implicit universality, the singular life passes away.[40] It has risen above its singularity only in the *Gattungsprozess* wherein it comes forth "again" only to pass away "again" as singularity in the endless repetition of the "negative infinity." [41] Implicit in this ceaseless coming to be and passing away of the singular, however, lies the "coalescing" of the universal with itself as universal. The realized genus "has posited itself as identical with the Notion." In the genus-process the singular life perishes but "the death of this life is the procession of Spirit." Nature's overcoming of the "immediacy of its reality" in the singular life means the sublation of its "last externality." The Notion, which in nature has been present only "in itself" (*an sich*), in the realized universal has become "for itself" (*für sich*).

With this, nature has passed over into its truth, into the subjectivity of the Notion whose *objectivity* is itself the sublated immediacy of singularity, is *concrete universality*; so that the Notion is posited as having for its *determinate being* (*Dasein*) the reality which corresponds to it, namely, the Notion—and this is *Spirit.*[42]

From the "dead husk" of nature, says Hegel, "proceeds a more beautiful nature, Spirit." This attainment of Being-for-self in its determinate Being as "its own difference from itself" [43] means that the essence of

---

[37] *PhN* 440.
[38] The Idea "exists in nature only as a singular." (*PhN* 443)
[39] *PhN* 441. On old age and death, see also below, p. 74.
[40] *PhN* 279; *L* 361.
[41] *SL* 774; *L* 362; *PhN* 414. The "negative" or "spurious" infinity is the iteration *ad infinitum* of the something that becomes other, which likewise becomes other, and so on without end. (*L* 174 ff.) Implicit in the passage of something to other, however, is the Being-for-self in otherness that marks the "affirmative" or "true" infinity. See, for example, the alternating states of sleep and waking, below p. 81.
[42] *PhN* 443.
[43] *SL* 775.

Spirit is freedom: "the Notion's absolute negativity as identity with itself." [44] But this "identity with itself" is no flight from otherness. Spirit's freedom is actualized only through the overcoming of otherness by positing it within itself as the negative of itself and preserving itself in this its negativity. As free, says Hegel, Spirit can "abstract from everything external, including its own externality," but at the same time Spirit can bear "infinite pain, the negation of its individual immediacy, i.e., preserve itself affirmatively in this negativity and be identical with itself."

Hegel is clear that the demonstration of Spirit's emergence from nature has the opposite meaning from that of a reductionism. In Spirit, nature "attains its goal and its truth," while at the same time Spirit does not remain merely "a world beyond nature" but takes it up "as absorbed in itself." [45] The Philosophy of Nature has purportedly demonstrated the emergence of Spirit as nature's own movement through its succeeding stages of mechanism, physics, and organism, where finally "soul" proves to be the simple inwardness in which nature sets itself aside as the spatial and temporal "asunderness."

Thus in the emergence of Spirit from nature we see the speculative principle that every advance is a going back towards the beginning, every unfolding an inwardization. [46] That Spirit "has become" as the "truth" of nature means that the progression is simultaneously a going back to the *arche*. Hence Hegel says, while "for us" in our investigation Spirit has nature as its "presupposition," Spirit as nature's "truth" is also its "absolute *prius*." [47] In the same way we shall see in the investigation of Spirit that each later stage is the "truth" of the preceding and never the reverse—as with those thinkers, for example, who would see in fear the source of religion, so that moral and religious principles "may seem to call for treatment as species of sensation." [48]

As Being-for-self, Spirit is the self-differentiating and self-determining universal whose determinations are at once an inner self-distinguishing and a revealing (*Offenbarung*). But what is revealed, says Hegel, is inseparable from the revealing process itself. By virtue of the absolute

[44] *PhM* 15.
[45] *L* 180.
[46] See above, p. 37.
[47] *PhM* 8. In all speculative demonstration, "what appears as sequel and derivative is rather the absolute *prius* of what it appears to be mediated by." (*PhM* 283; see also *L* 377; and above, p. 37)
[48] *PhM* 7.

inwardness of spirituality, revelation in the realm of Spirit is ever self-revelation and self-creation. Hence the revealing is not the word of the investigator, as in the Philosophy of Nature, but Spirit's own revealing of itself to itself.

Even in the organic world, says Hegel, the germ of the plant brings forth an actuality equal to itself; and in Spirit too its development reaches its goal when the notion of Spirit has completely actualized itself, when Spirit as the self-knowing has arrived at the full consciousness of its notion. But this coinciding of beginning and end is far more perfect in Spirit than in organism. While the seed generated is not the same as that from which it sprang, what is brought forth by the self-knowing Spirit is one and the same with what brings forth.[49] The principle that Spirit is the truth of nature and its "absolute prius," becomes a truth "for" Spirit in its advance to philosophic knowing. Hence Spirit's self-revelation includes its positing of nature as its world.[50] This positing we shall see as the culmination of the development of the soul to consciousness. Insofar as Spirit is subjectivity and "reflection," however, Spirit's positing becomes a "presupposing" of this world as an independent externality, which Spirit then proceeds to sublate as an otherness in obtaining the "affirmation and truth of its freedom." [51]

Where in nature the animal life attains to the universal only implicitly in the genus, in man as rational subjectivity Spirit actualizes itself as the universal that is "for itself" the universal. In man's modes of feeling, perceiving, and understanding, in his forms of knowledge and self-knowledge, Spirit becomes "for itself" as knowing subjectivity. Here Spirit is *erkennend* or cognitive, referring to itself within the "ideal" totality of the Idea.[52] In this its medium of ideality, Spirit moves freely and is with itself. Yet its freedom is still only implicit; as cognitive, Spirit appears to itself only as "subjectivity," only as "one side of the relation." The world presupposed as an independent externality, still stands as an

---

[49] *PhM* 6; *HPh* I, 22-23.

[50] *PhM* 18.

[51] *PhM* 18. For the logical meaning of "positing" and "presupposing" as forms of self-relation in other constituting the movement of "reflection," see *SL* 399 ff. See also the recapitulation of the entire system of philosophic science as "the self-thinking Idea" in *Encyclopedia*, paragraphs 574-77 (*PhM* 313 ff.). Since our interest lies in the realm of Subjective Spirit, we shall not seek to follow the total movement of Spirit in any detail beyond the ensuing brief outline.

[52] *PhM* 20; see also *SL* 775.

"other" over against the subject. Hence the doctrine of Subjective Spirit deals with Spirit in its finitude.

As Objective Spirit, Spirit knows itself not only as subject but as "person," and becomes free "for itself" through its own volitional activity. In the realms of right, ethical community, state, and history, Spirit overcomes its onesided theoretical attitude. Where before it attained a cognition of "the true," now it moves to add the dimension of "the good." Where before Spirit presupposed a world as given to its knowing, now it posits that world as its own doing, objectifies itself and becomes for itself in its own works and deeds. Yet this mode of Spirit is still but a "posited" objectivity. Objective Spirit is not aware of its freedom in its absolute form, and hence is also finite. Positedness must be overcome and objectivity freely released in order that Spirit may grasp the truth as at once its own creation and directly and immediately Being.

Spirit's grasping itself as the truth that is directly its own creation takes place first in art, where Spirit produces its own intuition of itself in sensuous shapes. In religion, Spirit reveals to itself the essential and actual in the forms of representational and figurative thinking. Finally in philosophic science, Spirit knows itself as the self-producing Idea in the form of Notion. In philosophy, Spirit possesses its absolute certainty and truth, that

The eternal Idea, in full fruition of its essence (*an und für sich seiend*), eternally sets itself to work, engenders and enjoys itself as Absolute Spirit.[53]

The above brief outline both affords us a glimpse into the Hegelian transition from nature to Spirit, and enables us more closely to locate ourselves within the total system of philosophic sciences. As our particular area of investigation, the science of Anthropology lies within the first of the three main divisions of the Philosophy of Spirit and one of the two realms of Spirit in its finitude. Hegel sees the stages of finite Spirit as stages of its "liberation," and throughout our study of the soul we shall note that the development of the soul to consciousness has the form of a "liberation struggle" (*Befreiungskampf*). But just as the command Know Thyself does not come to man as an imperative from without, Spirit's liberation is from no overlord standing outside and above it. For Spirit there just is no "complete other" [54] as in Manichaean

---

[53] *PhM* 315.
[54] *PhM* 1.

or other dualisms.[55] Spirit's liberation struggle, its own bringing itself forth from its "other," is ever in the striving and pain of the negative.[56] Spirit's freedom is not "natural" but must be "won." [57] Yet Spirit is eternal and "essentially and actually is and forever produces itself," and therefore there can be no doubt about the outcome of the struggle.[58] The "finitude" of Spirit consists in the discrepancy (Unangemessenheit) between its reality and its notion.[59] But this is the contradiction that produces all dialectical advance. Precisely in the advance the discrepancy proves to be but a "show" (Schein),[60] wherein Spirit imposes upon itself its own "limitation" (Schranke) [61] as its "ought," in order, through overcoming of the limitation, to return to itself in explicit knowledge of its freedom.[62] Hence the stages of finite Spirit, Hegel tells us, are stages of its Scheinen, stages on which it is Spirit's destiny to tarry and to pass through as steps in its winning of freedom. The absolute truth of this freedom is that Subjective Spirit's "finding" of a world as "presupposed,"

---

[55] Regarding the problem of good and evil, Hegel demands that the positive and negative be "discovered in one another" instead of being represented in "their succession and juxtaposition," as though it is "from outside that the negative comes to the positive." (PhR 255; see also Phen. 98.)

[56] Spirit is "at war with itself"; what in nature is peaceful growth is in Spirit "a severe, a mighty conflict with itself." Spirit seeks the realization of its notion but "hides that goal from its own vision, and is proud and well satisfied in this alienation from it." (PhH 55)

[57] PhH 41; HPh I, 23.

[58] While the issue is never in doubt as regards Spirit as such, the finite individual spirit can meet defeat. Only here, for Hegel, may we say with Kierkegaard: "as long as there is struggle there is the possibility of defeat."

[59] FPhG 27.

[60] Schein as "show" is the unstable, the transient, the unessential, and hence no longer the mere immediacy of determinate Being (Dasein) but an immediacy that is "in and for itself null"—thereby pointing beyond itself to essence, in which show has its nullity. But the determinations that distinguish show from essence are just the determinations of essence itself, and the aspect of essence as show is sublated within essence. (SL 397) Hence essence is "its showing within itself," whereby Scheinen becomes the "forth-shining" (Er-scheinen) or "appearing" of essence. (L 239) These logical categories will be important for the notion of consciousness as Spirit in its "appearing." (See below, pp. 159 ff.)

[61] Schranke is the limit of something posited of it as a negative and at the same time essential determination. Hence Schranke and Sollen (ought) are dialectical opposite moments of finitude. (SL 131 ff.) Limitation "ought" to be overcome. "Precisely in the fact that the limit is for it [i.e. Spirit], it stands beyond the limit." (FPhG 28)

[62] FPhG 29.

Objective Spirit's "positing" of that world as its own, and Absolute Spirit's liberation from and in it, are one and the same in the eternalness of Spirit.[63]

With this brief discussion of the meaning of Spirit's finitude and the illustration of certain logical categories that will be important to us later, we are finally in a position to speak directly of Hegel's notion of Subjective Spirit. We have noted Hegel's claim of access to this area in the context of the contemporary—particularly the Critical Philosophy's—problematic of knowledge. We have also located the area of Subjective Spirit within Hegel's total system of philosophic science. We now need to see in preliminary outline the doctrine of Subjective Spirit that represents Hegel's final statement with regard to the subjective consciousness and the problem of epistemology. The Anthropology, or science of Spirit as soul, is the first of the sciences of Subjective Spirit and presents the first moment in the notion of Subjective Spirit.

Spirit developing itself in its "ideality," says Hegel, is Spirit as knowing or cognitive.[64] Spirit cognitive is Subjective Spirit.[65] As long as Spirit stands "in relation" to itself as to an "other," it remains finite Subjective Spirit, Spirit arising out of nature and having to overcome its own forms of naturalness. Although, as we have seen, sentient animal life is already implicitly the overcoming of nature's spatial and temporal asunderness (*Aussereinandersein*), the subjective consciousness's higher idealized modes of overcoming that externality are in terms of the spatio-temporal *Aussereinandersein* itself.[66] The entire activity of Subjective Spirit, therefore, is toward grasping itself as Spirit by proving itself to be the

---

[63] *PhM* 22; see also *PhM* 181-182.

[64] *PhM* 25.

[65] In the logical Idea of cognition, the self-distinguishing of subjectivity is its repelling itself from itself and presupposing itself as an external universe. (*L* 362) For the subjective Idea, the objective is "the immediate world found ready to hand" (*die vorgefundene unmittelbare* Welt). (*L* 363) Just as in the Idea of life the living individuality in its organic processes proceeds to overcome the opposition between itself and its inorganic nature the spiritual individuality as "subjectivity" proceeds to do this in cognition. The decisive difference that marks the higher ideality of Spirit over natural life is that: "Subjective Spirit *makes* for itself the *presupposition* of an objective world; life *has* such a presupposition." (*SL* 760)

[66] Prior to its attainment of notional thinking, Subjective Spirit in its finite modes of thought allows the content which lies before it "to drop into the sphere of sensuous representation, into time and space, where the contradictory terms are held apart in spatial and temporal juxtaposition and thus come before consciousness without being in contact." (*SL* 835)

ideality of its immediate reality.[67] This endeavor characterizes Spirit up to the final moment of its overcoming of its finite subjectivity. Thus in the concluding and highest science of Subjective Spirit—Psychology as the science of "Spirit proper"—Subjective Spirit is still engaged in overcoming its spatially and temporally conditioned modes of "pictorial thinking" just prior to its attainment of notional thinking (begreifendes Denken). It is still striving to control and direct the natural "drives" within itself just prior to its attainment to free objective will.[68]

Since all of Spirit's knowing is implicitly or explicitly a form of Spirit's Being-with-self (Beisichselbstsein), the notion of Subjective Spirit divides itself into the three moments whereby Spirit makes itself "for itself" what it is "in itself." [69] In its first moment, Spirit is "in itself," Spirit in its "immediacy" and implicitness. Here Spirit is in the form of soul (Seele) or natural Spirit (Naturgeist). Its development comprises the subject matter of the science of Anthropology.

In a movement that will constitute the main focus of our inquiry, Spirit sunders itself from its natural Being as soul and becomes "for itself" mediately as identical reflection in self and other—"other" consisting in an objective outer world to which Spirit holds itself "in relation." Spirit is here "consciousness," and its movement of self-manifestation in other marks it as Spirit in its "appearing." The science of consciousness, or Spirit in its appearing, is Phenomenology.

Overcoming the externality of the subject-object relation in consciousness, and determining itself within itself as subject "for itself"—or identity of subject and object—Spirit has attained to "reason" (Vernunft). Within the compass of Subjective Spirit as finite individual intelligence and will, Spirit as reason provides the subject matter of Psychology.

The doctrine of Subjective Spirit thus demonstrates a development of finite Spirit from soul through consciousness to reason. But "development," Hegel want us to know, is not to be conceived as in "ordinary psychology" in terms of a narrating of what the mind or soul is, "what happens to it, what it does." [70] The notion of Subjective Spirit is not a presupposing of the soul as "completed subject" (fertiges Subject) that exhibits "expressions" from which we infer the "faculties" and "powers" it possesses. Such an external approach misses the point of all spiritual

---

[67] PhM 21; SL 781-82.
[68] PhM 234.
[69] PhM 25.
[70] PhM 25. See also above, p. 8.

development: that the soul's very "expression" of what it "is" is implicitly posited as what it is "for *it*," whereby the soul is already movement, has already won for itself higher determination. The notional development of Subjective Spirit also does not have the sense often connected with the singular subject's mental cultivation (*Bildung*) and education. Such education, to be sure, has as its purpose to bring the universal to existence in the individual through training and guidance. But in philosophical science, Spirit is viewed in its self-formation according to the necessity of its notion as Spirit. Its formations are precisely the moments of its "bringing itself forth to itself" that are simultaneously its "closing together with itself"—the very process whereby it is first actually Spirit.

In its immanent development according to its own notion, Subjective Spirit displays the three moments of the Notion as such: abstract universality, particularity, and individuality or concrete universality.[71] As soul, Spirit is in the form of abstract universality, for its determinations are but implicit and "within" the soul itself. In consciousness the determinations are as distinctions of "reflection," coming to the subjectivity as from its "other," the external world. For this reason consciousness is the moment of sunderance (*Besonderung*) in the subject-object antithesis, and particularization of the single self-consciousness as against other self-consciousnesses. In reason, which is the actualization of Subjective Spirit as finite individuality, the distinctions of the subjectivity are once more, as in soul, "within" the subject. But now they are also distinctions "for" the subject as universal rational self-consciousness—distinctions in which the subject is explicitly "for itself" in its determinations. Reason, or Spirit proper, is thus the return to self of Subjective Spirit in its notion, and the actualization of the universal as in-and-for-self individuality.

Since the doctrine of Subjective Spirit begins with the emergence of Spirit from nature as its "result," the first science of Subjective Spirit—Anthropology—deals with man in his "universal natural Being," the universal "basis of man."[72] As soul, Spirit is "newly born" out of nature as it were; it is immersed in its physical Being or corporeality and hence is not yet for itself or free. The development of Spirit as soul is therefore only "for us," the observers, not yet for Spirit itself. But the essence of Spirit is to be "for itself." In this contradiction of itself,

---

[71] *PhM* 26.
[72] *PhM* 27; *SL* 781.

Spirit turns negatively against itself in its natural Being and raises itself to consciousness.

In consciousness, Spirit has become ego, "for itself" mediately in its opposition to "other." Spirit as consciousness is no longer sunk in its natural Being but related negatively to it as an outer world which it knows as an independent externality structured in terms of such objective categories as cause and effect. Here Spirit's Being-for-self in its other is not yet the Being-in-and-for-self of its notion; rather its own determinations appear as a "showing" through the other, and therefore the realm of consciousness comprises the Phenomenology of Spirit.[73] Spirit permeates its object with its own subjectivity and at the same time renders its subjectivity objective, thereby attaining to reason.

As rational intelligence, Spirit knows that it has to do with its determinations as at once subjective and objective. This Being-in-and-for-self of Subjective Spirit comprises the highest science of Subjective Spirit, Psychology. Divesting its content of its aspect of givenness and immediacy, intelligence raises itself through its forms of intuition and representation to notional thinking. Having thus attained to a thinking of Notion, Spirit has actualized its own notion as theoretical, and passes over to practical Spirit. Beginning now with a content it knows to be its own, Spirit takes up its impulses, passions, inclinations as a "material" which it proceeds to raise out of its contingency and singularity to necessity and universality. Hereby Spirit has made unto its own those impulses formerly coming to it from the dark recesses of its selfhood in its natural Being. Spirit has thus returned from its sunderance as consciousness to its unity with itself as soul. Now, however, its determinations are no longer those of its unconscious psychical life as universal natural Being but its express knowing and doing as concrete free individuality.

In presenting the three sciences of Anthropology, Phenomenology, and Psychology as dealing with the inner self-division and return to unity of Subjective Spirit, Hegel puts forward a number of audacious and far-reaching philosophical claims. In the first place the demonstration purports to show the liberation of Spirit from its engrossment in nature and attainment, within the realm of finite subjectivity, to free intelligence and free will. Further, in showing that consciousness "awakens" in the soul and proceeds of its own necessity to raise itself to reason, Hegel

---

[73] *SL* 781.

claims to release philosophical thinking from the subject-object antithesis in which all of post-Cartesian philosophy had been caught.[74] This is purportedly done not by bypassing the Critical Philosophy but by fulfilling its demands in the most radical manner possible. Indeed, as we have tried to show, the enterprise of the "speculative method" arises largely out of and in response to Kant's posing of the problem of knowledge.

The sciences of Subjective Spirit form a circle within the circle of the philosophical sciences. Reason proves to be the ground and truth of soul and consciousness. Once again the advance is a return to the beginning: the notion of Spirit as the "truth" of nature. In this way the sciences of Subjective Spirit present both the development of the finite individual spirit to freedom and—since the development is Spirit's own overcoming of the inadequate and "untrue" forms of itself—a genetic epistemology in the form of an immanent self-critique of knowing. The critique is one in which Spirit employs as its "instrument" only its own modes of bringing itself forth.

At this conclusion of our introductory chapters a general statement would seem to be in order. For almost any student of the Hegelian philosophy, the almost desperate question is: how to gain entrance? Elaborated in one difficult work after another, the Hegelian position seems armed on all sides to keep out the intruder. In seeking to penetrate the redoubtable fortress, we have made use of issues concerned with Hegel's *Auseinandersetzung* with the Critical Philosophy. Here the giant of the castle to some extent has had to leave his inner fastness and display himself in public combat. We have utilized Hegel's criticisms of Kant

---

[74] Of all the thinkers from Descartes to Kant, perhaps Leibniz alone sought to view consciousness and reason in terms of an inwardly necessitated "emergence." In the purely internal development of the monad, "apperception" arises out of the lower level of "perception." The activity of the soul prior to apperception is conceived in terms of *petites perceptions,* and the movement to self-consciousness is viewed as a progress from "obscure" and "indistinct" presentations to "clear," "distinct," and "adequate." We have seen how Kant criticized this position as lacking a logical principle, and how he turned his back on the effort to show apperception in terms of an emergence. Hegel, as we shall see, claims to show at once the emergence of consciousness *as* the rule-giving or logical principle. Hegel criticizes Leibniz for showing no necessity in the monad's development. While the monad of Leibniz evolves its ideas and representations "out of itself," says Hegel, "it is not the power that generates and binds them together, rather do they arise in the monad like bubbles; they are indifferent and immediate over against one another and the same in relation to the monad itself." (*SL* 396)

not as though it were the main aim of Hegelian idealism to refute Kantian transcendentalism but to enable us to see better what Hegel himself was trying to do. We believe that this approach is not misleading but in fact close to Hegel's own intentions and development of basic problems.[75] For this reason we shall continue to pay attention to aspects of Hegel's doctrine of the soul that are important both with reference to the Critical Philosophy and as establishing the Hegelian position in its own right. Primarily we shall note Hegel's claim to demonstrate a subjectivity prior to the "I think": a psychical subjectivity that permeates its corporeal manifold without the aid of the Kantian categories of the understanding and in ways not yet objective but nevertheless meaningful. The implications of this demonstration will prove important in many ways.

In contrast to the Kantian claim that we shall never fathom the common source of our faculties,[76] Hegel will purportedly show how the psyche—as a germinal spiritual life—produces not three faculties or two separate stems of knowledge but organically brings itself forth as a spiritual totality. The psyche's gathering of spiritual strength in the course of its development, and its liberation from its baser natural drives, will prove inseparable from the subjectivity's attainment to the level of objective consciousness and objective knowledge. Since in actualizing itself the psyche will "posit" its content as an independent outer world, the demonstration of this development will purportedly reveal how the "thing-in-itself" is generated by the very activity of the thinking consciousness. In showing the subject-object relationship as arising from a development of the soul, the demonstration will claim to yield a new science—Phenomenology—which will deduce the objective categories not formalistically but out of the subjectivity's living encounter with the natural and social world that is implicitly the subjectivity's own universal selfhood.

Hegel's doctrine of the soul will thus purportedly rebut the Kantian limitation of theoretical self-knowledge to the findings of a "physiology of inner sense." It will supposedly establish the basis of a philosophical psychology as a speculative science in the great classical tradition. It will claim to remove the Kantian dichotomy of a knowledge of ourselves

---

[75] The Kantian philosophical position, says Hegel, "constitutes the base and the starting-point of recent German philosophy and this its merit remains unaffected by whatever faults may be found in it." (*SL* 61)

[76] "For all faculties or capacities of the soul can be reduced to three, which cannot be any further derived from one common ground: the faculty of knowledge, the feeling of pleasure and pain, and the faculty of desire." (*CJ* 13)

as sensible natural beings, or phenomena, and supersensible moral beings or noumena. It will pave the way for a rejection of the unknowable transcendental x both within and without us.

Without embarking on a far greater extension of our study, we cannot properly assess these far-reaching Hegelian claims. At certain places we shall raise questions with regard to the program's fulfillment of its own demands. Here and there—as in Hegel's somewhat dubious treatment of trance-like knowing (*schauendes Wissen*)—we shall seek to insert a "sobering" consideration or two from the side of Kant. On the whole, however, our endeavor will be to capture the thrust of the Hegelian treatment of the soul as a forcing open of the Critical Philosophy's narrowly sequestered approach to epistemology, and the replacement of a search for the a priori elements of cognition by a search for the spiritual roots of man even in his natural being.

PART II

SPIRIT AS SOUL:
THE SCIENCE OF ANTHROPOLOGY

The soul is the existing Notion, the existence of the speculative.

(*PhM* 93)

In the soul is the awakening of consciousness.

(*PhM* 25)

CHAPTER FOUR

THE NATURAL SOUL

In the Hegelian speculative approach, as we have seen, Spirit in its first appearance as concrete Spirit is that which it has become as the "truth of nature." Hegel's Philosophy of Spirit thus begins with a "result," whose meaning and necessity within the total system of philosophical science has been discussed in our introductory chapters. In thus beginning with a result, we start out neither with a notion of mind as a *tabula rasa* nor as a *res cogitans* to which stands opposed a *res extensa*. This is not to say that such problems as the relation of mind and body have been solved before we begin, but that the preconditions of the solution have been made available in the preceding systematic exposition.

The Cartesian mind-body dualism, Hegel tells us, emerges wherever the two sides are taken as independent subsistents related externally to one another as "materiality" and "immateriality" or the physical and the spiritual. Viewed in this fashion, the question of the soul-body "community" cannot but arise and cannot but remain an incomprehensible mystery.[1] But the mystery, according to Hegel, is a consequence of the improper posing of the question. The soul-body relationship cannot be comprehended in terms of cause and effect, reciprocal action, or pre-established harmony.[2] The soul as the immaterial is not related to the material as one particular to another but as the simple universality in which the "this-beside-this" is sublated to an ideal moment.

Hegel notes that even in the concept of God in Descartes and Malebranche, in Spinoza's doctrine of substance, and in Leibniz's monadology, the unity of the immaterial and the material is affirmed. But these

---

[1] *PhM* 30.

[2] See *Phen.* 356 *passim*. Such categories as cause and effect, and reciprocal interaction, which still belong to the Kantian categories of the understanding, have purportedly been overcome in the logical movement from essence to Notion (see above, pp. 36-37).

thinkers' respective demonstrations of this unity are in the form of abstract definitions and external reflections.[3] In the speculative system of philosophic sciences, the *Naturphilosophie* has shown the sentient animal soul to be the omnipresence of the one soul in all points of its corporeality [4] and thereby nature's own overpassing of itself as material *Aussersichsein* (Being-outside-self). In the realm of Spirit, the singular subjectivity is the "absolute negativity" in whose simple universality the *partes extra partes* of materiality is but a vanishing moment. Hence in the investigation of Spirit that begins with this "result," the question of the soul-body relation can no longer be a question of how "community" is possible but only of the advancing ways in which the soul as simple universality comes to power in its manifold corporeal determinations by rendering the body the soul's external expression of its subjective inwardness.

Even in its initial determination as soul prior to the objective consciousness, says Hegel, Spirit is immaterial "for itself." The singular soul in its Being-for-self (*Fürsichsein*) is at the same time the universal immateriality of nature and the latter's "simple ideal life." Hegel here undoubtedly makes use of a Leibnizian conception but he will develop it in a manner which he claims Leibniz was unable to do.[5] Hegel also indicates his debt to Aristotle.

Soul, says Hegel, is the "substance" of Spirit, the basis of all further particularization of Spirit as consciousness and rational intelligence. In soul, Spirit has all the material (*Stoff*) of its determinations. In its first moment as "natural soul," however, soul is but the "sleep" of Spirit. It is not a *tabula rasa* but, like the passive *Nous* of Aristotle, it is "potentially all things." [6] As passive *Nous* the soul is both abstract and concrete, though, as Aristotle would say, not in the same sense. The soul is "concrete" in respect to what it has "become." As the truth of

---

[3] For example, Spinoza, says Hegel, tells us that substance is the unity of thought and extension "without demonstrating how he gets to this distinction, or how traces it back to the unity of substance." (*L* 275. See also Kant's somewhat similar critique of Spinoza in *CJ* 270-271, 290.) For further Hegelian criticisms of the efforts of Spinoza, Malebranche, and Leibniz to unite the material and the immaterial, see *PhM* 30 ff; *SL* 161 ff., 536 ff.; and Hegel's discussions of these thinkers in *HPh* III.

[4] See above, p. 44.

[5] See above, p. 54 n. 74.

[6] *PhM* 29. See "Eine Ubersetzung Hegels zu *De anima* III, 4-5," presented and interpreted by Walter Kern, *Hegel-Studien*, I (1961).

the *Gattungsprozess,* nature's highest point of development, the soul is "concrete universality," [7] and this its universality is also its "determinate Being" (*Dasein*) in which it is for itself.[8] But in its aspect as the first emergence of Spirit, however, the soul has not yet differentiated its determinations as specifically spiritual determinations on the new level as spirituality. In this respect it is still "abstract."

The "natural soul" (*naturliche Seele*) in its development will constitute the first "syllogism" (*Schluss*) of the Anthropology.[9] Natural soul is soul "in itself" in its immediate unity with nature, soul in its implicitness and its unconsciousness (*Bewusstlosigkeit*). Its own determinations, of which it is itself unaware, belong to it in the manner of properties: the purely natural "qualities," "alterations," and "states," such as racial traits, phases of the individual's maturation, and the alternating rhythms of sleep and waking. Hegel's discussion of the soul's development through these determinations will constitute our present chapter on the natural soul.

From its immediate unity with its natural being, the soul divides itself to become "for itself" in its determinations. Here, we shall see, the soul enters into active opposition to its own natural being, a struggle with self, evidenced, for example, in mental illness. This constitutes the

---

[7] See above, p. 45.

[8] *SL* 775.

[9] For Hegel the *Schluss* or speculative syllogism is the Notion's self-distinguishing and return to unity, whose moments of universality, particularity, and individuality are expressed in corresponding forms of judgment united to constitute a self-moving, self-mediating "closing together with self." The speculative syllogism, according to Hegel, is not merely a subjective form of inference, any more than the Notion is a merely subjective form of thought. The *Schluss* is "the completely posited Notion; it is therefore the *rational.*" (*SL* 664; see also *L* 314) Viewed philosophically, "every process has the form of the syllogism." (*PhN* 412) The Hegelian syllogism is not the same as the Aristotelian which, according to Hegel, "is not a knowledge through itself in accordance with its content." (*HPh* III, 179-180) But, Hegel tells us, Aristotle never allowed his syllogistic to "intrude" in his higher philosophy. (*L* 322) For a brief discussion of Hegel's syllogism in contrast to those of Aristotle and certain other thinkers, see Mure, *A Study of Hegel's Logic, op. cit.,* pp. 224-227. An important part of our effort in the present study is to grasp Hegel's demonstration of the soul's development in its syllogistic structure. In the Hegelian syllogism, says Mure, "the middle term develops into the totality of the genus particularized to individuality." (Mure, *op. cit.,* p. 224) We shall see how this movement takes place as moments of the "natural soul," the "feeling soul," and the "actual soul," each of these moments themselves comprising syllogisms.

Schluss of the "feeling soul" (*fühlende Seele*), the second syllogism of the Anthropology. In this struggle the soul gains mastery over its corporeality, reducing the latter to an outer sign of the soul's own inwardness and ideality.

Hereby the soul becomes "in and for itself" in its physical reality, and is now "actual soul" (*wirkliche Seele*). This liberation from its natural being is at the same time its return to unity with itself. Now, however, it has "made" itself this unity. It posits itself as ego of consciousness and its content as an external world to which it holds itself "in relation." The attainment of consciousness marks the goal and conclusion of the movement in the Anthropology and the commencement of the movement of consciousness demonstrated in the Phenomenology.

a. The Natural Qualities

As the "immediate" universal substance, soul is termed by Hegel "world soul" (*Weltseele*).[10] Hegel's notion here seems far from clear. World soul, Hegel explains, is not to be taken as also "subject," i.e. as having existence apart from and independent of individual souls.[11] It is soul merely as abstract universality that has its "actual truth" only as individuality, subjectivity.[12] As subjectivity it is in the first instance soul in its "mere being" (*nur seiende Seele*), having its natural determinations merely "in it" (*an ihr*).[13] These determinations have "free existence

---

[10] *PhM* 35.

[11] In the logical Idea of life, the "creative universal soul" is to be viewed as "the *side of the universality of the Notion,* consequently as *abstract* universality, essentially only *inhering* in the subject and in the form of immediate *Being* which, posited on its own account, is indifferent to the subject." (*SL* 764-765) Geological nature, says Hegel, is not "veritable subjectivity" but only "*implicitly* organism" and does not exist "as a living creature." (*PhN* 275, 277) The description of *die Seele der Welt* in the *Phenomenology* (see above, p. 36) seems to be far more that of an actuality than in the *Naturphilosophie* or the Philosophy of Spirit.

[12] Whatever else we are to think of the *Weltseele* it surely is not to be equated with Plato's soul of the world (*Timaeus* 37; *Laws* X, 896), which is "the best of things created." For Hegel, the individual soul as "object and end of the love of God" and possessing "an absolute relationship to God as Spirit," is infinitely higher than anything in nature. (See *PhM* 240; *PhN* 18).

[13] In the logic Hegel distinguishes *an sich* and *an ihm* (or in the case of the soul as feminine gender, *an ihr*) as different determinations of the "something" (*Etwas*). *An sich* can usually be translated as "in itself" in the sense of latent, implicit, potential. But, says Hegel, "something also has *in itself* (here the accent

behind its ideality," i.e., they are objects of nature for the rational consciousness, like the sun, but the soul as such does not relate itself "for itself" to them *as* externalities. The soul has the determinations only *an ihr selbst* as belonging to it in the form of "natural qualities." [14]

Thus in its first moment, Spirit as natural soul is to be understood as universal natural "substance" and at the same time as "subjectivity" in its utmost abstract immediacy and implicitness. Soul is yet but spiritual life in "dumb communion" with nature's planetary cycles, ebb and flow of seasons, etc. Hegel describes this moment of Spirit as but a simple "pulsating," a self-within-self stirring of spirituality. Although the universal is actual only in the individual, in this moment of immediacy there is yet no "posited" distinction between individuality as against universality, or of soul as such against nature. Nevertheless, in its having become as the "truth" of nature, this first moment of spiritual life has distinctions implicit within it in the form of natural determinations. These determinations are in physical nature as "freely released spheres, a series of independent forms," but in the simple ideality of soul are set down (*herabgesetzt*) to "qualities" of the soul.[15]

As natural soul, Spirit lives in a kind of primitive attunement *(Mitleben)* with the universal planetary life.[16] The differences of climate, the cycle of the seasons, the alternating times of day come to the soul as but dim moods. This elemental affinity of soul and nature, Hegel claims, is to a certain extent still visible in the ways of primitive peoples. Some of our own holidays and festivals have an aspect of seasonal rites.

---

falls on *in*) or *within it*, a determination or circumstance in so far as this circumstance is outwardly *in it*, is a Being-for-other." (*SL* 120) Josiah Royce puts the distinction thus: "*An ihm* refers to a character which is, in a more external and overt fashion, so *in* a subject, or rather, as one might say, attached *to* this subject, as to determine the subject's relation to others." ("Hegel's Terminology," *Baldwin's Dictionary of Philosophy and Psychology*, ed. James M. Baldwin, New York, 1901, vol. I, pp. 454-464.) In the present context, the soul's relation to other (nature) is present in the soul as its determination (*Bestimmung*) but in such a way as to be entangled (*verwickelt*) with its other.

[14] Quality, in the logic, is one of the "earliest" determinations of Being, hence one of the most abstract and least rich of the categories. (*SL* 111) According to Hegel, quality has a subordinate place in Spirit and belongs more properly to the realm of nature. (*L* 171) The soul's first determinations are "qualities" because they "belong to the mere Being" of Spirit. (*FPhG* 30)

[15] "The soul, when contrasted with the macrocosm of nature as a whole, can be described as the microcosm into which the former is compressed, thereby removing its asunderness." (*PhM* 36)

[16] *PhN* 102.

At times in our life, often in youth, we feel mysteriously drawn to nature. Our humors and dispositions to a degree reflect the seasons and times of day. Winter, says Hegel, inclines us toward a going within ourselves, spring touches off a rebirth and outflow of energies. There is the "sober light" of morning, the "objectivity" of broad day calls us to our appointed tasks, the mellowness of evening disposes toward relaxation and the free flow of imagination. Yet, says Hegel, none of this in man is merely instinctual or without his will.

Hegel sees no great importance for man's actual life in this first moment of the natural soul's abstract attunement to the universal planetary life. He shows rather little sympathy for that *Mitempfinden* with nature that formed an important theme in the romantic literature of his time.[17] We need waste no time on the alleged sidereal and telluric forces that were once supposed to exert important influences on man, says Hegel. Astrology, Hegel holds, is superstition—not because the planets are remote from us but because the planetary life of the solar system is a life of external movement in which mere space and time are the determining features. Even in the natural organism, that externality is subordinated. The natural life, as we have seen,[18] begins to make its own time and space. Its physical alterations, life span, forms of sickness and health, movement in space are determined by its own life process and end (*Selbstzweck*). The plant of course is dependent on the change of seasons, and even the animal life is to some extent bound to this cycle, as in hibernation, migration, periodicity of mating. But the activity of Spirit consists essentially in raising itself out of its entanglement in nature in order to grasp itself in its freedom and independence.[19] Through his culture, man has emancipated himself from nature's mindless cycles. He has taken over the alternations of nature and made them to his own rhythms and routines of work and rest, his habitudes and styles of life. Man employs nature against nature,[20] for "nature does not itself contain the absolute, final end." [21] Man's destiny as Spirit is to negate the self-externality

---

[17] *FPhG* 45.

[18] See above, p. 44.

[19] "Everything which is human, however it may appear, is so only because the thought contained in it works and has worked." (*HPh* I, 4)

[20] *PhN* 5; *PhH* 27.

[21] *PhN* 4. For Kant too "the purpose of nature must itself be sought beyond nature." (*CJ* 225) Unlike Hegel in the *Naturphilosophie*, however, Kant does not seek to demonstrate how nature sublates itself to Spirit as its "truth." Any such endeavor for theoretical purposes would be an illegitimate employment of reason.

of planetary space and time, create his own time in history, and make the natural world but a room for his own universe of reason.

The abstract universal natural soul "binds" its universal natural determinations more truly unto itself in articulating itself into the particular natural spirits that correspond approximately with the earth's main land divisions and constitute the chief races of mankind.[22] These broad racial divisions are further differentiated into the national and local spirits that distinguish peoples and groups in their ways of life, body build, traits of temperament, and, more significantly, in Hegel's eyes, capacities for intelligent and ethical organization.

Hegel sees the main continental divisions as not merely accidental.[23] The respective human communities of the great land divisions, according to Hegel, express the three moments of Spirit in its notion as *Naturgeist:* immediacy or abstract universality, sunderance, and free concrete individuality. Black Africa, cut off from the Mediterranean by mountain chain and desert, has remained a natural fastness closed up within itself. The Africans, who have hardly separated themselves from the immediacy of natural life, are "childlike," show a spontaneity and vitality in their ways of life but lack perseverance toward remote and impersonal goals.[24] Their social and political organization hardly goes beyond the ties of kinship and tribalism, their religious beliefs beyond animism and fetishism.[25] The land mass of Asia is divided by a mountain

[22] Here (*PhM* 40 ff.) and more especially in other works, Hegel deals with the principal geographical factors in human community, particularly with regard to those peoples he views as decisive for world history. The treatment here is marginal to the notion of soul and Subjective Spirit generally, and we shall note only a few high points of Hegel's presentation.

[23] The three continents that comprise the Old World have an essential relationship to one another corresponding to the moments of the Notion. (*PhN* 285) The area of main importance for world history lies around the Mediterranean. Eastern Asia is of little importance, according to Hegel, and the New World is outside the process of general historical development. (See "The Geographical Basis of World History," *PhH* 79 ff.)

[24] Hegel, however, rejects the view that racial differences justify overlordship or deprivation of freedom. "Man is implicitly rational; herein lies the possibility of equal justice for all men." (*PhM* 41)

[25] Hegel's understanding of fetishism may be cited as an example of his meaning of the "immediacy" of the African spirit. The fetish has an apparently objective independence, but the "objectivity" here, says Hegel, "is nothing other than individual arbitrariness bringing itself to self-intuition (*Selbstanschauung*), the individuality remaining master of the image." But where such arbitrariness is the

chain which cuts off the vast flat steppes and plains from the seacoast, and the Asian spirit swings from the violent extreme of the Mongols to the quiescence of the Chinese and Indians. The Asiatics have gone beyond the immediacy of the Africans and have attained to the universal, but in the contradictory form of immediate singularity (the man-god of the Lamas) on the one hand, and abstract universality (Indian pantheism) on the other. In this unmediated opposition the Asian spirit has never arrived at concrete individuality, the consciousness of free personality. This consciousness has first come to the fore in Europe, which has afforded the best possibility of the free mingling and movement of its peoples, full access to the sea, and the stimulating intercourse of commerce. The Europeans alone, according to Hegel, have attained to the confidence that nothing in the world is alien to thought, to the unity of free individuality and concrete universality in religion, the state, and philosophy.[26]

Even the treatment of particular national minds, which Hegel says must go off into the empirical and the descriptive, is approached by him in some measure as showing features of the Notion. For example, in southern Europe, particularly southern Italy, Hegel says, individuality is mainly in the form of immediate singularity, the individual character having no desire to be other than what he simply is.[27] There is a consequent laxness and lack of interest in impersonal spheres, such as government, and a disinclination toward universal goals, and at the same time a vivaciousness in gesture and a spontaneousness in personal relations and expression. Almost at the opposite extreme, says Hegel, the German spirit is inclined toward brooding and inwardness, seeks universal grounds for all actions, and in its passion for systematization

only "substantial objectivity that is realized," the spirit cannot be conscious of any universality. (*PhH* 94-95)

[26] Hegel's treatment of racial and national spirits has been frequently criticized and no doubt with justification. Fun has been made of his "deduction" of the continents (see Morris R. Cohen, "Hegel's Rationalism," *Philosophical Review*, vol. 41, no. 3, May 1932), at his omissions of what is not "convenient" to the Notion, at his sweeping pronouncements on civilizations of which he could have known relatively little (see Bertrand Russell, *A History of Western Philosophy*, New York, 1945, p. 735). Many of the critics, however, have not seriously sought to come to grips with Hegel's endeavor to view the manifold phenomena of geographical and ethnic communities in terms of universal determinations of mind. Our example of fetishism is meant as but one small indication of the suggestiveness of Hegel's approach.

[27] *PhM* 48.

often drives toward mere formalism, as when it honors the title and office above the individual man.[28]

From its particularization in the various racial and national spirits, the universal natural soul is singularized in the individual subject. Subjectivity at this point is but natural individuality, whose determinations are yet in the form of inborn dispositions, aptitudes, traits, insofar as these have a largely hereditary element. In this first appearance of the natural individuality, the abstract universal soul "takes back" the natural qualities into itself from the manifold group spirits in which it seemed to have lost itself, and is now concrete as the individual soul of man. The natural qualities of the individual soul are broadly divided by Hegel into those of "talent," "temperament," and "character."

Talents display the form of immediacy or "merely positive Being" (*blosse Seiendes*). Of the three forms of the individual's natural endowment, they seem most of all to have the nature of something merely "found" or "there" in the individual. Talents retain a certain lastingness through the lifetime of the individual, but at the same time, as immediate, refer for their eliciting and development to something outside themselves. A child may show an early fancy for drawing, but until this is purposefully developed it is impossible to say whether the child possesses a genuine talent or a mere penchant for dallying.[29]

Those traits we regard collectively as making up the individual's "temperament," says Hegel, include the often vague, almost infinitely varied shadings of disposition, sometimes proceeding to idiosyncracies, which fall into the realm of the contingent and offer little of essential interest to philosophy.[30] The traits of temperament, sometimes bordering on mere "humors," do not have the "fixed being" of the talents, and an individual may gravitate from one kind of temperament to another during the course of his life. Temperament in general, says Hegel, comprises the

---

[28] *PhM* 51.

[29] In art, both talent and genius, according to Hegel, require a specific aptitude "in which unquestionably natural endowment plays an essential part." For, since beauty is the Idea in sensuous form, the artist must discover and embody the content of his art "within the sphere of sensuous perception and feeling" and "in relation to a given sensuous material." Hence artistic creativeness necessarily contains the "aspect of immediacy," and "it is this appearance, which the individual is unable to evolve from himself, but has to find it, if he finds it at all, as immediately presented to him." (*The Philosophy of Fine Art*, trans. F. P. B. Osmaston, 4 vols. (London, 1920), vol. I, p. 385)

[30] On Hegel's view of *Menschenkennerey*, see above, p. 4.

ways in which the individual tends to relate himself to the outer world. In accordance with this notion of temperament, its distinctions may be seen as following along the lines of whether the individual in his activity tends to be directed "outwardly" (*in die Sache hineinbegibt*) or "inwardly" toward himself in his singularity.

Hegel notes the fourfold classification by Kant,[31] but cautions against any rigid application of this schema to individuals. Speaking of extremes, Hegel suggests that opposite temperaments are in fact dialectical opposites. The sanguine man often exhausts his substance in his manifold "projects." But his opposite, the phlegmatic man who also goes *in die Sache,* may likewise lose himself in the rut of his one pursuit. Both these extremes of outer directedness can be said to display a onesided objectivity, a loss of self in externality. On the other hand, the choleric's frenetic mobility derives from an inner restlessness that makes him unable to stay with the *Sache,* while the melancholic's inner brooding is but another expression of self-preoccupation. In the former pair, there is a loss of self through disrelation to objectivity, in the latter, a loss of touch with objectivity through a disrelation to self. In fact both pairs display the nature of extremes inasmuch as they express in a onesided and deficient way the essence of Spirit as self-relation in and through relation to other.

In character, the natural talents and endowments lose their immediacy as mere *Seienden,* while the traits of temperament become something more than dispositions. Both are negated in their immediacy and taken up in the enduringness of character as developed by will. Insofar as will is here essential, the fuller treatment of character belongs not on the present level of natural subjectivity but on the much higher level of free rational intelligence.[32] Hegel therefore contents himself with a few general remarks. There is no "talent for virtue," says Hegel, for a man's character is essentially his own creation rather than an inheritance. Nevertheless, on its "formal" side, says Hegel, character has a certain natural basis in the energy with which the individual pursues his goals and retains the sense of himself in his manifold undertakings. Here, Hegel says, we must distinguish between character and obstinacy

---

[31] Kant stresses the physical basis of temperament as making either for a heightening (*Erregbarkeit*) or lowering (*Abspannung*) of the individual's life-activity. He divides the temperaments into those of feeling (sanguine and melancholic) and those of activity (choleric and phlegmatic). (*APH* 286 ff.)

[32] *PhM* 228 ff.

(*Eigensinn*). In obstinacy—a "parody of character" [33]—the individual's activities are an outlet for his subjective peculiarities. In genuine character the goals of the individual's activity are of a substantive and universal content, yet at the same time freely the individual's own in which he obtains his self-satisfaction.[34]

The soul's individuation in "character" concludes the first moment of the Anthropology. This moment of the "natural qualities" has meant the "coming to be," as yet in the most abstract sense, of the individual soul. As yet the soul has only the complement of determinations sufficient to establish its *Dasein* as natural individuality.[35] The qualities of the natural soul purportedly derive from the universal *Naturgeist* in its particularization in the racial and national minds, and its actualization as universal in the individual soul as its determinate Being.

At this point it may be profitable to raise a few considerations regarding method. The opening presentation thus far in the Anthropology has, by Hegel's own admission, tended toward the descriptive. The natural soul's movement from the universality of world soul to the particular racial spirits and the individual soul seems to lack explicit negation,[36] and the treatment of the individual soul itself in terms of talent, tem-

---

[33] *PhM* 53. Cf. Aristotle's comparison of the obstinate and the self-restrained man in *Nicomachean Ethics* 1151b5 ff.

[34] *PhM* 53. See also *PhR* 83.

[35] Determinate Being (*Dasein*), or, literally "there-Being," is "Being with a determinateness (*Bestimmtheit*), which is as immediate or *seiende* determinateness: quality." (*L* 170)

[36] The emergence of the racial minds is presented as a "breaking up" (*Zerfallen*) of the universal planetary life of the *Naturgeist* (*PhM* 40; see also *PhN* 273); and the individuation (*Vereinzelung*) as a kind of "proceeding further" (*Fortschreiten, Fortführen*). Hegel also speaks of the latter movement metaphorically: "As light bursts asunder (*zerspringt*) into an infinite host of stars, so does the universal natural soul burst into an infinite host of individual souls; only with this difference, that whereas light appears to have an existence independently of the stars, the universal natural soul attains actuality solely in individual souls." (*PhM* 35)

Regarding the national and local minds or spirits, Hegel says, we are in an area where deduction is impossible. As in the physical realm, where we have to take account of the "impotence of nature" (*PhN* 23), the Notion here does not have the power to preserve itself in its pure moments and goes over into "contingent and external determination." (*Ibid.*) According to Hegel, contingency prevails wherever it makes no difference to the Notion whether a particularity exists or not. (*L* 11) Contingency has its "due office" in the world of phenomena, and it would be foolhardy for philosophy to seek to show an a priori necessity in all existences. (*L* 265; *PhN* 23)

perament, and character does not appear to be meant by Hegel as a rigorous *Schluss*. In the light of Hegel's own methodological claims, should we demand more by way of a deduction? Perhaps it would be incorrect for us to do so on these early stages, beyond noting, as we have done, the appearance in the material of certain moments of the Notion. Purportedly as the development of the individual soul proceeds and its shapes develop in determinateness, the moments of negativity and hence mediation will give the movement its genuine *Schluss* form.[37]

Before proceeding with the next moment of the natural soul, let us briefly note another point regarding method. At this bare beginning, we are yet far from the level of conscious subjectivity. Nevertheless Hegel has introduced material that we ordinarily associate with conscious life, e.g., the exercise of a talent, the expression of temperament and character. These and other determinations of the Anthropology are meant to be understood as "moments" of consciousness—logical steps in the "unfolding" of subjectivity "to" consciousness—which can nevertheless hardly be discussed except in terms of the content of conscious life. It is in this sense, says Hegel, that our method requires a certain "anticipation" of stages of development that have not yet made their appearance in the deduction.[38]

b. The Natural Alterations

In the preceding first moment of the natural soul, that of the natural qualities, the individual soul emerged as the actualization of the abstract universal *Naturgeist*. With this coming to be of the singular soul, the determinations take on a different logical character from that of the qualities. They now derive from the opposition of the universal and the singular within the singular soul itself. The soul as individuality steps into opposition to its own inner universality or "substance." [39] In the individual soul the distinctions in the first instance take the form of "alterations" (*Veränderungen*).[40] The alterations are "in" the individual (*an ihm*), which abides as permanent subject in these moments of its development according to the universal life of the species. From the logical

---

[37] Negation in the logic does not become explicit until the category of Being-for-self. In mere determinate Being as such, the moment of negation is but implicit (*als eingehüllt*). (L 172) In the category of quality we have not reached Being-for-self.

[38] *PhM* 55; see also above, p. 42.

[39] *PhM* 55; *FPhG* 33.

[40] *PhM* 55.

point of view the natural alterations have a higher, i.e., more ideal relation to the subject than the natural qualities. The alterations are succeeding phases of one and the same subject, as compared with the qualities, which are more or less fixed *Seienden*.[41] The alterations are in the first instance the growth and maturation stages of the individual constituting the course of the "life ages" (*Verlauf der Lebensalter*).

The course of the life ages begins with the contradiction of the universal in this immediate singularity, the foetus, and ends with the victory of the universal in the death of the individual. As a natural life, the individual succumbs in death, the "abstract negation" of his singularity. To be sure, even in nature there is more than this abstract negation of the singular, since the genus process means that "subjectivity has coalesced with itself." [42] The animal subjectivity, however, cannot actualize the universal for itself. What is genus in the realm of animal life is objective rationality in the realm of Spirit.[43] As Spirit, says Hegel, the human individual has the power of actualizing the universal for himself, and the course of the life ages is not only a biological development but more essentially a laying of the foundation for the education (*Bildung*) of the individual in his universality as Spirit. Since the process of Spirit here is still on the natural level, however, the stages of the development fall asunder in time as a series of successive states (*Zustände*).

In its speculative consideration, according to Hegel, the ages of man constitute a movement whose course is a closing together of beginning and end. From its "envelopment within self" in childhood, the individual soul sunders itself into the opposition of particular and universal in youth, overcomes the opposition in the man's encounter with and acceptance of the universal, and returns to the simple unity of childhood in the dulling habituation of old age that marks the coming of death.[44]

The foetus, says Hegel, is the immediate, abstract unity of singularity and universality, the genus-life as mere implicitness or potentiality.[45] At this first moment of individuality, the foetus is but the soul's simple

---

[41] Hegel defines "alteration" logically as follows: "In so far as something alters, the alteration falls within its constitution; it is that *in* the something which becomes an other. The something itself preserves itself in the alteration, which affects only this unstable surface of its otherness not its determination." (*SL* 124)

[42] See above, p. 45.

[43] *FPhG* 33.

[44] *PhM* 64.

[45] " In the grain of seed the plant appears as a simple, immediate unity of the self and the genus." (*PhN* 323)

unity with itself, Spirit closed up within itself. The unborn child is hardly yet an individuality, hardly yet relates itself to particular things in particular ways. Surrounded by the amniotic fluid, it absorbs an unbroken stream of nourishment, draws as yet no intermittent breath.[46] Its coming to birth—a "tremendous leap"—is the first sundering of this oppositionless unity, the first step in the individual's particularized relation to otherness. The newborn's first independent act, breathing, is a taking in and expelling of the surrounding material at one definite point in the body. But even in this first act of intussusception, according to Hegel, the infant shows itself different from the animal life. The body of the infant is of far greater fineness than that of the animal cub, and the higher nature is revealed in the greater need. Where the cub's first breaths are drawn in silence, the infant's are accompanied by an imperious bawling, which "ideal activity" already shows the child's implicit certainty that it has the "right" to satisfaction, that the independence of the external is but a nought as against man.[47]

Infancy and childhood are seen by Hegel as mainly a time of natural harmony. The child's needs are satisfied in the bosom of the family, and he lives in simple innocence, enveloped by the love and care of parents. The child is not yet fully a subjectivity; it is for itself "through another subjectivity," that of the parent. The child's destiny as Spirit, however, is to actualize itself as subjectivity for itself. It grows teeth, stands upright, learns to walk and orient itself toward external reality, and this directing itself outwardly is also its gaining of individuality.[48] The child's learning to say "I" is a sensing of its own universality and simultaneously a beginning to grasp things as universals.[49] As a boy he becomes more and more aware of the adult world as one different from his own, the feeling dawning in him that he is not what he ought to be. He begins to worship heroes, dream of great deeds, imitate models of behavior. Still standing within the framework of immediacy, he intuits the "higher"

---

[46] PhN 367, 353; FPhG 35.

[47] PhM 59. Cf. Kant, who views the human infant's first cry as a protesting of its inherent freedom in the face of its present helplessness. (APH 268, 327 n.)

[48] FPhG 35.

[49] According to Kant, before the child can say "I," it "merely feels itself; now it thinks itself." (APH 127) Schelling tells us: "Kant in his Anthropology finds it noteworthy that as soon as the child begins to speak of himself through the pronoun 'I' a new world seems to rise up for him." (System des transzendentalen Idealismus, Hamburg, 1957, p. 42)

in the form of individual personages. Boyhood ripens to youth when in puberty the life of the genus stirs in him and seeks satisfaction.

The youth turns from boyish imitativeness and hero worship to ideals in their form of universality. But the idealism of youth, says Hegel, has the form of a onesided subjectivity. For the youth, society is philistinism. He sees himself called upon to remake the world, and since his ideal remains unrealized he feels himself shut out and unrecognized. His actual entrance into civil society, where each man seems bent on his personal interest,[50] comes as a painful shock. The contradiction between the youth's lofty sentiments and his enforced preoccupation with what he regards as demeaning particularities may plunge him into hypochondria—a condition of self-sunderance, according to Hegel, that consists in the youth's unwillingness or inability to give up his onesided subjectivity.

The man recognizes the objective necessity and rationality in the world, at least to the extent of being able to engage himself with it in some particular sphere of activity. Often the reconciliation appears at first in terms of mere need. The world seems only to offer the alternative: Give up your ideals or perish. Yet, says Hegel, the world is not some static and dead thing, but like the life process itself it is ever bringing itself forth anew in its self-preserving. In this *erhaltende Hervorbringen* consists the work of man, says Hegel, though in appearance his activity may have the aspect of a pursuit of private interest. In his role in family and community the mature man brings to actuality what was true in the ideals of the youth and "works off" what was empty and untrue. In every field of endeavor, claims Hegel, there is the underlying substantiality of the ethical, the political, and the religious, wherein the individual can find wholeness and unity with the universal.[51]

Over the years there emerges for the man a universal perspective on all his doings. Every particularity finds its place in the pattern, and soon it appears that there can be hardly anything new. The old man lives in release and freedom from entangling interests. He hardly any longer looks ahead, for he believes that whatever the future may bring it will wear the mien of familiarity. His detached wisdom means also a

[50] In "civil society," according to Hegel, individuals are "private persons whose end is their own interest." (*PhR* 124)

[51] It is not on the "slaughter-bench" of history, where "individuals in general are regarded under the category of means," but in "morality, ethics, religion" that the individual has his highest relation to the universal, to the "essentially eternal and divine." (*PhH* 33)

loss of touch with the incidentals and particulars of the present. This coming together of the subjectivity and its objective world, says Hegel, is in effect a return to the oppositionless unity of childhood. The "process of life has become the inertia of *habit*," [52] and the dulling habituation of the organism is the sinking back of the individual life into the power of the universal in death.[53]

Thus, for Hegel, a man's life-span has its meaning as a movement of Spirit. Although as "natural," the process takes place in time, its essential meaning as a whole, as well as the meaning of the particular stages, derives from the moments of the Notion. While the "life ages" theme is one beloved of poets and writers, a speculative consideration may ask the question, what is an "age"? why this "stage" as a particular demarcation in the whole? If the part is to have more than an external relation to the whole, its very meaning as "this" part must refer immanently to the others and to the whole. Not only must the part be in the whole, but the whole must in some fashion be in the part. In the realm of Spirit, as in the present notion of the life ages, Hegel conceives each stage as expressing the notion in a manner peculiar to itself that is at the same time an expression of the whole.[54] This is more than saying the part is in the whole, or even that "each part can only be understood through the whole"—which is already true for certain areas in inorganic nature. Rather, as in organism, and even more eminently in Spirit, "in each part the whole of the form is manifest." [55]

In Hegel's presentation of youth, for example, the particular stage is "this" particularity precisely as an expression of the whole. Youth, according to Hegel, marks the sunderance and particularization constituting the break from the abstract identity of singularity and universality in childhood. At the same time this break makes possible the unity of concrete individuality and universality in manhood. The sunderance of youth is the moment of "first negation," and surely it would be hard

---

[53] *PhN* 441. "The living being, as a singular, dies from the habit of life, in that it lives itself into its body, into its reality. Vitality makes itself, for itself, into the universal, in that the activities become universal; and it is in this universality that the vitality itself dies; for since vitality is a process, opposition is necessary to it, and now the other which it should have had to overcome is for it no longer an other." (*PhN* 442; see also *PhR* 260-61)

[53] *PhM* 64.

[54] "Every stage is really the Idea, but the earlier stages contain it only in rather an abstract form." (*PhR* 253)

[55] *PhN* 161.

to find a more compelling instance of the dialectical meaning of negativity than the period of youth. The youth takes up a defiant and challenging attitude toward parents, tradition, self—toward all that he had formerly accepted with the implicit faith of childhood. Everything is put to the test and found wanting. The youth will have none of the pretense of the adult world. He will brook only the truth, which he knows to be the pure ideal contained within himself. This negativity, Hegel indicates, is essential to the youth's becoming an independent individuality. His pushing off the "found" world from himself is necessary for a new union with it, not the simple unity of the unawakened child but one posited by himself and made unto his own through his own overcoming of the negative both within himself and without. Thus the universal is in him precisely in his negativity toward it. The stage of sunderance is a moment of the whole, contains implicitly the whole and, sublating itself as "this" stage, becomes the whole.

The course of the life ages constitutes the first moment of the *Schluss* of the natural alterations. It marks the completion of the individual soul as a natural life insofar as the universal is actualized in it through the succeeding stages of childhood, maturation, and death.

The second moment of the natural alterations is that of the "real opposition" (*reeller Gegensatz*) of the individual toward himself. It is his seeking and finding himself in an other individual: the sex relationship.[56] Once again on this level of the *Naturgeist*, it is important to see the determination as essentially spiritual and not merely natural. The plant life, according to Hegel, displays only "an analogue" of the sexual relationship, "for the sides of the relation are not two individuals"[57] and the genus-process is only "formal."[58] The sex relationship of animals is that of two individuals, but, as we have seen, the animal singularity only senses the universal in the immediate form of another singularity. In the notion of natural organism the process of propagation "spends itself in the spurious infinite" and the genus preserves itself "only through the destruction of the individuals who, in the process of generation, fulfil their destiny and, in so far as they have no higher destiny, in this process meet their death."[59] In the realm of Spirit the individual has a higher destiny. Here, where the universal as universal can be for

[56] *PhM* 64.
[57] *PhN* 344.
[58] *PhN* 346.
[59] *PhN* 414.

the individual, the sex relationship is a way the individual soul proceeds to become for itself in its universality as Spirit.

In this second moment of "real opposition," the self-relation of the soul as singularity and universality is different from that of the course of the life ages. Where the determinations in the life ages were alterations of the individual, who remained the "one abiding subject" in them, the sex relation sends the individual "out of himself" to seek and find himself in a "real" other. By virtue of this real opposition, there is attained a higher, more ideal relation of the singular soul to itself as universal substance, since there is now negation and mediation. Instead of taking the form of passing alterations in the one abiding subject, the opposition and unity of the singular and universal now consists in a movement whereby the singularity relates itself negatively to itself and returns to itself in and through another singularity.[60]

Thus in the realm of Spirit the sex relation brings forward the universal as for itself the universal.[61] To be sure, the distinction of the sexes has its natural basis, as everywhere in the Anthropology. For Hegel as for Aristotle, the masculine is the active form-imparting nature, the feminine the passive form-receiving material.[62] But in Hegel's notion of Spirit as subjectivity, the Aristotelian distinction of matter and form takes on a somewhat different meaning. Male and female become the complementary moments of the universal as "Being-for-self subjectivity."

As femininity, says Hegel, the singular subjectivity remains in feeling-unity with itself as universality in moral life, love, and family—without striving toward the wider expressions of the universal in political, scientific, and artistic endeavors. The masculine nature goes forth actively, bending to the task of applying universal objective aims to the merely existent conditions—within its own nature and in the world—thereby at once shaping the world and transforming itself, and in this way bringing itself to unity with the universal.[63] The feminine spirit, in Hegel's view,

---

[60] "The first moment in love is that I do not wish to be a self-subsistent and independent person and that, if I were, then I would feel defective and incomplete. The second moment is that I find myself in another person, that I count for something in the other, while the other in turn comes to count for something in me." (PhR 261; see also JR 200 ff.)

[61] PhN 414.

[62] PhN 413.

[63] PhM 64. Along with the "real opposition" of masculine and feminine, the "nature of each permeats both; and both exist within the sphere of this universality." (PhN 412)

is fulfilled in home and children, intuitively perceptive rather than intellectually powerful, most at home in immediate personal matters rather than abstract affairs. The masculine mind is free-ranging in imagination and strong in conceptual thinking, directed toward the broader goals of public life and intellectual pursuits.[64] Love, as uniting these opposites, is the "feeling unity" of Spirit with itself.[65]

Out of the "real opposition" within the soul, which sends it out beyond itself, there arises a new distinction of the soul within itself. The new distinction is not only "in" the soul but "for" it. In the third and concluding moment of the natural alterations, the soul attains to its first Being-for-self as subjectivity in the proper sense.[66]

This first appearance of *Fürsichsein,* Hegel terms the soul's natural "awakening" (*Erwachen*).[67] As still a natural determination, the soul's Being-for-self has here the form of a "state" (*Zustand*), opposed to and opposed by the state of "sleep." The soul's awakening, says Hegel, is not only "for us" the observers; it is the soul's own "immediate judgment," [68] the soul's own dividing of itself from itself by setting itself opposite its own substantial being which now becomes "for it." Thus the distinction is not only within the singular subjectivity as such, but at the same time marks a new relation of the soul to itself as singularity to universality.

In this its natural awakening, according to Hegel, the soul for the first time takes on the character of subjectivity. Up to now the soul's determinations have been distinctions "in it" (*an ihr*), i.e., belonging to it, but not yet "for" the soul itself. We the observers distinguished the determinations, such as the stages of the life ages. To be sure, even here the soul was in a certain sense "for itself," since, as we noted, the universal was ever implicitly present in each particular stage. Yet the succession of distinctions went on blindly as a natural process. Hereafter

---

[64] *PhR* 114-115.

[65] *PhR* 110. In love, "life is present as a duplicate of itself and as a single and unified self." (*Early Theological Writings,* trans. T. M. Knox, Chicago, 1948, p. 305)

[66] Though we are still far from the level of the objective consciousness.

[67] *PhM* 65.

[68] See above, p. 16. While for Kant judgment belongs to the faculty of understanding, Hegel sees *Urteil* as belonging not to a faculty but the essential *Scheidung in sich* of Spirit as Notion. Thus in the movement of the soul we shall see what may be called a germinal development of understanding. In Hegel's notion of *Urteil* (here and at later stages of the soul) we may note his endeavor to overcome the Kantian dualism of the "two stems" of knowledge: the understanding, which can "intuit nothing," and the sensibility, which can "think nothing." (*CPR* A 51 = B 75)

the soul will be "for itself" in its distinctions in a manner not yet encountered in its development. In this first "awakening," however, it would be more correct to say that the soul attains its Becoming-for-self. On the present natural level the awakening has the character of a mere "happening," the soul's first "finding of self" (*Sichfinden*) that is yet far from the level of the rational consciousness, whose emergence will also be termed an "awakening" but in another sense.

Within the waking state of consciousness falls the whole gamut of self-conscious and rational activity of the mind. On the level which we now take sleep and awakening, we prescind from that activity as such in order to consider the most primary Being-for-self of subjectivity as a dimension of natural soul. Hence the present awakening is the soul's wholly abstract distinguishing of itself from itself as merely being (*nur seiend*). The self-dividing of the soul in its awakening is its stepping opposite itself (*gegenübertreten*). But this dividing remains within the soul itself as a self-enclosed natural life: it is not yet the positing of its content as an external world that will mark its emergence as consciousness. The soul opposes itself to its own *seiende* selfhood as its sleep and has its Being-for-self in this opposition.

Sleep, according to Hegel, is the state of the soul's sunkenness in its undifferentiated substantial unity or universality. Waking is the state of the soul as having entered into opposition with this its universal Being. Sleep and waking, however, do not have the character of mere alterations but "alternating states" (*wechselnden Züstande*), the one going over into the other. Sleep is the soul's return into its universal natural Being and undifferentiated unity with itself. Hence, says Hegel, sleep is not merely rest as cessation of activity. It is the soul's return within itself in its simple universality, the restoration of its wholeness from its dispersion in the particulars of waking life.[69] In relation to the later rational consciousness, sleep will signify a surrendering of the active subjectivity and a "healing" of the diremption of self in consciousness. Sleep is a retirement to the natural subjectivity from the rational consciousness which grasps the outer world as a connectedness structured by the objective categories of the understanding. Hence, according to Hegel, in order to answer the old poser: how do I know I am not dreaming? Hegel says [70] that one need

---

[69] "Man cannot tarry long in his conscious mind; must take from time to time refuge in his unconscious, there his being has its roots." (From a fictive monologue by Goethe in Thomas Mann's *The Beloved Returns*.)

[70] *PhM* 66; see also *JR* 180, 184.

only employ the Kantian distinction of the "congruence" of a representation with "the criteria of all real experience,"[71] namely, its necessary connectedness, as against the contingent play of images that flow through the mind in the dream state.[72]

Wakeness and sleep take up into themselves the qualities and other determinations noted earlier in the soul's development. The two states express, for example, the planetary alternations of day and night. The soul's retiring to the undifferentiated uniformity of sleep, says Hegel, corresponds with the fading distinctiveness of things in the darkness of night.[73] The soul's awakening to self-distinction is also its awakening to the distinctiveness of things in the light of day and to the call of its manifold tasks. In sleep those organs and functions that are outwardly attuned, such as the senses, become inactive or subdued, while those concerned with the soul's concentration "within self" proceed with their work. When in the waking state a content takes on a uniform and undifferentiated aspect for the mind, Hegel notes, we become bored and sleepy, for "the opposition and unity of the mind with its object" makes for the liveliness of the waking state.

The soul's alternate gathering itself within its immediate substantial Being and its going outwards in the broad daylight of objective activity may be seen in a very loose way as corresponding with the spiritual distinctions of sex: the immediacy of inner moral feeling (feminine) as contrasted with the wider-ranging goals of purposeful activity (masculine); the power of the "nether world" (feminine) as against the "daylight of conscious existence" (masculine); the "law of the inward life" (feminine) as against the "law of the land" (masculine).[74]

---

[71] *CPR* B 278.

[72] Kant makes frequent reference to the "play of representations" in dreaming by way of contrast with the structured experience of objective consciousness. He does not set himself the problem of explaining how representations as such are possible. In the notion of the soul's *Urteil* of sleep and waking, Hegel seems to be trying to show how "awareness" of a particular content as such—on whatever level— is possible.

[73] "Night is the mother who nourishes all that is, and light is the pure form which first possesses being in union with night." But "the truth," says Hegel, is "the unity of both." (*PhN* 201)

[74] See *Phen.* 482, 739; *PhR* 115. At the risk of reading too much into Hegel here, we would say that the *Urteil* of sleep and waking, following upon the "real opposition" that sends the soul out beyond itself to find itself in "other," is Hegel's accounting, on this primitive level of the natural soul, for the elemental power of the psyche that produces the primary "awareness" as such of any content. See Aristotle on the "common sense" in *On Sleep and Waking* (455 a 15 ff.).

Hegel's notion of the natural alterations—comprising the second moment of the natural soul—cannot but strike the reader on first sight as strange. From the point of view of commonsense the three moments of the life ages, sex relationship, sleep and waking, surely comprise an odd kind of sequence for which to claim "immanent connection." [75] But it is Hegel's contention that commonsense is to be educated to the philosophic viewpoint, not philosophy accommodated to commonsense. We have been warned in the speculative consideration of a subject matter not to expect the kinds of sequence and connections we are accustomed to in everyday experience. According to Hegel the sequence of the natural alterations form a *Schluss,* whose logical movement we may briefly try to make clear.

Viewed in terms of the logic of the development of the natural soul, the awakening is the union of the two previous moments: the life ages and sex relationship. In both the latter, we recall, the relation of the soul as subjectivity to its substantiality as a genus life or universal was a relation of opposition and identity of singularity and universality. In the soul's awakening, this relationship attains a higher spiritual plane: namely, the newly emerging ideality of Being-for-self as subjectivity in a particular content. But in what sense, we may ask, has the soul attained a higher plane? The answer is, the ascension in ideality of the logical relation of singularity and universality. In the life ages, we saw the soul as simple subject persisting through its distinctions as passing alterations (*fliessende Veränderungen*) brought about in it by the universal as genus life; in the end the individual succumbs to the universal in death. In the sex relation, on the other hand, the genus or universal acts in the individual through a "real opposition" within himself. The "fixed opposition" (*feste Gegensatz*) is a determination of higher ideality than the *fliessende Veränderungen* for it is a distinction at once of the individual in his totality [76]—the felt lack in the individual that impels him out of himself to seek and find himself in another. Here the universal's power of death over the natural singularity is "contained" or "stayed" by the individual soul itself, which unites itself spiritually with another. The awakening, finally, is a still higher determination, for here again the individual distinguishes himself in his wholeness, yet not in the form of a *feste Gegensatz* but through relation to an opposite that is but an "alternate state" of his own self. The fixedness of opposition has been overcome,

---

[75] See *PhM* 66.
[76] See the story of Aristophanes in Plato's *Symposium.*

and the soul has returned to unity with itself—not back to the passively abiding subject of the transient alterations, but as "for itself" in its opposite.[77]

The individual soul as subjectivity is now related to itself as universal in the relation of waking and sleep. The ascension in ideality is marked by the movement of the determinations from 1) passing alterations, to 2) real opposition, to 3) alternating states. The constant passage into one another of sleep and awakening is the way, on the present level of natural soul, that the unity of the Being-in-self substantiality of the soul with its Being-for-self subjectivity first comes to expression.

c. Sentience (Empfindung)

Sleep and waking, as we have just seen, are not simply alterations but alternations, the one calling forth the other, the one going over into the other. As natural states, each has its "limit" outside itself in the other, which is therefore its own other.[78] Each implicitly contains the other in itself, for both arise out of the real opposition of the individual within himself: his going forth into the self-dispersion of waking life and his self-renewal through return to the primal sources of his natural Being in sleep. Hence each state in its separateness is but a onesidedness and untruth of the soul, and the ceaseless passing over of one state into the other and back is but the deficient expression of their implicit unity. In the apparently "bad infinity" of endless alternation lies the positive significance that the truth of each state is not merely its passing over into its opposite but the unity of both.[79]

---

[77] Hegel of course has been leading up to sensation or sentience, as we are about to see, and the demonstration of the natural alterations is the deduction of sentience. The role of the sex relation in this demonstration may be seen on the level of natural organism in Hegel's distinction between animal and plant. Reproduction in the plant is "not mediated by opposition" in the sense of the "veritable separation of the sides" in the sex-relation. The plant has no feeling inasmuch as "the Being-within-self is not yet self-subsistent in the face of the outer world" as it is in the animal. "Only that which possesses sensation (Empfindung) can tolerate itself as other, can, with the hardiness of individuality, assimilate it and venture into conflict with other individualities. The plant is the immediate, organic individuality in which the genus has the preponderance, and the reflection is not individual, the individual does not as such return into itself but is an Other and therefore has no self-feeling." (PhN 309, 312; see also below, p. 84)

[78] See L 172 ff.

[79] For the meaning of the spurious and the genuine infinity, see above, p. 45 n. 41.

The unity of wakeness and sleep is not a third "state": it is no longer a distinction of the soul in the form of a *Zu-stand,* a something beside or outside an other in time.[80] It is a determination in which the soul is at one and the same time "in itself" and "for itself," hence an instance of the soul's overcoming of the this-after-this (*Nacheinandersein*) of nature.[81] The substantial being of the soul, from which the soul in its awakening abstractly distinguished itself as its opposite state of sleep, is now "held in" (*enthalten*) as ideal moment in the soul's own self-distinguishing. Thus, says Hegel, the content-determinations of its sleeping nature "are *found* by the waking soul in its own self, and, be it noted, for itself." [82] Hereby distinction no longer has the status of a "quality" in the soul (*an ihr*) as a determination of its mere being. The content found is both distinguished *from* the identity of the subjectivity and at the same time *contained simply in* the simpleness of the subjectivity.[83] As thus "finding" its content within itself, says Hegel, the soul is "sentient" *(emp-firtdend).*

The sentient soul's finding of a content in this its first awakening, however, is not yet accompanied by an awareness of an objective outer world as source or locus of the content found. Externality in this sense has not yet arisen for the psychical subjectivity. The content found, says Hegel, comes from the soul's own "dark" side, which is the "other" to it in its awakening. The content found is "immediate," something merely "given" through the soul's own other; hence sentience as such is "the contradiction of the reflection of the soul within itself and its externality." [84] The "given," however, is given by an "other" that is but the soul itself in its natural substantiality—the soul, as we have seen, having "come to be" as the truth of nature as self-externality. Hence the given is implicitly negated in its immediacy and singularity, implicitly constituted as ideal by the fact that it is in the soul. In sentience, says Hegel, the Being-for-self of the soul in its awakening obtains its "first filling." For the first time, we may say, the soul is the ideality of its determinations as subjectivity. The sentient soul is that stage in the soul's development "where the universal constituting its nature becomes explicitly for it in an immediate determinateness." [85]

---

[80] *PhM* 67.
[81] See above, p. 41.
[82] *PhM* 71.
[83] *Ibid.;* see also *FPhG* 37.
[84] *FPhG* 37.
[85] *PhM* 72.

Sentience, however, is but the first appearance of subjectivity, the "worst" form of the spiritual, as Hegel would have it. Sentience is the "form of the dull stirring (dumpfes Weben) of Spirit in its unconscious and unintelligent individuality." [86] The sentient soul is natural soul, undeveloped and mainly passive, determined largely by the contingent externalities of space and time, not yet master of its material as it will be in the higher forms of thinking.

The sentient soul is subjectivity in its immediate singularity. No doubt, says Hegel, we can say that everything is in Empfindung, everything that arises in conscious intelligence has its source in sensation. Even morality and religion are not for my intellect alone but must be rooted in feeling, whereby I first make a content "my very own." But can any experience be more "trite," asks Hegel, "than that feelings and hearts are also bad, evil, godless, mean?" If the modes of feeling precede rational willing, the latter, according to Hegel, is nevertheless the truth of the former. Since the speculative study of Spirit is a going forward toward the beginning,[87] Hegel can accept the dictum: Nihil est in intellectu quod non fuerit in sensu," [88] and at the same time maintain that its deeper significance and truth lies in the converse.

The determinations of the sentient soul, according to Hegel, may be distinguished as 1) those coming from the "outer" senses, and 2) those coming from the "inner" of the soul. What the sentient soul finds in itself is on the one hand the "natural immediate" as in it ideal and "made unto its own," and on the other hand those passions and emotions belonging to the soul itself as Being-for-self and which are "specified to natural corporeality." [89] Thus sentience, for Hegel, is not to be under-

---

[86] PhM 73.

[87] See above, p. 37 "It is precisely the contradiction within sentience that impels Spirit to go beyond it, or rather to sublate it, just as the higher always emerges through the fact that the lower, as contradiction within itself, sublates itself to the higher." (FPhG 38)

[88] "If speculative philosophy refused to admit this maxim," says Hegel, "it can only have done so from a misunderstanding." But philosophy will no less assert that nothing is in sense that was not in thought; and this, says Hegel, may be taken in two ways: 1) "that Nous or Spirit (the more profound idea of Nous in modern thought) is the cause of the world"; and 2) that the sentiment of morals and religion is of such a kind that "it can spring from and rest upon thought alone." (L 15) With regard to the latter, Kant and Hegel are at one. But for Kant it is not through an Aufheben but an Erheben above the sensuous through our moral freedom that we attain to the supersensible.

[89] The distinction of "outer" and "inner," Hegel wants us to know, are as yet

stood merely in terms of passive receptivity. In the first sphere the determinations of the corporeality (e.g., the eye and other sense organs) must be "inwardized" (*erinnert*) in the Being-for-self of the soul, whereby alone they can be "sensed." In the second sphere the determinations arise *im Geiste* and, in order to be "found" and thereby sensed, must be "corporealized." It is in this way, says Hegel, that the content is in the subject as "posited" in the soul.[90] The specification of the first sphere consists in the system of the five senses. The second sphere is also systematically specified, mainly in the inner organs of the body.

Thus although the sentient soul obtains its first filling through a "finding," nevertheless Hegel wants us to understand that there is an essential moment of activity in sentience, as there is in all phases of the life of Spirit. Sentience for Hegel is not the faculty of pure receptivity and passivity in the way *Sinnlichkeit* is for Kant [91]—for it is not to be viewed as a faculty properly speaking but as a selfhood: "the sentient soul." The meaning of the sentient soul's "positing" of its content in itself, as we have just seen, derives from its self-dividing (as *Urteil*) and return to self in the states of sleep and waking. Yet in order to see the full dimension of the Hegelian notion of sentience, we need to look back once again to the Philosophy of Nature. For Hegel links his doctrine of sentience with that of his notion of natural materiality, and in so doing he puts forward certain far-reaching claims for his concept of the sentient soul.

In the science of Organics, Hegel tells us that the animal individual exists "as subjectivity" insofar as the organism "in its process outwards preserves inwardly the unity of the self." [92] In this process outwards the sentient organism differs from the vegetable organism; in its very exter-

---

only for us, the observers, and not yet for the soul itself which has not yet posited its content as an objective outer world.

90 *PhM* 76.

91 *APH* 140. For Hegel, what comes to existence in Spirit can do so only through the self-determining Spirit's positing it in itself. (*FPhG* 41-42) Speaking of Schelling's concept of "stimulation by external potencies," which Hegel regards as an improvement over that of "the action of external causes," Hegel nevertheless regards the former as inadequate: "But of all the concoctions of external reflection in the sciences, none is more unphilosophical than the introduction of such formal and material relationships in the theory of stimulation as have long been regarded as philosophical, the introduction, for example, of the wholly abstract opposition of receptivity and active capacity, which are supposed to stand to each other as factors in inverse ratio of magnitude." (*PhN* 385-386)

92 *PhN* 351.

nalization the sentient organism returns to itself in the form of "self-feeling." [93] Whereas the plant's relationship to other is only that of "assimilation," the animal has in addition a "theoretical relation." To be sure, the theoretical process itself is to be understood organically as a moment of assimilation,[94] an advanced development in the animal of assimilation. Assimilation, as an essential life-process, consists in that the organism "posits" its non-organic nature "inwardly as ideal." [95] In the theoretical process, however, the organism does not do this physically, as in nutrition, but ideally, so that in being related to its other the organism is "at the same time related to self, preserving its own freedom in face of the object, while the freedom of the object, too, is left inviolate." [96] In the plant the return-into-self in assimilation does not result in self-feeling. Such a result can only occur where, in the process outwards, the animal nature "in the actuality and externality of immediate singularity," is equally "the *inwardly reflected* self of *singularity, inwardly* present *subjective* universality." [97] It is this inward reflectedness that makes possible the theoretical relation of sentience. Thus light, in the plant's color, can only be a "being-for-other." [98] In the plant "the selflike character (*Selbstischkeit*) of light as an objective presence does not develop into vision." The plant's relation to light "does not become a union-with-self, but a fashioning of itself into a light-plant (*Lichtpflanze*)." [99] Thus while light in a sense has been assimilated in the plant, it remains as "color" but a property of the plant, which is not "for itself" in this determination. The plant does not contain the theoretical process. The color "in" the plant is "not the light which has been reborn in the midnight of sleep, in the darkness of the pure ego —not this spiritualized light as existent negativity." [100]

Thus we see in the sentient organism's theoretical relation of the life-process a continuity with the notion of the sentient soul as Spirit. While the sentient soul's "positing" of its determinations in itself derives directly from its *Urteil* in sleep and awakening, this positing by the sentient

[93] See above, p. 81 n. 77.
[94] *PhN* 380-81.
[95] *PhN* 356.
[96] *PhN* 180.
[97] *PhN* 351.
[98] *Ibid.*
[99] *PhN* 336.
[100] *PhN* 337. On this "midnight of sleep" and "darkness of the pure ego," see below, p. 104 n. 4.

subjectivity as Spirit is also to be understood as a further specification and development of the more elemental and purely natural inner reflectedness of the sentient organism in its life-process.

Hegel claims to have shown in his Philosophy of Nature that "the animal organism is the microcosm, the center of nature which has achieved an existence for itself in which the whole of inorganic nature is recapitulated and idealized." [101] If this is so for the animal organism, it must be *a fortiori* true for the "perfect animal, in the human organism." [102] Therefore, although in outer sensation, as Hegel says, our body is determined externally,[103] we do not begin here with a notion of a *tabula rasa* that obtains a filling through "impressions" from outside, nor do we begin with a notion of abstract receptivity or passivity. For Hegel the sentient soul is nature "knowing itself," though indeed not the higher kind of knowing that belongs to Spirit in its intelligent modes.

Sentience in general, says Hegel, may be termed the healthy living-together (*Mitleben*) of the individual soul in its corporeality. "My body is the middle term by which I come together with the external world as such." [104] The outer senses, according to Hegel, constitute a simple system of specified "bodiness" (*Körperlichkeit*). As the soul is in general the simple ideality of its body, it is also, in its ways of sensing, the ideality of external body. Hence, says Hegel, why we have the five senses and just these five is demonstrable according to the nature of natural body in its notion.[105]

In Hegel's division, the five senses comprise three classes: 1) sight and hearing; 2) smell and taste; and 3) feeling or touch. These classes, Hegel maintains, correspond with the three moments of natural body as abstract physical ideality, real difference, and solid reality—or, as formal moments of the Notion: abstract universality, particularity, and concrete individuality. Each class of the senses presents a moment of material body in its notion. Why the threefoldness of the Notion goes over into the five-foldness of the senses will become evident shortly. Why the moments have separate existence at all for the ideality of the soul, Hegel tells us,

---

[101] *PhN* 356. "In general, the existence of the organic being is the act of the whole earth, in which it individualizes and contracts itself, the reflection-into-self of the universal." (*PhN* 302)

[102] *PhN* 357. "Through myself, nature, do I first of all know thee, through myself feel thee most profoundly." (From Goethe's "monologue" in Thomas Mann, *op. cit.*)

[103] *PhM* 77.

[104] *PhM* 146; see also *SL* 766.

[105] *PhM* 76, 77; *PhN* 382 ff.

lies in the fact that the sentient soul is itself still a natural subjectivity whose forms of unifying activity go over into particular existences, i.e., the various senses.[106] The order in which we consider the senses is not important. The main point is that the senses, "as rational, constitute a totality," [107] and as this sensuous totality the sentient soul is the truth of external materiality.

Sight and hearing, according to Hegel, present particular body in its manifestation as abstract universality. For sight the ideality of body manifests itself in the form of simple self-relation. Sight is the sense of the material in its moment of abstract ideality: light.[108] In sight, the particular body shows itself spatially. Light itself, in which all things are seen, is "physicalized space" (der physikalischgewordene Raum).[109] Like space, light is unseparated extension lacking all inner determination and inner difference, hence "simple Being-outside-self." As at once self-external and abstractly identical with itself, light is "material ideality," the "immaterial matter," the "absolutely light" (das absolut Leichte).[110] Light contains no limit within itself, offers no resistance, extends on all sides to the immeasurable. It is only with this ideal element and its "obscuration" (Trübung) through "the dark"—that is, with color—that sight has to do.

Basing himself in large part on the researches of Goethe, Hegel argues at length against the Newtonian view that white light (sunlight) is composed of many different colors.[111] Light, according to Hegel, is simple. Color only arises as a combination of light and darkness, where the two "are in such a relationship that while they are held asunder they are just as much posited in unity; they are separate and yet each also shows in the other." [112] For this reason, darkness "is present in all color phenomena." The relation of light and darkness in color involves the basic principle for Hegel that all determination is negation. Light is

---

[106] PhN 382 ff.; PhM 76 ff.

[107] PhN 384.

[108] Light is matter as "pure identity-with-self, unity of reflection-into-self," the "existent, universal self of matter." (PhN 87) In showing the relation of the respective senses to the moments of the notion of body, we can only deal briefly with certain main points in the presentation of body in the Naturphilosophie.

[109] PhM 78.

[110] PhN 91.

[111] PhN 198 ff.

[112] PhN 198.

"the pure making manifest which is nothing but a making manifest." [113] As "abstract identity," light has its difference "outside it, as the Not of light" existing as physical corporealities. The determinations manifested must come from elsewhere as the "limit" of light. Light as such is invisible: "in pure light nothing is seen, just as little as in pure darkness." [114] It is first in limit that the moment of negation—"and therefore of determination"—arises. Limit is present in the dark body as "heavy matter," "specified matter," to which *das absolut Leichte* stands in relation as to an "other" that is yet external to it. Material specification is here the merely spatial difference of surfaces. The corporeality is rough, smooth, pointed, thus placed, etc. The difference of things visible is hence in the first instance a difference of spatial shapes; "only thus do light and shade arise." In this first moment of manifesting as such, the determinations are "merely spatial."

The element of darkness, however, also brings color. Darkness, while the negative of light, is for Hegel not simply absence of light but also "positive," something on its own account.[115] But the dark first becomes "real" as "physical, individualized corporeality" in its "interior existence." [116] Darkness is an "active principle" of corporeality in its moment of brittleness (*Sprödigkeit*),[117] a distinction from body as "pure crystal," which is "transparent and a medium for light." [118] The active principle in brittleness develops into "the abstract, one-sided extreme of compact solidity, of passive cohesion (the metallic principle)." [119] The "manifestation of color" is the positing, through the intermediation of transparency, in a "concrete and individualized unity," of the "dark element and the bright element, each separately existent." [120] Thus on the one hand, material individuality is an "inward darkening" inasmuch as it "shuts itself off from ideal manifestation to an other"; at the same time, however, the individual form which, as totality, "has pervaded its matter,"

---

[113] *PhN* 91.
[114] *PhN* 89; *Phen.* 192.
[115] *PhN* 95.
[116] *PhN* 195.
[117] *PhN* 194.
[118] *PhN* 182.
[119] *PhN* 195. The "fundamental principle" in the process of darkening, which accounts for color, is that, "loss of brightness is bound up with specific gravity and cohesion." These determinations (which include brittleness), in contrast to the abstract identity of pure manifestation (light as such), are "the peculiarities and specifications of corporeality." (*PhN* 196)
[120] *PhN* 195.

in the various determinations of specific gravity, including brittleness, "has thereby entered into manifestation and advances to this ideality of definite being (*Dasein*),[121] which includes the determination of color. In this way, color is a property: a unity of the moments of body's "showing" or being-for-other, and its remaining with itself in its own proper determination.[122]

Since sight has to do only with the ideal element, light, and its obscuration in color, the properly material character of body, its solidity, is not manifested to vision. As pure sensation, our seeing is a seeing of surface.[123] We perceive depth and solidity only after experience with touch.[124] We see the "same thing" with two eyes because they "make their sight of the object into one sight," the "unity of direction" sublating the "diversity of sensation."[125] If the eyes are focused on something else in the field of vision, however, it is possible to see an object "doubled."

Sight, however, is but one of the two senses to which body in its ideality is manifested. Since the ideality, in this first moment of the notion of body as universality, is that of body in its abstract self-relation, it cannot be "concrete" totality, says Hegel, but falls apart into two mutually indifferent determinations: the outer manifestation of simple self-relation presented to sight; and the inner manifestation of self-negation presented to hearing.[126]

Whereas light is space become physical, sound is time become physical.[127] Where light is physical ideality as unbroken extension, sound is this ideality as concentrated inner movement. Sound is thus also the "immateriality of the material" but as the pure oscillation of body within itself, a mechanical quivering (*Erzittern*) wherein body, without changing

---

[121] *PhN* 184.

[122] "Now color as a property presupposes a subject, and is held (*gehalten*) in its subjectivity; but as a particular property, color is also for an other—and every property, as such, exists only for the sense of a living creature. We are this other, the sentient subjects; our sense of sight is determined by colors.... Color is for an other, but this other must leave color to the body; thus the other has only a theoretical, not a practical relationship to color. The sense (of sight) leaves the property as it is; true, the property is for sense, but the latter does not seize the property for itself." (*PhN* 216)

[123] "Only colors are for sight; shape belongs to touch and only discloses itself to sight through the alternation of light and shade." (*PhN* 216)

[124] *PhM* 78.

[125] *PhN* 383.

[126] *PhN* 382, 384; *PhM* 78.

[127] *PhN* 137, 384.

its relative place, moves only its parts. In sound, body posits its "inner spatiality" timewise.[128] In letting its "pure inwardness" step forth and immediately recovering itself out of the mechanical vibration of its parts, body negates ideally its self-externality as materiality.

Hence while sight is "the sense of ideality as a manifestation of the *outer* for the outer," [129] hearing, says Hegel, is the sense of "inwardness." Hegel links hearing with voice as the "sense of the manifestation of the organism's *inwardness* expressed as such in its utterance, the sense of sound." [130] While in sight the external object is "an indifferent self," in hearing it is a "self-sublating self." In voice, says Hegel, sense "returns to inwardness." The voice, as "active hearing," is the pure self positing itself as universal in expressing its particular feelings.[131]

Thus for Hegel, in sight and hearing, as well as the other senses, as we shall shortly note, our nature is to be the truth of nature. Our system of outer senses comprises not only the fundamental modes of our relating ourselves to physical externality but embodies the implicit truth of that externality in the moments of its notion. To be sure, our sense of sight does not tell us that light is "space become physical," or our sense of hearing that sound expresses "the flight from materiality" and the "transition to the immaterial and ideal." Our senses contain the implicit truth of nature but are not philosophers of nature. Nevertheless, in the general relation of the senses to external body, we may see certain spiritual aspects that are of interest for a philosophical anthropology.

Our seeing, Hegel points out, is a seeing of body in its pure extendedness suggestive of a timeless quiescence. We see at a distance,[132] we "look on," our attitude is a detached beholding in which we take the object wholly on its ideal side, leaving it eternally unaltered.[133] In vision we do not encounter body in its properly material aspect—which for

---

[128] Sound is the "at first *inward form*, emerging from its submergence in material asunderness" which "becomes *free* in the *negation* of the self-subsistence of this its asunderness." (*PhN* 136-37)

[129] *PhN* 382.

[130] *Ibid.*

[131] "Every animal suffering violent death has a voice, and thereby declares its own supersession." (*PhN* 384)

[132] Cf. Aristotle's *De Anima* 419a13.

[133] "In treating of visibility we are in the field of ideality, for visibility as such is the positing of something as ideally present in an other." (*PhN* 189) The Platonic *eidos*, perhaps the first of philosophy's pure concepts, means literally, that which is seen. "The eye lends distance to things, it makes them into objects." (Bruno Snell, *The Discovery of the Mind*, trans. T. G. Rosenmeyer, Harper Torchbook, 1960, p. 33)

Hegel is weight—and for this reason, according to Hegel, sight is called the noblest of the senses. In our hearing of sound—this "mechanical soul" (*Seelenhaftigkeit*) of materiality—we are "caught up" in a way that is different from a detached beholding. In sound we encounter "the emergence of the specific inner being freed from gravity," for sound is "the plaint of the ideal in the midst of violence, but also its triumph over the latter since it preserves itself therein." [134] Sound affects our innermost feelings. "It speaks to the inner soul since it is itself inner and subjective." [135] The "natural man," says Hegel, "marvels at sound since in it an inner being is revealed; he does not presuppose a material basis for it but rather something psychic" (*ein Seelenhaftes*).[136]

In Hegel's treatment of sight and hearing we see further his endeavor to view man as the truth of nature—not merely in his explicit knowing but in his very being. Where Kant would permit a reading of our subjective purposiveness into nature only in the aesthetic or teleological judgment but never "constitutively" for scientific knowledge, Hegel rejects this sort of demarcation.[137] He does so on the ground of a different notion of sensation from that of Kant. Our senses, Hegel seeks to show, do not cut us off from nature but establish our continuity with nature. If the primitive perceives a *Seelenhaftes* in what sounds, he is not so wrong, according to Hegel, for sound is indeed the "mechanical soul" of materiality. While Kant rejects any scientific view of nature beyond mechanism as anthropomorphic hyperphysics, Hegel would perhaps reply that it is no less anthropomorphic to maintain that no doctrine of nature can be scientific except insofar as it can contain mathematics.[138]

The senses of the second class, smell and taste, relate to natural body in the second moment of the notion of *Körperlichkeit*: real difference or opposition.[139] This moment is body in its process of dissolution or decomposition, its becoming other. To understand smell and taste as the "senses of difference" which pertain to the "self-developing process"

---

[134] *PhN* 139.

[135] See Heinz Heimsoeth, "Hegels Philosophie der Musik," *Hegel-Studien*, bd. 2, 1963, pp. 167 ff.

[136] *PhN* 138.

[137] It is "the perpetual contradiction in Kant's philosophy," says Hegel. (See *HPh* III, p. 472; *L* 114)

[138] For Kant, "in every special doctrine of nature only so much science proper can be found as there is mathematics in it." (*Metaphysical Foundations of Natural Science*, trans. J. Ellington, New York, 1970, p. 6)

[139] *PhN* 382; *PhM* 76, 79.

of materiality as such, we must note briefly Hegel's concept of the "elements" and their role in the process of difference.

Whereas light is the abstract "universal self" of matter and its indeterminate ideality, the determinations of "the elemental totality" that have "an immediate existence as free, independent bodies" are the four "universal, physical elements": air, fire, water, and earth.[140] Odor and taste are among the determinations of "physical specification" wherein the individual body, as "subject" of these determinations, "contains them as properties or predicates" but in such a manner that they are at the same time a "relationship towards their unbound, universal elements and form processes with them." [141] In the case of odor, the elements are fire and air; in the case of taste, water.

The "combustible fiery element" [142]—which is fire in the "violent" process of consumption and air in the pervasive "insidious" process [143]—is the body's smell: "the permanent, unsuspected process of its consumption." But consumption, says Hegel, does not have here the chemical sense of oxidation, but "air individualized to the simplicity of a specific process." [144] Odor thus presents "specific individuality as a simple theoretical process, the volatilization of body in air." [145] Smell is our sensation of "this silent process, immanent in body, in which body is consumed in the air, which itself has no odor for the very reason that in it everything passes off in odor." [146] Odor is the specific individuality of bodies "concentrated in their difference," it is their "entire specific character turned outwards and consuming itself in the process."

---

[140] PhN 105 ff. The term "elements" for Hegel does not have the usual meaning of incomposites in the chemical sense. Hegel's "physical elements" are "universal matters particularized solely in conformity with the moments of the Notion," which here has to do "only with the becoming of individuality and at first, only with that of the universal individual, the Earth: the elements are the differentiated matters which constitute the moments of this becoming of the universal individual." (PhN 107)

[141] PhN (178).

[142] Fire is "materialized time or selfhood (light identical with heat), the absolutely restless and consuming element." (PhN 110)

[143] Air as such "is already this wasting activity." "Air is slumbering fire." (Ibid.)

[144] PhN 179. Air is "purely corrosive, the enemy of all that is individual which it posits as a universal element." (PhN 108) Air "renders bodies odorous; for being odorous is only this invisible ceaseless process between what is individual and air. Everything evaporates and turns to fine dust, and the residue is odorless." (PhN 109)

[145] PhN 217.

[146] PhN 218.

Fire, the "absolutely restless and consuming element," in consuming an other "also consumes itself" and "thus passes over into neutrality." [147] The "neutral element" is water, in which the opposition has "returned into itself." Water does not have "the unrest of process in itself" but is "only the possibility of process, namely, solubility." [148] The moment of neutrality is "individualized to the specific physical neutrality of salinity and its determinations, acid, etc.;—to taste, to a property which, at the same time, remains in relationship with the element, with the abstract neutrality of water, in which body, as merely neutral, is soluble." [149]

Here we see that "taste" is defined by Hegel quite apart from our sensibility. Like color and odor, taste is a determination of the particularization as such of individual body and thus part of Hegel's notion of materiality in general. For this reason, although our sense of taste is surely not of preeminent importance epistemologically, let us utilize Hegel's presentation to note more explicitly his position that the properties of body manifest to our senses are not "merely subjective" but also in "the things themselves."

As a "neutral" property, says Hegel, taste "has also again sublated this relationship to the element [water] and drawn away from it." That is to say, the process of taste does not always have "immediate existence" as has odor, but depends on a "contingent encounter of the two sides." [150] The two sides (which are not here subject and object but water and the soluble) "consequently exist in a state of mutual indifference." Taste is therefore not only a process between bodies and elements, as is the case in color and odor, where the relation is of particular and universal as dissolution of the particular through the all-penetrating power of the universal.[151] Rather taste is also "real process among individual bodies," and hence with taste, body "passes over into chemical, real process." [152] The neutral body is decomposable into acid and base. As "abstract" neutrality, water is tasteless. Taste

[147] PhN 110.

[148] PhN 111.

[149] PhN 219. The Zusatz contains the following note: "Solution and resolution are chemically different. Resolution is separation into elements, solution occurs simply in water."

[150] PhN 219.

[151] Ibid.

[152] Hitherto we have been discussing bodies in relationship with the elements. "In chemical process, we shall come across these same bodies, but as independent existences in process with one another, no longer with the elements." (PhN 220)

first appears with "individualized" neutrality, "the unity of opposites which have collapsed into passive neutrality." Hence only neutral bodies such as salts, which decompose into their opposites, "have a definite taste." We call it taste with reference to our sense, says Hegel, "but the other moment here is still the element; for the solubility of bodies in water simply means that they can be tasted."

In the Physics of the Particular Individuality are demonstrated those properties of weight, cohesion, and heat, yet to be discussed, and sound, which we already discussed. In the Physics of the Total Individuality are demonstrated the properties of color, odor, and finally taste. The physically individualized bodies, "as the totality of their properties," now "behave differently towards one another." [153] Since the "two sides" in taste can exist in a state of "mutual indifference," taste forms a moment of transition. From bodies standing in relationship "with the elements," says Hegel, bodies as wholes now enter into relationship with each other as "physical individualities." [154] This takes place first "superficially" in electricity, and then as the "real relation" of the "passing of these bodies into one another" in the chemical process. Thus we see the role of "taste" in the Philosophy of Nature even apart from the notion of sentient organism and sentient subjectivity.

With regard to the notion of organism, the senses of taste and smell are termed by Hegel the "practical senses," [155] since their object is "the real being of things for an other by which they are consumed." Smell and taste have a close affinity for the sentient subjectivity and with regard to the location of their respective organs. They are also closely connected in their organic roles. Smell belongs to the inner organism as the principle of air,[156] and receives external body in its abstract process of evaporation. Taste is the sense of digestion; it receives body in the concrete process of physical dissolution and through those chemical determinations of sweet, bitter, caustic, sour, and salty, which emerge in this process.[157]

The third class of the senses, touch or feeling, is the sense of "earthly totality." In the doctrine of the elements, earth is the "individual ele-

---

[153] *PhN* 221.

[154] *PhN* 220.

[155] *PhN* 383. Cf. Kant, *APH* 154, where the distinction is between touch, sight, and hearing as the "more objective" senses, and taste and smell as the "more subjective."

[156] *PhN* 384.

[157] *PhM* 79.

ment," [158] and in the doctrine of the senses, touch is the most "concrete" of the senses, for it relates to body neither in its abstract ideality (sight and hearing) nor in its real difference (smell and taste) but in its solid reality (*gediegene Realität*). Of primary consideration for touch is the object as a "self-subsistent other" expressed in its specific gravity, body's "first indication of individuality." [159] To touch, therefore, belongs the sensation of heaviness: the "sought unity" of body with its center outside itself, whereby it offers "resistance." [160] In my sense of touch, says Hegel, I, as immediately existing individuality, encounter otherness as existent individuality, "a material object existing independently, which is how I, too, feel it." [161] To the sense of touch as thus taking the object as "persisting for itself," belong the determinations of cohesion,[162] such as elasticity,[163] hardness and softness,[164] brittleness,[165] roughness and smoothness.

Heat, according to Hegel, is the negative of self-subsisting materiality, the return of materiality into its formlessness and fluidity.[166] For this reason, and as connected with specific gravity and cohesion, hot and

[158] *PhN* 113.

[159] *PhN* 128.

[160] "Matter yearns for a center, a yearning which is first satisfied in the animal, which has its center within itself. It is just this drivenness of matter, lacking a self, towards an other, which I sense." (*PhN* 383; see also *PhM* 79)

[161] We recall Plato's apt characterization of materialists as those who believe "nothing is real save what they can grasp with their hands." (*Theaetetus* 155e)

[162] Cohesion is "the identity of body in the mutual externality of its parts" but as showing this only as a "mode of resistance to an other." (*PhN* 132)

[163] Elasticity is cohesion "displaying itself in motion," "the retreat of body into itself so as immediately to reinstate itself." (*PhN* 135)

[164] "The cohesive body when struck, pushed, or pressed by another body, suffers a negation of its material being as occupying space, and so of its occupation of a particular space. We are thus in the presence of the negation of material asunderness, but equally, too, of the negation of this negation, of the reinstatement of materiality." (*PhN* 135)

[165] *PhN* 131, 194.

[166] Heat and sound are related as opposites, according to Hegel. "Heat is the consummation of sound, the manifestation in matter of matter's negativity." Where in sound, body displays itself specifically as preserving itself, in heat it is now manifest "rather as negating itself." Whereas sound is "only ideal ideality of specific asunderness of the material parts," heat is the "real ideality of specific gravity and cohesion." (*PhN* 147) The senses of touch and hearing are therefore the two senses of the mechanical sphere. The determinations of cohesion, sound, and heat are ways whereby the "inwardness" of particular body in its specific gravity reveals itself. (*PhN* 154)

cold also belong to touch. So too does shape as three-dimensionality, since touch is essentially the sense of mechanical determinacy.

Thus we see how the notion of sentience in the doctrine of Subjective Spirit is linked with the notion of material body in the sciences of nature. Every "property" as such, says Hegel, "is only for the sense of a living creature." [167] Yet this does not mean a distinction of primary and secondary qualities, or a divorce of the sentient subjectivity from the truth of external reality. While the color of the rose implicitly distinguishes it from the lily, the distinction is explicit for us. In the same way, the properties of body manifested in sound, odor, taste, and touch are determinations whereby bodies are really distinguished from one another —the determinations belonging to the bodies intrinsically and specifying them in the process of the elements, while at the same time they are "for us" explicitly. Hence one cannot say of Hegel's concept of *Empfindung,* as for Kant's, that a sensation is "a perception which relates solely to the subject as the modification of its state," [168] or belongs merely to our "subjective constitution" and "cannot be rightly regarded as properties of things." [169]

For Hegel, as for Aristotle and Leibniz, there is no gap in principle between subject and object, sensing subjectivity and nonsentient externality. The healthy sense organ, the healthy soul, is the "measure." [170] In Aristotle's doctrine of *aisthesis,* the activity of the sensed and that of the sentient are one *energeia* located in the sentient.[171] For Leibniz, perception is "the interior state of the monad representing external things." [172] But in neither thinker is there an effort to demonstrate the identity of sentient subjectivity and external nature by linking the forms of sentience with a doctrine of the necessary specifications of material body as such. Neither in Aristotle's *Scala Universi,*[173] nor in Leibniz's

---

[167] See above, p. 89 n. 122. From Hegel's detailed and subtle discussion of "property" in the logic, we may note the following: "Quality is especially *property* only when, in an *external* relation, it manifests itself as an *immanent* determination." (*SL* 114) "Property is not only an *external* determination but an *intrinsic* existence." (*SL* 493)

[168] *CPR* B 377.

[169] *CPR* A 28 = B 44.

[170] Aristotle, *Metaphysics* 1063a3. Leibniz, *Nouveaux Essais,* in *Philosophischen Schriften,* ed. C. J. Gerhardt (Hildesheim 1960), vol. 5, p. 120.

[171] *De Anima* 426a11.

[172] *Principes de la Nature et de la Grace,* 4, *Schriften, op. cit.,* vol. 6, p. 600.

[173] "The scheme of things entire is to [Aristotle] a hierarchy of substances and not a whole of dialectical moments." (G. R. G. Mure, *Aristotle,* New York, 1964, p. 183)

concept of nature as continuity,[174] are we shown a movement from natural materiality to sentient subjectivity. Hegel, as we have now seen, claims to show one line of development from the necessary forms of physical materiality to the emergence of the animal organism in which "the whole of inorganic nature is recapitulated and idealized,"to the "awakening" of Spirit as sentient soul in whose "midnight of sleep" the properties of external natural body are reborn as specified modes of the subjectivity's Being-for-self in the external affections of its corporeality.

Although we noted that, as compared with the higher forms of thought, the content of sentience is in the form of immediate data, even the sensations are not to be viewed in atomic fashion like the simple impressions of Hume. Not only does each sense express a universal possibility of becoming determined, each encompasses a spectrum of possible sensations of its kind.[175] If I could see only blue, says Hegel, this limitation would be a "quality" of myself in the way blue is a quality of colored water: it would not be "for me" but for an external observer. As Spirit, however, I am the universal that is for itself as universal even in its particular determinations.[176] My seeing blue, says Hegel, is implicitly a seeing of "color," or rather the collective varieties of the colored. The single sensation is an actualization of a universal possibility, hence not abstractly simple, as in Hume, but implicitly containing difference and reference to other. Further, the fact that sensations have an "intensive magnitude" and thereby a certain "measure" signifies a relation of the particular affection to the "in-and-for-self determinateness" of the subject, a "reaction" of the subjectivity in its inwardness, as against the externality.[177]

Apart from the feeling of pleasure and pain and the stimulation of the inner drives—whose discussion comes later, in the Psychology— the various outer affections also have an implicitly universal aspect for the "spiritual inner" of the soul in the form of "mood" (Stimmung). No doubt we can discern analogous states in animals. But mood, says Hegel, has something characteristically human insofar as the outer affec-

---

[174] Hegel rejects Leibniz's formulation of continuity: "The old saying, or so-called law, non datur saltus in natura, is altogether inadequate to the diremption of the Notion. The continuity of the Notion with itself is of an entirely different character." (PhN 22)

[175] PhM 77. Cf. Aristotle's doctrine of the senses as a "mean" (De Anima 424a5).

[176] FPhG 37.

[177] PhM 80.

tion is invested with something like a symbolical character.[178] The relation
of colors and moods is a familiar one. We speak of the solemnity of
black, a reposeful blue, the regal purple. To be sure, says Hegel, there
is much arbitrary convention in the "meanings" of colors. Nevertheless,
Hegel maintains, such meanings are not wholly matters of fashion or
accidental association. They are not merely subjective but also in the
nature of things.[179] Tones also evoke meaningful "natural" responses in
us, those of the human voice especially affording the widest range of
nuances. Thus even on this primary level of the sentient soul we find
"meanings," for the soul, says Hegel, is no indeterminate emptiness but
a *geistige Innere*.

The external sensations are thus "outer" affections of the soul's
corporeal being that are "inwardized" and "made unto its own" as
posited by the awakened soul in its inner spirituality. In the ways we have
seen, the determinations "found" by the sentient soul in its "sleeping"
nature are both distinguished from the identity of the subjectivity "and
at the same time contained simply in its simpleness." [180]

The course of the inner affections is the reverse of the outer. The inner
affections do not derive from external natural body but are the soul's
"own" to begin with. Only in becoming corporealized, however, are they
first "found" and thereby sensed. The inner affections take on a determinate Being (*Dasein*) in the body, the soul's own other. For the inner
affections to be sensed, says Hegel, they must no less be "distinguished"
from the subjectivity as posited identical with it: but this takes place
"only by making outward (*Entaüsserung*), by the corporealization (*Verleiblichung*) of, the inner determinations of the sentient subjectivity." [181]

The inner affections are in the first place those natural impulses of
rage, shame, envy, etc., which in any particular instance are occasioned
in me as referring to my immediate singularity. Secondly they include

---

[178] "Symbol" here does not have the sense of standing for a distinct object but
rather a penumbra of *geistige Sympathien* that clothes the outer affection.

[179] Black, for example, expresses not only the sadness and gloom of our grief-
darkened spirit but also a solemnity and dignity wherein the "play of contingency,
manifoldness, and mutability finds no place." Purple is for us the "kingly" color as
the most forceful and striking to the eye: "the penetration of the bright and the
dark in the full intensity of their unity and opposition." (*PhM* 81; see also *PhN* 210)

[180] See above, p. 82. See also Hegel's discussion of the senses particularly with
reference to space and time as forms of intuition on the level of the rational intelligence, *PhM* 197 ff.

[181] *PhM* 82.

those universal sentiments of right, morality, religion, the beautiful, and
the true, which become the more strongly distinguished from the natural
impulses the more they free themselves of the contingency they possess
as belonging to the natural subjectivity. The full treatment of these
affections would take us beyond the present level of the natural soul.
Hence we shall have little to do at this point with the higher mental
content of the passions and emotions.[182]

Just as external body can be "for me" only through the mediation
of my own body,[183] the inner affections can be for me only insofar
as they obtain embodiment: for, belonging to the natural soul, they must
obtain an immediate determinate Being wherein alone the subjectivity
as natural can be "for itself." The inner affections are in different ways
corporealized in the body as a whole, as well as localized in certain
organs in accordance with their meaning for the psychical totality. For
example, sorrow, worry, distress (*Kummer*)—this powerless burrowing of
the soul into itself—Hegel says is mainly localized in the "reproductive"
system, which constitutes the "negative return" of the animal subject
to itself.[184] Courage and anger, directed outwardly against an alien
power, have their place in the breast and heart, this midpoint of the
"irritability" system, the "reactive" outer drive.[185] Shame is seen by Hegel
as an anger directed against the self, my reaction to the contradiction
between my appearance for other, and that which I ought and want to
be—hence a defensive reaction of my inner self as regards my unsuitable
outer appearance.[186]

---

[182] Again we must keep in mind that Hegel is dealing with what undoubtedly goes
on in conscious life, yet is not entirely explicable in terms of consciousness. When
Hegel speaks of the blush, for example, he does not deal with the kinds of social
embarrassment that might occasion it but only with its character as a psychophysical
reaction.

[183] See above, p. 86.

[184] By reproductive system, Hegel means here mainly the digestive system (see
PhN 359 ff.) Thus we sometimes say of the worrier that he is "eating himself up
inside." Aristotle says of concealed anger and bitterness: "it takes a long time to
digest one's wrath within one." (*Nicomachean* Ethics 1120a24) On Hegel's view of
the digestive process as involving an "anger towards the object," see *PhN* 397, 402, 403.

[185] Hegel notes the rise in heartbeat and blood pressure, tensing of muscles, etc.
In discussing mental illness, he suggests that persons of different temperaments are
prone to different ills. (*PhM* 124)

[186] In his interpretation of the Biblical story of the Fall, Hegel says that the
sense of shame—"the first reflection of awakened consciousness in men" which told
them that they were naked—"is a naive and profound trait." "For the sense of

·We need not follow Hegel's further discussion of the inner affections beyond noting its main bent: to show an immanent connection between the content as a *geistige* determination and its specific corporealization in the organs and functions according to their respective roles in the organism as a physical *Gestalt*.[187] While in physiology the organs and viscera are studied as moments of the animal organism, at the same time, says Hegel, they comprise a system of "embodiment of the spiritual," whereby they obtain a more than merely physiological significance and one that would be the province of a "psychical physiology." [188] Such a science, Hegel says, would be no doubt in large part empirical. But it would operate within the general philosophical concept that the corporealization of the inner affections is the manner whereby the soul is for itself as sentient—as "finding" those determinations in the form of an immediate *Dasein* of its own body as the "other that is present" (*vorhandene Anderes*). But this "other" is of course the soul itself in its substantial Being, the "dark side" of itself, in whose determinations the soul is "for itself" as sentient subjectivity.

Since the notion of the sentient soul is its Being-for-self as "simpleness" in its manifold determinations, the corporealization of the inner affections is only consummated in their "removal" (*Wegschaffung*)—or rather sublation—as *daseiende* particularities, i.e., determinations on their own account. This takes place, for example, in laughter and tears. Laughter is seen by Hegel as a triumph of subjectivity. We break out into a laugh, says Hegel, when something of a sudden shows itself as a nought against our Being-for-self; when· *das Lächerliche* deflates and collapses before us as something "immediately self-nullifying." [189] Like the ex-

shame bears evidence to the separation of man from his natural and sensuous life. The beasts never get so far as this separation, and they feel no shame. And it is in the human feeling of shame that we are to seek the spiritual and moral origin of dress, compared with which the merely physical need is a secondary matter." (*L* 54 ff.) The meaning of our feeling of shame for our nakedness, according to Hegel, is thus (as one commentator puts it) "the emergence of the reflection of the tension between the sensuous aspect of our life and our spiritual destiny." (Nathan Rotenstreich, "On Shame," *Review of Metaphysics*, vol. xix, no. 1, Sept. 1965, p. 75)

[187] *PhN* 357 ff.

[188] *PhM* 76.

[189] "For in laughter, the subjectivity which has attained to the serene enjoyment of itself, the pure self, this spiritual light, corporealizes itself as a lighting-up of the face, and at the same time finds a physical expression in the forcible intermittent expulsion of the breath." (*PhM* 86; see also *Philosophy of Fine Art, op. cit.*, vol. 4, pp. 301 ff.)

pulsion of the breath in laughter, tears both "express" (*äussern*) and "outwardize" (*entäussern*) in the sense noted of a "removal." Tears, Hegel says, are a healing. In weeping, the pain of inner tornness is rendered an indifference in the "neutral" element of water.[190] In both laughter and tears, therefore, the subjectivity returns to wholeness with itself in its corporeal *Dasein*.[191] But in voice there is an even more complete *Wegschaffung* of the inner affection that is straightway one with its very corporealization. In voice, says Hegel, there is brought forth an incorporeal corporeality, a materiality in which the inwardness of the subjectivity retains throughout the character of inwardness. The very diffusion of tone is directly one with its vanishing. The Being-for-self ideality of the soul obtains here a *Verleiblichung* whose very arising is a disappearing. In voice, says Hegel, the inner affection is posited in the body in such a manner that its positing is one with its *Wegschaffung* as this particular embodiment.

The sentient soul is the concluding moment of the natural soul, whose movement constitutes the first main *Schluss* of the Anthropology. Now we may see better the speculative development in its character as a demonstration. In the movement thus far, Hegel has purportedly demonstrated the emergence of the soul in its first actualization as individual subjectivity. In the first moment, that of the "natural qualities," the soul's determinations were "in it" (*an ihr*), not yet truly "for it." These were the racial, ethnic, and hereditary traits in which the universal world soul is first actualized as natural individuality. With this first emergence of the soul as individuality, the movement took on the form of an opposition and identity of the singular and universal: the "natural alterations" of the life ages, the real opposition of the sex relation, and the alternating states of sleep and awakening. In the sentient soul we return to the immediacy of the beginning, but on a higher level of ideality. Where we began with the abstract attunement of natural soul to the universal planetary life, the individual soul as sentient lives in attunement with its own corporeality, which mediates it with outer natural body. The healthy soul as sentient is nature in microcosm in a new and higher sense. In its outer as well as inner affections, the soul as individuality meets with itself in its universality or substantial natural

---

[190] *PhM* 86.

[191] Kant too sees laughing and crying as affects whereby nature "mechanically furthers health," but not explicitly as the psychical subjectivity's *Wegschaffung* of the particular and return to unity with itself. (See *APH* 261 ff.)

Being. Sentience thus proves to be a first form of the soul's "closing together with itself"—proximately from the *Ur-teil* of its awakening, more generally from its self-division as singularity and universality comprising the notion of the natural alterations. This closing together (*Schluss*) or Being-with-self is, as sentience, for the first time a Being-for-self, or the soul's emergence as subjectivity.

To be sure, in sentience as such the soul is for itself in determinations that have the character of immediacy, of something "found," of singular and passing affections. Yet, as Hegel has purportedly shown, the soul's "finding" of its determinations proves to be its healthy dwelling together with itself in its own natural Being, its substantiality. The passing affections, in the ways we have tried to show, implicitly carry for the soul the sense of its own totality. But as thus "for itself" as totality in its particular determinations, the soul is no longer *emp-findend*. Its determinations are no longer the singular and transient affections which it happens to find crossing its ken. The soul has attained to a presentiment (*Ahnung*) or feeling of its wholeness, its "selfness" (*Selbstischkeit*)—whereby it has come to be "feeling soul" (*fühlende Seele*).

CHAPTER FIVE

THE FEELING SOUL

Although the soul as *emp-findend* comes back to itself in its "findings," the soul is only for itself in its totality as feeling soul (*fühlende Seele*). The feeling soul, says Hegel, is the "simple ideality" of sentience. The determinations of the feeling soul are no longer transient sensations but are retained in higher form (*aufbewahrt*) in the "inner" of the soul. This idealization of the manifold of sentience is the soul's "making" unto its own of the determinations that come to it from its own natural being. Hitherto the soul has been "natural" individuality. As feeling soul it becomes "inner" individuality, obtaining the feeling of itself (*Selbstgefühl*) in its totality.

The goal of this inner individuality, which is indeed the central theme of Hegel's demonstration in the Anthropology, is to "posit" its natural or substantial being "for itself" as conscious subjectivity or ego.[1] The soul's development henceforward may be described as its taking itself "in possession," its positing as for itself what it thus far as had "in itself" abstractly as a natural heritage. Thus we may say of the task of the soul, as Goethe says in *Faust:*

> Was du ererbt von deinen Vätern hast,
> Erwirb es, um es zu besitzen.'

The feeling soul in its Being-for-self is but the presentiment or intimation of self, not yet self-consciousness. Nevertheless Hegel speaks of the feeling soul in a way that seems to invite comparison with Kant's identity of apperception, which Hegel, as we saw, regarded as one of Kant's "most

---

[1] *PhM* 152. The soul of man "does not merely possess natural differences, it differentiates itself inwardly, separates its substantial totality, its individual world, from itself, sets this over against itself as subject. Its aim in this process is that what Spirit is in itself is to become explicitly for Spirit, that the cosmos contained *an sich im Geiste* is to enter into Spirit's consciousness." (*PhM* 91)

profound" insights. Nothing of the feeling manifold, says Hegel, can
stand as a barrier to the psychical subjectivity, any more than there can
subsist a manifold of representations uninformed by the identity of the
ego of consciousness. [2] This manifold is not that of the objective consciousness but the soul's substantial being which now comes before it as
a dream world, an inner life. In it the soul is "for itself" abstractly, as
compared with the ego's Being-for-self in its objectively structured manifold. Nevertheless, Hegel will claim to show, the feeling soul permeates
the manifold of its feeling-life (Gefühlsleben) as its ideal unity. A great
part of the interest in the present chapter is to see how Hegel views the
relation of the psychical subjectivity to its manifold where there is yet no
distinction of "I" and "object" but rather "what I feel I *am*, and what
I am I feel." [3]

As such a self-enclosed subjectivity, the feeling soul as individuality
is termed by Hegel a "monad". The term monad, however, does not have
here the metaphysical sense that it has for Leibniz. The feeling soul is a
monad insofar as, on the present level of subjectivity, its world is not yet
distinguished by the soul as objective but is "wrapped up" within the soul
itself. The content of this inner world is in the first instance the manifold
of the sentient soul. But the feeling soul is not limited to the sensuously
present. The determinations of sentience, says Hegel, are sublated in the
"timeless undifferentiated inwardness" of the soul.[4] As sublated, they
possess no explicit existence or "being-there" (Dasein) in the soul; yet
they have not tracelessly vanished but can arise for the psychical subjectivity as in dreams. There is thus a kind of memory in the feeling soul,
though not yet memory proper, which presupposes intuition on the level
of the objective consciousness.[5]

[2] *PhM* 93. Such a statement is far more than Kant would commit himself to.
See the discussion of a possible nonobjective consciousness in Kant, in H. J. Paton,
Kant's Metaphysic of Experience, 2 vols. (London, 1970), vol. 1, pp. 332 ff.

[3] *PhM* 89-90. Condillac in his *Treatise on Sensations* (I, i, 2) says: "If we give
the statue a rose to smell, to us it is a statue smelling a rose, to itself it is a smell
of rose."

[4] *PhM* 90. In dealing with imagination on the level of the rational intelligence,
Hegel speaks of "this night-like mine or pit in which is stored a world of infinitely
many images and representations, yet without being in consciousness." (*PhM* 204)
"Man is this night, this empty nothing that contains everything in its simplicity,
a wealth of infinitely many representations, images, none of which may appear
or be present to him. This is the night, the inner nature that exists here—pure self."
(*JR* 180; see also *FPhG* 42)

[5] See *PhM* 219.

There is a deeper content in the feeling soul, however, than that which *Empfindung* as such can present. The feeling soul, says Hegel, is the concentrated inner life of the individual in all his conscious activities. Thus the notion of the feeling soul must in part anticipate that of conscious life.[6] As an actual individual, I am within myself a world of concrete content with an "infinite periphery," a world of innumerable ties and interconnections that can grow and alter within me even without my explicit awareness, a world that to an extent has a life of its own. It is this inner world as a feeling-life (*Gefühlsleben*) that now constitues the individual soul's substantiality and that now, in contrast to such previous forms as the life ages, is the way the universal is present in the individual.

In the feeling soul's Being-for-self in its inner world, distinction is wholly "within" the soul itself: this constitutes the soul's "monadic" character at this stage. Distinction here, says Hegel, is the soul's own judgment (*Urteil*), in which the soul is ever subject, and its object is its own substantial being that is at the same time predicate.[7] In this monadic

---

[6] See above, p. 42.

[7] *PhM* 94. Here it is essential for us to recall Hegel's critique of Kant's argument that the ego can never know itself, since it can only be subject and never predicate of its judgment (see above, p. 17). We have now encountered the term *Ur-teil* several times, and its meaning for Hegel's position, as well as for seeing his difference from Kant, cannot be overstressed. One might say that Kant's Copernican revolution in philosophy can be stated briefly in terms of his meaning of "objective judgment." Such a judgment, says Kant, "is nothing but the manner in which given modes of knowledge are brought to the objective unity of apperception. This is what is intended by the copula (*Verhältniswörtchen*) 'is'". (*CPR* B 142) Now for Hegel, as we shall see, this is also the case. But for Hegel the *Verhältniswörtchen* in the first place is not to be understood only with relation to the subject, as in the Kantian "subjective idealism." Rather, says Hegel, "the copula 'is' springs from the nature of the Notion, to be self-identical even in parting with its own" (*in seiner Entäusserung*). (*L* 298) It is thus not only consciousness but "the Notion" that distinguishes itself into subject and predicate, and whose very forms of self-distinguishing comprise the necessary senses of the word "is," namely, the logical categories. Now it is indeed the task of a doctrine of Subjective Spirit to demonstrate consciousness *as* the Notion, or rather as one form of the Notion. For the soul too is Notion. We have already seen how the soul as Notion makes the "immediate" *Urteil* in its "awakening." In the present *Urteil* of the feeling soul, the subject-predicate relation is still a form of the soul's self-enclosedness. The most important *Urteil* in the Anthropology will be that comprising the emergence of consciousness itself and its relation to its content in the form of the subject-object relation. Since, for Kant, we cannot know the transcendental ego, we can never know any such *Urteil* that produces consciousness itself. Though for Kant every objective judgment must entail a self-relation of the subjectivity, it must also depend in some manner

inner distinguishing, the feeling soul is yet only a "formal" subjectivity, only abstractly an individuality. It is not yet an individual "as itself" (*als Es selbst*). Though it is "active" compared with the earlier levels of the natural soul, it is "passive" as compared with the self-possessed waking consciousness. The feeling soul has but the presentiment (*Ahnung*) of its selfness (*Selbstischkeit*); it has not yet "posited" itself as a self "for itself." Because it is thus "formal" and "passive"—or as we would perhaps say in nonscientific terms "weak"—the individuality here, says Hegel, can have the subjectivity of an "other" as its controlling "genius." Hegel will claim to show the feeling soul's relation to its feeling-life in the following main forms: the dream life, the foetus in the womb, the peculiar "inner genius" of the individual, and in certain sickness and trance states. Before we take up Hegel's discussion, let us note a few points regarding the structure of the demonstration.

In the overall *Schluss* movement of the Anthropology, the feeling soul constitutes the second main stage of the soul's development, the state where opposition is pre-eminent. On this stage the soul will proceed from abstract unity with itself in its universal natural being or substantiality to self-sunderance and opposition. This is the stage of sunderance that is at the same time particularization (*Besonderung*). In contrast to the natural soul's healthy *Mitleben* with itself in its naturalness, the feeling soul will display those features of diremption and negativity that are essential for its liberation from its naturalness. Through this liberation struggle, the soul will posit its substantiality as its own, thereby raising itself from abstract feeling-subjectivity to subjectivity that has itself in possession. Our task in the present chapter will be to follow Hegel's demonstration of the movement of the soul's *Besonderung* both in its logical aspect and in the empirical forms that Hegel claims embody the movement of the Notion.

a. The Feeling Soul in its Immediacy

Hegel begins his discussion of the feeling soul by reminding us of the importance of the category of "ideality" for the study of the soul and Spirit generally.[8] The feeling-subjectivity knows itself in the manner of a

---

on the transcendental object as thing-in-itself. In Hegel's demonstration of the final *Urteil* of the soul, we shall purportedly see the emergence of consciousness in whose notion is included the *Urteil* that makes for the "thing-in-itself."

[8] Ideality is "negation of the real, which, however, is at the same time *aufbewahrt*, retained *virtualiter* without coming to existence." (*PhM* 92; see also *SL* 154 ff.; *L* 178)

dreaming-through (*Durchträumen*) and presentiment (*Ahnung*) of its inner world. It is the ideal unity of that world, though its ideality is not yet on the objective plane of the ego, whose unity of the manifold is a "mediated" one. The "immediacy" of the feeling-subjectivity's idealization of its feeling-life is termed by Hegel the "magical relation" (*magisches Verhältnis*).[9]

The magical relation, says Hegel, is not something unfamiliar to us. The "most immediate" magic is the power which the individual subjectivity exercises over its own corporeality in employing it as the direct instrument of its will.[10] But the familiar, as Hegel is fond of saying, is not on that account better known. Throughout the realm of the psychical life, according to Hegel, we encounter phenomena that elude the ordinary intelligence and baffle the fixed distinctions of the understanding. Particularly in certain sickness states, which display a "sinking down" or regression (*Herabsinken*) of the ordinary waking subjectivity to the level of the feeling-life, a buried content emerges from the "indefinite pit" (*bestimmungsloser Schacht*) of the inner self. This regression, says Hegel, opens up before our very eyes the working of Spirit as ideality. [11]

The inner world of feeling, which the feeling-subjectivity knows in the immediate manner of dream and presentiment, comprises not only the individual's heritage as natural soul and the content of sentience, but also his deep-rooted ties to others that have sprung up in his conscious life and have been woven together with his own inner substance. This wealth of content comprising the individual's inner feeling-world stands as a manifold over against the soul's simple unity. But it is neither something apart from the soul nor the soul something apart from it. It is the soul's concrete life and substance. In its relation with this its substantial Being, the feeling-subjectivity knows its manifold in the form of a dream world passing before its ken. Despite its generally fragmented character, the dream content is not entirely contingent. Often the soul in dreams, says Hegel, attains to a "deep and powerful feeling of its entire individual nature," of the whole compass of its past, present, and future.[12]

But the subjectivity in dreams is not firmly in the saddle, not the controlling power over its manifold. Indeed it is destined to be sublated in the

---

[9] *PhM* 95.

[10] See the discussion of habit, below, p. 137.

[11] See above, p. 106.

[12] *PhM* 99. Hegel offers almost nothing here by way of substantiation or development of this claim. However, we may take certain material revealed in animal magnetism as relevant to the dream life (see *PhM* 119).

higher subjectivity of ego, which is therefore in a sense two subjectivities
in one. On the present natural level—or in a regression to that level from
the waking consciousness—the Being-outside-self of nature once more
displays itself in the phenomenon of two subjectivities existing in the same
selfhood, the one the controlling power over the other. The natural basis
for this "living in one another" (*Ineinanderleben*)—and also its most
immediate and in a sense prototypical example—is seen by Hegel to
consist in the relation of foetus and mother.

In the foetus-mother relationship, according to Hegel, the Being-for-self
of the individual soul (the foetus) and its Being-in-self are divided between
two individuals in a "psychical unity" (*Seeleneinheit*).[13] The soul of the
foetus is not yet an actual Being-for-self. The foetus, says Hegel, cannot
yet "bear itself for itself" and is for itself only through another subjectivity.
The subjectivity of the foetus is borne by that of the mother, to whose
permeating power the foetus lies "wholly open." The foetus is "thrilled
through" (*durchzittert*) by the infusing "genius" of the mother, which is
thus the single self of both.[14]

Hegel places some emphasis on this alleged psychical unity in the
foetus-mother relationship. It is just such a "unity of the distinguished,"
says Hegel, which constitutes the essence of Spirit. This kind of unity is
incomprehensible to the viewpoint that clings to the spatially and materially
"distinct."[15] To be sure, the relation has its physical side. But to take the
foetus-mother relationship merely as one between two natural organisms
linked by physical connections, says Hegel, is to miss the "immediate
action" (*unmittelbares Einwirken*) as a magical relation that is the essence
of this physical *Ineinanderleben*.[16]

---

[13] *PhM* 94 ff.

[14] By "genius," says Hegel, is meant here "the spiritual selfhood as totality,
as it has existence of its own, and constitutes the subjective substantiality of an
other, who is only externally posited as an individual and has only a formal
Being-for-self." (*PhM* 95)

[15] Hegel says the same about love as an instance of the magical relation in the
psychical unity of two individuals. Love therefore is "the most tremendous contradiction" for the understanding, since there is "nothing more stubborn than this
Punktualität of self-consciousness which is negated and which nevertheless I ought
to possess as affirmative." Love is "at once the propounding and the resolving of
this contradiction." (*PhR* pp. 261-62)

[16] Whatever truth may lie in Hegel's notion of the *unmittelbares Einwirken*
of the foetus-mother relation, what he has to say by way of empirical support
is largely of the caliber of old-wives tales, e.g., that a woman shocked in pregnancy
by the sight of a broken arm may give birth to a child with a damaged arm.

The feeling soul as subjectivity of the inner feeling-life is most fully developed in the individual as his own particular "genius." This genius is the individual in his inner personal particularity, which, as Hegel puts it, marks him off in any given situation from a hundred other men. I am within myself a "twofold being" (*ein Zweifaches*), says Hegel.[17] I am as I know myself in my everyday world and as I am known to my fellows. I am also an inner being with a particular *geistige Natur* that brings itself to bear on all my activities. This inner nature, Hegel says, can be termed my "fate," my inner oracle, my *daimonion*.[18] It is that "intensive form of individuality" that often has the last say in my decisions, however ready I may be to provide "reasons." As such a *Zweifaches*, says Hegel, I retain in my relation to myself a certain similarity to the foetus-mother *Inein-anderleben*. In its enveloping simplicity, this "concentrated" inner individuality absorbs into itself the ties and connections of deepest interest to the individual in his lifetime. At the same time it is distinct from the conscious selfhood that knows itself as objectively reflected in the individual's social relationships, activities, and outlook.

Yet the genius as the individual's "other selfhood" (*ein selbstisches Anderes*), says Hegel, is a "formal" subjectivity, normally but a "moment" of the active conscious life. As the inner voice behind the show of conscious intentions, the genius directs the individual along subjective and particular lines, rather than in accordance with objective and universal requirements. The inner genius partly appears in what we call "heart" or *Gemut*, and a *gemütlicher Mensch*, according to Hegel, is one who lets himself be led by his feelings. Thus Hegel does not see the feeling-subjectivity or inner genius as a great source of intuitive truth.[19] Genuine knowledge, Hegel is never tired of saying, has the form of universal thought determinations,[20] and genuine moral action is guided by canons accessible to all men.[21] The present level of the feeling soul is for Hegel

---

[17] "Zwei Seelen wohnen, ach! in meiner Brust." (*Faust*)

[18] Kant speaks also of this oracle but does not seek to place it within a notion of subjectivity as does Hegel. (See *APH* 145) For Hegel's view of Socrates' *daimonion*, see *HPh* I, 421 ff.

[19] Hegel is not speaking here about the genius of a Socrates or a Goethe, or of the hero in history.

[20] If a man appeals not to reasons but to his feeling, "the only thing to do is to let him alone, because by his behavior he refuses to have any lot or part in common rationality, and shuts himself up in his own isolated subjectivity—his private and particular self." (*PhM* 194)

[21] "In an ethical community, it is easy to say what a man must do... he simply has to follow the well-known and explicit rules of his own situation." (*PhR* 107)

mainly a level of "darkness," and it is properly sublated as a moment of
the rational consciousness. In the ordinary healthy development of the
individual, the inner feeling-subjectivity becomes formed and molded by
the rational selfhood, which in this manner becomes the true controlling
genius over the feeling-life.[22]

The self-possessed rational consciousness, however, does not always
retain its sovereignty. When a failure occurs, as in certain abnormal
conditions or sickness states, there is a relapse or regression to the level
of the feeling subjectivity. Such an *Herabsinken* is termed by Hegel the
"unhealthy magical relation," and in Hegel's view it reveals a largely
unexplored domain of Spirit whose investigation possesses intrinsic interest for a doctrine of Subjective Spirit. Indeed Hegel's discussion of its
various manifestations are fuller and more interesting than his sketchy
account of the healthy magical relation.

The subjectivity in the healthy magical relation, we recall, is but
"formal" and "passive." In normal waking life the feeling-subjectivity
does not arrogate to itself the role of the rational consciousness. The
dream subjectivity, for example, does not intrude its representations upon
the waking consciousness. The ego does not normally "lie open" to the
dominating subjectivity of another, as in the foetus-mother relationship.
In healthy sleep, as we have seen, there is a retirement from the dispersion of the outer world to the inner feeling-life of the monadic selfhood.
But in certain abnormal states, according to Hegel, the monadic selfhood
emerges as a "real" subjectivity.[23] At this time the self is no longer in
open-eyed encounter with an external world but has become a somnambulistic, inwardly turned consciousness. The inner genius steps forth as
a "clairvoyant" (*hellsehende*) subjectivity. The self-possessed conscious-

---

[22] In his lectures, Hegel seems to suggest a *Schluss* in the three moments:
dream, foetus, and genius (*PhM* 101). If this is indeed intended, it surely seems
difficult to take seriously. In dreaming, it would appear, the feeling soul has its
Being-for-self in the form of simple self-relation with its substantiality as the manifold of the dream world. In the foetus-mother relation there is sunderance in the
sense that the foetus has its Being-for-self in another subjectivity. The genius, as the
inner subjectivity of feeling, contains, on the one hand the moment of simple self-
relation, on the other hand the doubleness of the second moment inasmuch as the
genius is as "an other selfhood" vis-à-vis the waking subjectivity. Unlike the case of
the natural alterations (see above, pp. 80 ff.), it is difficult to see any intrinsic connection of the three moments. It might be noted that in the text written for publication there seems to be no attempt to show a *Schluss* in this first moment of the
feeling soul in its immediacy. Indeed nothing at all is said about dreaming.

[23] *PhM* 105 ff.

ness having abdicated before the passive and formal feeling-subjectivity, the individual is borne along by his tutelary genius, guided by voices, or lies open to the dominating subjectivity of an other, with whom he is in a relationship of "psychical unity."

The unhealthy magical relation is thus seen by Hegel as a diremption (*Entzweiung*) of the individual selfhood in its wholeness, a diremption whose possibility consists in that the self is a *Zweifaches*. In the unhealthy magical relation the psychical subjectivity is no longer a "sublated moment" of the integrated objective consciousness. It has set itself up on its own account. There is here, says Hegel, a "blocking" (*Hemmung*) in the universal fluidity—the ideality—which is of the essence of Spirit. In the transition from the waking to the somnambulistic consciousness and return, there is an alternation between two "selves," for, as we have seen, the feeling-subjectivity is also a selfhood, a totality, just as is the conscious subjectivity. At the same time, however, the lapse into the feeling-selfhood is a "regression," since the "two" selves are not on an equal plane of ideality, of Spirit.

The possibility for the "pulling loose" (*Losreissen*) of the "lower" self, says Hegel, consists in the fact that the psychical (*das Seelenhafte*) is "distinguished from Spirit no less than it is implicitly identical with it." [24] In the notion of Spirit as the "unity of the distinguished," says Hegel, we can grasp the dialectical character of the phenomena of the somnambulistic regression. In the notion of the regression, we have two "selves" that are nevertheless one, and whose relation to one another cannot be expressed except in the speculative forms of the Notion.

A self, for Hegel, is a simpleness that is at the same time concrete insofar as it is "for itself" as identity of its manifold determinations. It is this identity, however, not abstractly but in "coming back" to itself as absolute negativity or ideality of its manifold. This manifold, however, is of a different character on the different levels of subjectivity, and the ways of the latter's negating and thereby being for itself in its manifold are different. The feeling-subjectivity is the unity of Being-for-self and Being-in-self—of subjectivity and substantiality, individuality and universality—in the form of "immediacy." Consciousness is that unity as "mediated" through objective categories, such as cause and effect, and the linking of determinations in space and time. To the substantiality or concrete being of the individual, says Hegel, belongs the collectivity of his interests and relations to others and to his world: his family ties, his deep-

[24] *PhM* 106.

rooted loyalities, his attachments to home, soil, and community. As the totality immanent in him, it has grown together with his inner feeling-life and his particular inner genius. On the level of consciousness all this content is known to him objectively, mediately. On the level of soul, this manifold has the immediacy of the feeling-form. It is to this level that the selfhood "sinks down" in the unhealthy magical relation of the "somnambulistic" consciousness.

The somnambulistic consciousness is thus, in Hegel's terms, a "self," a totality, a subjectivity that is "for itself" as simple ideality of its manifold as a *Gefühlsleben*. Its Being-for-self, however, is but a relation to its immediate inner world. This is not to say that it is a "partial" self in the sense that, in its somnambulistic withdrawal into self it has discarded its ties to the outer world. It cannot do this, since these ties constitute its own substantial being. Rather the outer ties and relations are taken in by the somnambulistic subjectivity as "concentrated" and "enveloped" (*eingehüllt*) within its inner world. It is this concentrated content that the somnambulistic subjectivity "knows" in the immediacy of the feeling-form.

As such an immediacy, according to Hegel, the feeling-selfhood is an "inappropriatness" of Spirit. Its world of feeling is not the world of free spirituality, of rational willing and thinking. The somnambulistic retirement to the private inner world, according to Hegel, is the individual's giving up of his existence as "spirituality that is at home with itself." It is for this reason that the unhealthy magical relation is a "regression"—not so much from whole to part as from one selfhood to another, each of which is in a sense the whole. If the parts-whole terminology is to be employed in the realm of Spirit, it must be in just such a sense of a relationship of the immediate feeling-totality to the mediated totality of consciousness, which contains the former within it as a moment.

It is in this sense that Hegel uses the terms parts and whole in his conception of mental illness, to which Hegel devoted considerable attention in his lectures on the feeling soul. The *Losreissen* of the feeling-subjectivity from the integrated rational consciousness means that the part has become for itself the whole. Physical illness, according to Hegel, consists in the "becoming fixed" (*festwerden*) of a particular organ or system, as against the fluidity (*Flüssigkeit*) of the organism in its totality.[25]

This fixedness may proceed to the point where the particular becomes the concentrated focal point of the organism's entire activity. Sickness of

---

[25] *PhN* 428.

the psyche has essentially this meaning, in Hegel's view. When the psychical subjectivity, normally but a moment of the waking consciousness, separates itself from the latter, it becomes a Being-for-self on its own account.

Psychical sickness is not only similar to physical in its notion, says Hegel, but generally comes bound together with it. The corporeality, which is the "empirical existence" at once of the "two selves," with the separation of the psychical from the conscious selfhood becomes likewise divided between the two, thus losing its healthy fluidity. Almost any sickness, says Hegel, can show signs of this separation of the psychical life. There are certain illnesses, however, that manifest interesting forms of this separation. Such forms show especially well the nature of the magical relation, wherein the individual is "the monad which is inwardly aware of its actuality—the genius which beholds itself." [26] This inner self-intuiting (*Selbstanschauen*) of the monadic subjectivity is not a knowing that proceeds to the discursive judging of consciousness and connects appearances mediately according to objective categories. Rather, claims Hegel, it is a "gazing-knowing" (*schauendes Wissen*), an immediate knowing on the part of the monadic subjectivity of its own substantial being as a feeling-life.[27]

Since the monadic subjectivity lacks the active self-distinguishing of consciousness in knowing its content as objective, the self in the feeling-life is passive. In somnambulism, cataleptic seizures, trances, religious and other forms of ecstasy, the self appears as possessed rather than self-possessing. It is an automatic self, borne along as by some inner spirit that dictates its doings and utterances. Along with this aspect of passivity, according to Hegel, there is a characteristic loss of articulateness and differentiation in the content of the gazing-knowing. For since the inner self-intuition means withdrawal from the external world in all its manifold

---

[26] *PhM* 103.

[27] The gazing-knowing that Hegel is talking about would seem to fit into neither of the Kantian "two stems" of knowledge. It does not belong to understanding, since it nonconceptual and nondiscursive. It cannot come from the senses alone, which for Kant yield only a rhapsody of impressions. In speaking of the kinds of knowing supposedly exhibited, for example, in Socrates' oracle, Kant says: these pronouncements do not come from the senses "but rather out of real, albeit obscure, reflections (*Ueberlegungen*) of the understanding." (*APH* 145) But how there can be reflections of any sort by the understanding that do not come under the rule-giving identity of apperception would seem to pose a problem for the Kantian position.

expansiveness, there is a reorientation of the modes of perceiving. The outer senses are dimmed, as in sleep. Their specificity is blurred, and particular functions tend to become fused.[28] The specific roles of the outer senses, says Hegel, are taken over by a "common feeling" (*Gemeingefühl*) purportedly located in the organism's more primitive digestive system.[29]

Thus Hegel puts forward the notion that our normal everyday perceiving in fact rests on a certain psychical health and attainment. There is more to objective perception than the uniting of impressions through association. Indeed Kant had already pointed out that objective experience rests on a spontaneous act of the ego as self-identity, and this notion was also implicit in Leibniz's distinction of perception and apperception.[30] As we saw, however, Kant was interested in the logical aspect of consciousness and did not believe its psychological or anthropological genesis could be demonstrated scientifically.[31] Hegel, however, now points out that objective experience presupposes a psychical development whereby the subjectivity becomes sufficiently self-possessed to maintain a posture of disinterestedness—and that in certain sickness states or other moments of weakness this posture can be relinquished or surrendered. To perceive as an "objective" consciousness, the self must be able to "hold itself" toward a content as an independent other. Indeed this theme is implicit in Hegel's whole conception of the soul's development to consciousness as a liberation struggle. In the present context, Hegel is interested in the regression to the feeling-life as indicating a kind of perceiving and knowing that is not yet that of the objective consciousness. Hegel's claim is that the various sickness states and other unusual phenomena of the psychical life manifest different forms of the monadic subjectivity's "self-intuiting."

In the first place, says Hegel, there is an immediate knowing of the presence of outer objects in which there is no employment of the external

---

[28] As an objective consciousness, says Hegel, the knower knows the world "as an objectivity *external* to him, infinitely *manifold*, but in all its parts necessarily interrelated and containing nothing unmediated within it" and to which consciousness relates itself in a correspondingly "manifold, determinate, mediated, and necessary" way. Whereas the conscious subject is able to see only with the eyes, in certain forms of the gazing-knowing the subject can perceive things "without the help of the eyes or without the mediation of light." (*PhM* 107) Hegel does not seem to concern himself greatly with evaluating the empirical evidence for such sightless seeing.

[29] *PhM* 105 ff.

[30] See above, p. 54, n. 74.

[31] See above, p. 110.

sense organs. Such is the case, Hegel claims, with the so-called diviners
(*Metall- und Wasserfühlern*), persons whose organism reacts to the subterranean presence of water or certain metals by virtue of some special
sensitivity. The second kind of immediate knowing is manifested in sleepwalking and catalepsy. This has in common with the first that "an object is
sensed without the mediation of the *specific* sense with which the object
is mainly connected." [32] Here, however, there is not a wholly mediation-
less perceiving, as in divining, but a taking over of the function of a
specific outer sense, such as sight, by the more primitive sense of touch,
or, says Hegel, by the "common sense" (*Gemeinsinn*) active mainly in
the pit of the stomach (*Herzgrube*).[33] The significant aspect of the sightless seeing in sleepwalking, according to Hegel, is that the sense for which
objects in the normal relation of consciousness must be at some distance
from us, "in this condition of nonseparation of subjective and objective
ceases to be active." The third kind of immediate knowing, says Hegel, is
that termed "clairvoyance," whereby, "an undefined feeling gives rise to
an intimation or a vision of something not sensibly present but distant in
space or time, either future or past." [34] It is this kind of "gazing-knowing"
that Hegel is most interested in as allegedly affording empirical evidence
that the soul is not confined to the limitations of space and time.[35]

The possibility for this *schauendes Wissen*, according to Hegel, is the
nature of the soul itself, which is at once soul as universal and this individually determined soul. As "implicitly the totality of nature," soul as
such is the "all-penetrating" which "does not onesidedly stand over
against its other, but overarches it." [36] The soul is the ideality of all
materiality, the wholly universal in which all distinctions of the *partes
extra partes* of nature are taken up as ideal. As this individual soul, it is
"the existent Notion, the existence of the speculative." [37] It thus contains
within itself those manifold determinations which appear as instincts and
inclinations, universal in nature but obtaining in the individuality a particular content. Within me, for example, the love towards parents and
friends is individualized; for I cannot be friend in general but friend to
this friend, in this time, place, and circumstance. All such ties, which are

---

[32] *PhM* 108.

[33] *Ibid.*

[34] *PhM* 109.

[35] See Kant's rejection of all such forms of immediate knowing which "cannot
be based on experience and its known laws." (*CPR* A 223 = B 270)

[36] *PhM* 109.

[37] *PhM* 93.

universal soul-determinations individualized in me and lived in by me, constitute my actuality, are grown together in my substantiality, and belong as much to my actual being as my head or breast to my living *Dasein*. It is of this actuality, this my total inner world and inner being, that, as feeling-subjectivity, I can know in the self-intuiting gazing-knowing. Insofar as I am a monadic subjectivity, I know of this my inner world as a world not separated from myself, says Hegel, but in an immediate "wholly abstract, positive manner."

Hegel claims to distinguish three main forms of this gazing-knowing. The first is of a content already deposited in the inner of the soul. Under certain sickness or trance states, says Hegel, the feeling-subjectivity may bring forth a content buried deep in the "indeterminate pit" of the soul and apparently long forgotten. Often this is a content simply not accessible to the waking consciousness, as when a person under hypnosis produces details of an incident in early childhood and seemingly obliterated.

The second form of clairvoyance, according to Hegel, is the immediate knowing of occurrences that are external to the subject spatially or temporally (in future) but known in a manner not mediated by the forms of space and time. In our ordinary waking state, says Hegel, we can know what is spatially distant only under the condition that we sublate the distance in some mediated fashion.[38] This mediation, however, is not available to the monadic subjectivity, which has not posited its content as "outer" and whose knowing is "not yet mediated through the opposition of subjective and objective and the sublation of this opposition." In clairvoyance as prescience (*Vorauswissen*), Hegel claims that the soul shows its elevation above the condition of time. The occurrence will only take

---

[38] "Space pertains not to the soul but to outer nature; and this outer existence, in being apprehended by the soul ceases to be spatial since, transformed by the soul's ideality, it is no longer external to itself nor to us." (*PhM* 111) Space and time for Hegel are known by intuition on the level of the rational self-consciousness (see *PhM* 195). This does not mean that for Hegel space and time are merely subjective forms of our intuition, as in Kant. Rather they are forms of our rational intuition, which grasps external things in their self-externality, i.e., their truth.

As an example here of the "independence of the soul from space," Hegel cites the case of a girl, who, unbeknown to herself in her waking consciousness, had a brother in a distant country. In a moment of clairvoyance she envisioned him as ill and in a hospital, which turned out to be true. Though there is often mere charlatanry in these and similar accounts, says Hegel, there is enough evidence to render some of these phenomena credible.

place in the future and in this sense is "external" to the subject, yet it is a content bound up with the inner substantiality of the feeling-subjectivity.[39] The clairvoyant, says Hegel, is in a "concentrated" state and gazes upon this his "enveloped, pregnant life" in a concentrated way whereby the relations of time and space are not grasped on their own account. The quantity of time, for example, becomes a function of the content, and this, according to Hegel, accounts for the haziness and imprecision about time that usually marks the clairvoyant's utterances.

In the third kind of gazing-knowing, the subject in a trance becomes directly aware of his own psychical condition in a manner often more acute than the self-awareness of the normal waking state. In the trance, says Hegel, may be revealed the baser inner drives as well as the nobler impulses that motivate the individual and make up his "moral struggle with himself." The patient's reporting of his inner state, however, is often so "symbolic" and "bizarre," says Hegel, that it needs to be interpreted by someone specially trained.

As regards this *schauendes Wissen* as a whole, Hegel is not one of those who would regard it as something to be highly prized and esteemed. The monadic selfhood is not the developed individuality that has made itself sovereign over its manifold and heir to the fullness of its cultural heritage. In the immediacy of the gazing-knowing "the distinctions between subjective and objective, between intelligent personality and

---

[39] In this second form of clairvoyance, Hegel emphasizes the interwovenness of the clairvoyant's inner substantial being with the fabric of a closely knit communal life. Cases of clairvoyance, says Hegel, are most often found in areas where "the natural life" of men prevails to a marked degree. In the Scottish highlands, for example, Hegel says, there frequently occurs the phenomenon of "second sight," whereby the persons so gifted envision themselves in circumstances in which they will only later appear. Such phenomena, says Hegel, are not uncommon where people lead a narrowly circumscribed folk life, wherein their interests and goals are pursued in "indolent imitation of old traditions."

Kant, as we have seen, makes no claim to a notion of preconscious subjectivity as identity of its manifold as a feeling-life. Any alleged foresight (*Voraussehen*), says Kant, would be either a presensing (*Vorempfindung*), which would entail some hidden sense for what is not yet present, or a foreboding (*Vorhererwartung*), which is based on causal reflection. Thus "one easily sees" that all foreknowing or presentiment (*Ahndung*) is a phantasm (*Hirngespenst*), for "how can one sense (*empfinden*) what does not yet exist?" To be sure, says Kant, there are judgments based on obscure concepts of causal relation. But these are not presensings (*Vorempfindungen*) but can be explained by tracing and rendering explicit the concepts. Kant calls the alleged phenomena of second sight *Bezauberungen*. (*APH* 187)

objective world, and the finite relations between them, "are not present." [40]
The content is the feeling-life in its particularity and has the mark of
the contingent and particular, rather than the universal and necessary.
Hence, according to Hegel, it is silly to regard this kind of knowing as a
source of lofty and universal truths.

Nevertheless, the fact that there is such an immediate knowing, Hegel
maintains, has important implications for the philosophy of Subjective
Spirit. Spirit in its notion, according to Hegel, is to be absolutely identical
with itself in its determinations. Insofar as this identity is achieved on the
level of finite Spirit, it will only be truly actualized as reason, following
the overcoming of the separation of subject and object in consciousness.
The feeling soul's immediate knowing of its substantial being on the
present monadic level prior to consciousness, Hegel claims, is a fore-
shadowing of that unity of Spirit with itself to which it will return as
reason.[41] To understand the meaning of the present immediate knowing
is impossible as long as the subject-object antithesis of consciousness is
taken as an ultimate principle, as long as "we assume independent personalities, independent of one another and of their content as an objective
world—so long as we assume the absolute spatial and material externality
of one part of Being to another." [42] The significance of the gazing-knowing
is that it enables us to see consciousness itself as an *Urteil*, and its subject-
object relation as in fact a separation of what was originally one in the
feeling soul.

That the original feeling-unity of the soul is prior to the objective
consciousness and is taken up as a moment in the latter, Hegel sees as
strikingly manifested in the phenomena of the hypnotic trance.[43] In
"animal magnetism," according to Hegel, we are able to witness an
induced regression to the feeling-life. Hence in hypnosis there appear
various forms of the gazing-knowing evident in other instances of the
unhealthy magical relation. But the hypnotic trance displays in dramatic
fashion what was not quite so apparent in the sickness states. The nature
of the *Herabsinken* in the sickness states, we recall, consisted in the

---

[40] *PhM* 105.
[41] *PhM* 176 ff.
[42] *PhM* 105.
[43] The term "hypnosis" only came into use after Hegel's death. The terms
"animal magnetism," "magnetic somnambulism," and "magnetic sleep," which
Hegel mainly uses, were the current terms applied to the work of Anton Mesmer.
Hegel's view of this phenomenon, as will become evident, has nothing to do with
physical magnetism but rests wholly on his notion of Spirit as ideality.

emergence of a "real" subjectivity of feeling which has detached itself from the waking consciousness and taken over some of its functions. In the regression of the sickness states, the "second self" was the individual's own inner genius. In the hypnotic trance, the "second self" becomes the subjectivity of the hypnotist.

In the hypnotic trance, according to Hegel, the conscious subjectivity of the patient retires to the inner feeling-life, as in sleep, at the same time, however, surrendering its relation to the external world to the hypnotist. The patient's Being-for-self reverts to the passive, merely formal subjectivity of the feeling soul. Like the foetus, the patient does not "bear himself." He lies "wholly open" to the stronger subjectivity and is "thrilled through" by the infusing genius of the hypnotist.[44] The dominating subjectivity no longer has the character of an "other," as in the ordinary waking relationship of persons to one another but becomes one with the feeling-selfhood of the patient. In everyday waking life the self-possessed consciousness may be united with another in various ways. Normally this is a mediated unity—mediated, for example, by the requirements of a shared task or common goal—hence a unity in which the healthy consciousness retains its free Being-with-self even in uniting with another.[45] In the patient's relation to the hypnotist, however, there is an *Ineinanderleben* of two individuals where the one has surrendered his active Being-for-self and reverted to a lower foetus-like stage of the formal selfhood. The passive subjectivity of the patient, Hegel says, "has its contents in the sensations and representations of the other; sees, smells, tastes, reads, and hears in the other." [46]

Hegel regards the "new studies " [47] of hypnotic phenomena, as well as the psychical realm generally, as affording empirical confirmation of the

[44] *PhM 104*, 114 ff.

[45] This free unity of independent self-consciousnesses is possible only in the context of polity, which has overcome the master-slave relationship. (See *PhM* 176-177)

[46] *PhM* 104. But it is "undetermined," says Hegel, "which sensations and visions, the patient, in this formal perceiving, receives, beholds, and brings to knowledge from his own inner self, and which from the ideation (*Vorstellen*) of the person to whom he stands in relation."

[47] The work of Mesmer produced considerable stir in certain German circles around the turn of the century. Not only Hegel, but Fichte, Schelling, later Schopenhauer, and others took great interest in "animal magnetism" and saw in it any number of things, from a "spiritual matter" to sidereal and telluric forces. These views are spurned by Hegel (*PhM* 36 ff.) who, in common with Fichte, saw hypnosis as laying open a realm of mind underlying that of consciousness. See William

speculative approach to the study of Spirit. In the *Ineinanderleben* of two subjectivities that can be produced experimentally, as it were, in hypnosis, the soul, says Hegel, is revealed as the "truly immaterial," the "all-penetrating, the existing Notion," for which all distinctions are distinctions within itself. In hypnosis, even more overtly than in the other forms of the gazing-knowing, the immediate feeling-unity of the monadic subjectivity and its substantial being as a *Gefühlsleben* is manifested as the original identity from which consciousness and its mediated relation of subject and object first emerges as a self-dividing.

Hegel's notion of the *Ineinanderleben* of two souls deals with a theme almost as old as philosophy itself,[48] and one that is important to his effort to grasp man as Spirit. The treatment on the present level provides the "natural" or anthropological substratum for later and higher forms of spiritual unity, such as the ethical one of love.[49] But the *Ineinanderleben* of two adults can also betoken a regression from the level of the free rational consciousness and the morbid exercise of power by one subjectivity over another.[50] Hence, as in the case of the feeling-selfhood as inner genius, Hegel does not see in the natural *Seeleneinheit* as such an exaltation of Spirit but rather a psychical possibility that obtains its properly spiritual character only in its *Aufgehobensein* as a moment of the ethical realm and the mediated relationship of free, self-possessed subjectivities.[51]

b. *Self-Feeling*

The feeling soul in its notion, we recall, is the monadic subjectivity that is for itself in its feeling-life not yet distinguished from it as an objective outer world. The first moment of this notion, namely, the feeling soul in its immediacy, has shown the monadic subjectivity in undifferentiated unity with its substantial being as feeling-totality. The unity in this first moment is that of simple self-relation. The subjectivity

Wallace's introductory section, "Anomolies of Psychical Life," in his edition of *Hegel's Philosophy of Mind* (Oxford, 1894), pp. 123-31.

[48] A friend is "another self." (*Nicomachean Ethics* 1166a30)

[49] As a resolving of the contradiction of the unity of self-consciousnesses in their independence, "love is a unity of an ethical type." (*PhR* 262)

[50] In literature one thinks of such relationships as that of Uriah Heep and Mr. Wickfield in Dickens' *David Copperfield*, of Thomas Mann's *Mario and the Magician*.

[51] See Murray Greene, "Psyche and Polity in Hegel," *Man and World*, vol. 4, no. 3, fall 1971.

is for itself in its own fluid element: e.g., in its dream world in which it is passively borne along as by a power not its own. But this merely formal subjectivity, says Hegel, is "destined to raise its Being-for-self out of itself to subjectivity in one and the same individuality." [52] In the second moment of the feeling soul the monadic subjectivity moves to grasp itself in a *particular* manner and confirm its Being-for-self in a determinate content. This moment is termed by Hegel "self-feeling" (*Selbstgefühl*).

Self-feeling is the moment of the feeling soul's particularization (*Besonderung*), in which negativity will make its appearance in the strongest and most acute form thus far encountered in the soul's development. The negativity here is the "first negation," which is necessary to all determination.[53] This moment, therefore, is essential to the soul's actualization as controlling power in its substantial being. For the particular finite subjectivity, however, the negativity can also mean a schism in which the very selfhood is rent asunder. This takes place in extreme form in insanity (*Verrücktheit*). Insanity is thus viewed by Hegel within the context of the liberation struggle that the soul must go through to attain to the self-possession of the rational consciousness.

The feeling-totality as individuality, says Hegel, is essentially this: to distinguish itself within itself and to awaken to the judgment (*Urteil*) in itself in virtue of which it has particular feelings and is as subject in relation to these its determinations. The subject as such, Hegel says, posits these determinations in itself as *its* feelings. It is immersed (*versenkt*) in this particularity (*Besonderheit*) of its feelings, and at the same time "closes together" with itself as subjective one through the ideality of the particular. In this way, says Hegel, it is self-feeling—and at the same time is so only in the particular feeling.[54]

Hegel here has presented the second moment of the feeling soul in its bare notion, and it will help us to understand Hegel's meaning if we note the necessary advance—at once logical and spiritual—from the previous moment. In the *Urteil* as such of the feeling soul, we recall, the monadic individuality is "subject in general," and "its object is its substance, which is at the same time its predicate." [55] In the previous moment of immediacy, subject and predicate were in simple self-relation,

---

[53] *PhM* 95.
[53] See above, pp. 34 ff.
[54] *PhM* 122.
[55] See above, p. 105.

the monadic individuality having its Being-for-self in its feeling-life as abstract totality. In this immediate identity, the subject is not determinate in the predicate but in undifferentiated unity with it. The *Urteil* is thus tautological. It is for this reason that the subjectivity is merely "formal," having no particular content in which it is for itself "as itself." Such abstract identity, according to the speculative viewpoint, is itself a contradiction—in the realm of concrete Spirit, no less than in logic.[56] The soul is in contradiction to its notion when its Being-for-self is in the form of the abstract self-identity or "formal" subjectivity.[57] Hence the soul's "destiny"—meaning its essential nature according to its notion—is to "posit" its determinations as "for itself" in order that it may attain to its concrete Being-for-self as Spirit. The determinations seized, as it were, from the dreaming and *ahnende* subjectivity and "posited" by the soul in itself as *its* own are those of the feeling-life—now in the form of the particular feelings, drives, passions—which the soul lives through. The soul's obtaining its satisfaction or dissatisfaction [58] herein is its "idealizing" of the particular, whereby it "closes together" with itself in the particular and "is self-feeling."

In this second moment, however, the closing together with self in the particular as particular (*nur im besondern Gefühl*) is a onetime affair, or rather a plurality of such ones. The subject's coming back to itself in the particular as its predicate is not yet its coming back to itself in its universality. The idealization is yet but "first negation" and the subject's coming back to self is infected with diremption. Logically, the situation is such as to produce the "spurious" or "bad" infinity.[59]

---

[56] In the immediate unity of the monadic feeling soul, "the soul is already implicitly the contradiction of being an *individual*, a singular and yet being at the same time immediately identical with the universal natural soul, with its substance. This opposition existing in the soul in the contradictory form of identity must be made explicit as opposition, as contradiction." (*PhM* 125) In logic, according to Hegel, the proposition A=A is nothing but a law of abstract understanding. "The propositional form itself contradicts it: for a proposition always promises a distinction between subject and predicate; while the present one does not fulfil what its form requires." (*L* 213-14; see also *SL* 415)

[57] Similarly on the higher level of ego, Hegel says: the "I am I" is also an *Urteil*, the ego's distinguishing itself from itself. (See above, p. 24) But when there is nothing to distinguish subject and predicate except the abstract form of self-distinguishing, then, says Hegel, "the distinction *is* not, and self-consciousness is only motionless tautology, ego is ego, I am I." (*Phen.* 219; see also *PhM* 153 ff.)

[58] See above, p. 115.

[59] See above, p. 45 n. 41.

It is altogether necessary, according to Hegel, that a man actualize his individual capabilities in a determinate occupation or profession.[60] It is necessary that a man's will as "person" becomes objective to himself in the external and merely positive (*seiende*) form of property;[61] that his need for love be fulfilled in love for certain persons. Only through the particular can he close together with himself as concrete universality. But if he remains "sunk" in the particular, if his satisfaction remains "unmediated" or unsublated in its particularity, then the closing together in the particular does not mean a genuine concretization of the self in its inherent universality but only a form of self-sunderance. For in this case the particular remains "the simply affirmative" and hence "the first and immediate negation" that needs to regenerate itself endlessly in new particularities.[62]

The notion of self-feeling as the soul's necessary particularization—in which it can get "caught" in the particularity as "first negation"—forms the basis of Hegel's characterization of insanity as the mind's "Being-with-self in the negative of itself." [63] Hegel proposes to consider insanity

---

[60] *PhR* 133. "Man, if he wishes to be actual, must be-there-and-then, and to this end he must set a limit to himself. People who are too fastidious towards the finite never reach actuality, but linger lost in abstraction, and their light dies away." (*L* 173)

[61] "A person must translate his freedom into an external sphere in order to exist as Idea." (*PhR* 40)

[62] One finds no lack of illustrations in literature of this kind of spurious infinity. For Balzac's Gobseck, each new acquisition whets the appetite for an other. Similar to the miser's money-madness is the bad infinity of a land-madness (Tolstoy's *Land Enough for a Man*), Don Giovanni's *mille e tre* "already in Spain alone," or the kind of possessions-madness of the recluse whose home has become a labyrinth of miscellaneous accumulations. The particular craving has taken possession of the individual in his wholeness, and the selfhood as universality has reduced itself to a part of itself. Immersion (*Versenktsein*) in the particular may take another form, as in Goethe's *Werther*, where, when the particular passion cannot be fulfilled, the whole self must pine away; or in the spurned affection of Miss Havisham in Dickens' *Great Expectations*.

Regarding the "form of immediacy" that here characterizes the particular, Hegel says: "...It is the essential onesidedness of the category, which makes whatever comes under it onesided and, for that reason, finite. And, first, it makes the universal no better than an abstraction external to the particulars... Secondly, it invests the particular with the character of independent or self-centered Being. But such predicates contradict the very essence of the particular—which is to be referred to something else outside. In the form of immediacy, the finite is posited as an absolute." (*L* 136-37)

[63] *PhM* 126.

not merely as an anomoly but in terms of the notion of self-feeling and thus a moment in the soul's development toward the objective consciousness.[64] At the same time he regards insanity as a regression from the objective consciousness, which therefore needs to be "anticipated" in the discussion of insanity.[65] But how is it possible to view insanity at once in the movement toward consciousness and as a regression from it? To understand Hegel's notion of insanity we need to recall certain features of the speculative methodology.

The speculative development of Subjective Spirit is not a genesis in time but in notion.[66] The speculative consideration of Spirit shows a development from the abstract, incomplete, and therefore "untrue" forms of Spirit to the concrete, actual, and true forms. Hegel draws a parallel to the later level of Objective Spirit.[67] In the Philosophy of Right, for example, we deal with civil society before the state,[68] although we know quite well that the existence of civil society requires that of the state with its powers of administration, justice, etc. As an incomplete and abstract form of right, however, civil society precedes the state, which is the complete and actual notion. The order is logical, not temporal.[69] More specifically, the role of insanity in the doctrine of Subjective Spirit is compared by Hegel with that of crime in the doctrine of Objective Spirit. It is certainly not the case that every individual must go through the condition of extreme self-alienation, any more than that everyone must go through a phase of criminality because, in the notion of right, crime is a necessary form of appearance of will preceding

---

[64] Kant in his Anthropology, as we have noted, does not try to show a necessary development of the soul to consciousness. Unlike Hegel, he does not seek to view insanity as a sickness of the subjectivity in its wholeness. He views the different forms of insanity mainly as ways of malfunctioning of the respective mental faculties, e.g., judgment. (See *APH* 202 ff.) Kant does say, however, that even the powers of the deranged mind are organized into a system, and even in unreason (*Unvernunft*) nature strives to effect a principle of combination (*Verbindung*) in the faculties, whereby the thinking capacity, though not working in objective fashion to bring about a true knowledge of things, nevertheless does not remain inactive in bringing about a merely subjective knowledge on behalf of the animal life. (*APH* 216)

[65] "In considering insanity we must, as in other cases, anticipate the full-grown and intelligent conscious subject, which is at the same time the *natural* self of *self-feeling*." (*PhM* 123)

[66] See above, p. XI.

[67] *PhM* 130.

[68] *PhR* 122 ff.

[69] *PhR* 35, 233.

morality. Crime and insanity are extremes which do not always exist in every individual as extremes but may take the form of eccentricity, momentary loss of self-possession, noncriminal guilt. To ask the question: How can a responsible person stoop to crime? Hegel argues, means to have lost sight of the fact that only in the overcoming of the natural self does the morally responsible self first emerge.[70] Similarly, in the emergence of the objective consciousness, the self-overcoming of the subjectivity of feeling means that the self has acquired the strength and self-possession to "let go" its monadic content to acquire the higher form of objectivity.

As an objective consciousness, the self-possessed subjectivity is the ruling genius of its individual world.[71] Normally the special content of the particular feelings, desires, passions, are subsumed within an ordered whole and experienced in a manner consistent with that whole—which comprises the individual's concrete actuality. There are indeed times when this is not so, as when a person appears "beside himself" with rage, or when he clings to a onesided point of view with such a tenacity that we tend to say in exasperation: Why the fellow is mad! And indeed it is often not easy to draw the line between certain forms of eccentricity or extreme obstinacy and insanity as such. The essential consideration in insanity, according to Hegel, is that the feeling-particularity has taken on for the subjectivity the form of a fixity rooted in the very corporeality of the subject. The particularity has the immediacy of a positive Being (*Seiendes*) that resists mediation in the fluid totality of the body-soul relation of the rational selfhood.[72]

This taking on of a subsistence of its own by the feeling-particularity means that the ruling selfhood has relinquished its sovereignty. When the self-possessed consciousness is no longer the permeating ideality of the particular content of feeling, says Hegel, then there emerge the "dark, subterranean powers" which are otherwise "subordinated and kept

[70] For the speculative consideration of Spirit, says Hegel, the proper question should be: "How does the soul, which is shut up in its *inwardness* and is immediately identical with its individual world, emerge from the merely *formal*, empty differences of the subjective and the objective and attain to the actual difference of their two sides, and thus to the *truly* objective, intellectual and rational consciousness?" (*PhM* 129-130)

[71] See above, p. 109.

[72] "Spirit determined as merely *seiend*, insofar as such *Sein* is unresolved (*unaufgelöst*) in its consciousness, is sick." (*PhM* 124; see also above, p. 7 n. 22).

hidden" by the controlling rational selfhood.[73] The content unloosed
is a content of the natural state, the self-seeking impulses of vanity, pride,
hate, and other passions. Thus insanity for Hegel is not only a regression
to an abstract and "untrue" level of Spirit but to a baser level as well.
Nevertheless in its most complete form in which it has its essential notion,
insanity is a "tornness" (*Zerissenheit*) of Spirit, in which the self becomes
aware of its own state of diremption. Here insanity is not merely a
regression from a higher to a lower self but their confrontation and
conflict in the deepest pain of contradiction. It is this pain and contradiction, according to Hegel, which marks the difference between insanity
and the forms of the unhealthy magical relation.

Somnambulism in its various forms, as we have seen, is also termed
an *Herabsinken* from the objective consciousness to the monadic level
of the feeling soul. But the regression in somnambulism does not have
the same meaning as in insanity, according to Hegel. The regression in
insanity is not from a waking state, as in somnambulism. The deranged
person remains "awake." For this reason the regression in insanity has
the nature of a diremption (*Entzweiung*), while that of somnambulism is
but a separation (*Trennung*). In somnambulism there is a retirement from
the waking subjectivity's "mediate" unity with the objective world, to the
dream subjectivity's "immediate" unity with its substantiality as an inner
feeling-life. The psychical and the waking subjectivities remain on different levels, and the relation between the two is one of difference
(*Verschiedenheit*) rather than explicit opposition or contradiction. As in
the alternation of sleep and waking, daydream and alertness, trance and
self-possession, the *ahnende* subjectivity can alternate with the waking
subjectivity. The somnambulistic content does not retain for itself a
subsistence within the self's waking activities. In recovering from the
hypnotic trance, the patient recovers at once from his immediate relation
to his substantial being and his psychical *Ineinanderleben* with the hypnotist. The patient may not insist on the truth of his gazing-knowing,
indeed may not even remember what he said in the trance state.

In insanity, on the other hand, the content deriving from the feeling-life
is invested with "objective" status. Here, says Hegel, "the dream falls
within the waking limits." [74] What in somnambulism is but presentiment,

---

[73] Cf. Plato's treatment of the "tyrannical" soul (*Republic* 571 ff.).

[74] *PhM* 123. Kant also speaks of a *Träumen im Wachen* (*APH* 161) but does not
explicitly compare the subjectivity in somnambulism with that in insanity, as does
Hegel.

in insanity "belongs to actual self-feeling." The insane person is not in a trance state, not somnolent. The "tornness" of insanity, according to Hegel, consists in that the "two personalities" are "in one and the same state." Formally, the deranged subject is on the level of objectivity; the subjectivity relates itself to its content as a would-be objective consciousness. At the same time, says Hegel, the content is not truly objective, not mediated within the total *Zusammenhang* of the rational consciousness and structured by such objective categories as cause and effect. It is a content transposed from the monadic feeling-life, with its arbitrary and contingent associations, and as such insisted upon as "objectively" valid.[75]

Precisely because it is such a contradiction, according to Hegel, insanity in its speculative consideration marks an advance in the soul's development beyond the forms of immediacy in the magical relation and somnambulism. As a sunderance of the self, insanity is to be viewed both as a sickness state and as part of the soul's liberation struggle from its abstract identity with its natural being as monadic feeling soul. The positing of a particular content as its own is the soul's distinguishing it from the fluid wholeness of the feeling-life. In this positing, the soul relates itself negatively to itself in its substantial being: its closing together with itself in the particular is at the same time its breaking with itself as abstract identity of subjectivity and substance. It is this breaking with its own substantiality as self-enclosed monad that constitutes a step in the coming to be of genuine objectivity. As "first negation," however, the particular content has but the "formally" objective character of a mere *Seiendes* not yet sublated to a moment in the total interconnectedness of a genuinely objective content. It is "objectivity" in the abstract sense of the *idée fixe,* which has an implacable "thereness" for the deranged subjectivity. It is thus a parody of true objectivity, as obstinacy is a parody of firmness.[76]

In the content posited by the deranged subjectivity, says Hegel, the subject is "with himself in the negative of himself," for "the self-seeking determinations of the heart, vanity, pride, and other passions—imaginations, hopes—love and hate of the subject" are but his own "evil genius." [77] Insanity is thus at once a unity and opposition, a uniting of

[75] Cf. Kant, *APH* 219.

[76] See above, p. 69.

[77] *PhM* 124. "The negative endured in insanity," says Hegel, is one in which "only the feeling not the intellectual and rational, consciousness finds itself again." (*PhM* 127)

the self with itself and also a sunderance of the self in its fluid totality. This is the dialectical meaning of self-alienation: not abstract loss of self but a Being-with-self in a form directly contradictory to the *Beisichsein* of Spirit in its notion.

In the objective consciousness, according to Hegel, the identity and opposition of subject and object is a mediated relationship. Both sides have been raised to the level of universals: the ego of consciousness, as well as the content known by the ego. The particular content in insanity, however, is only "objective to me" (*mir gegenständlich*), an immediate and onesidedly subjective "objectivity." To raise myself to the level of rational thought, according to Hegel, I must sever myself from the content in its immediacy, set it opposite myself (*mir gegenüberstellen*) and in this way encounter it at a distance, as it were, or disinterestedly. This *Gegenüberstellen* that first enables the content to be *gegenständlich* requires a certain self-mastery on the part of the subjectivity, a liberation from itself as feeling-particularity. Only when I have come to power over myself in the particular am I capable of letting the content go free and attain to universality. Only then can I "find myself in the other" as a universal for a universal.

In insanity the merely contingent, that which can be as well as not be, is seized upon and clothed with a necessity deriving from an inner compulsiveness of the monadic selfhood, some blocking of the subject's implicit universality. The insane person clings to his imaginings—an isolated content of feeling—as undeniable in its immediate presence. In this merely subjective representation he has the certainty of himself. On it hangs his very being; he can see it in no other way. He is held captive by the fixed idea, which he is able neither to dismiss nor to resolve in the fluid totality of his consciousness.

Hegel views insanity in the light of Spirit as *Nous pathetikos*, the possibility of being all things. This abstract possibility is at once the glory and vulnerability of man as finite spirit. Like pain, insanity is seen by Hegel as a "privilege." Only man can grasp himself in that complete abstraction of "I", which is a condition for the possibility of insanity no less than of the objective consciousness. The fixed idea is an abstract imagining grounded on a mere possibility. Whatever might be the animal's feeling of itself, it cannot entertain the possibility of being other than just what it is. My claiming to be emperor has no other ground than the indefinite possibility that, since a man as such can be emperor, I, this man, am emperor. That I am able thus to imagine myself in a role so at odds with my concrete actuality, says Hegel, has its basis in that "I am, in the first instance, a wholly abstract, completely indeterminate 'I' and therefore open to any arbitrary content." [78] The regression in insanity is to this "powerless, passive, abstract ego," which, having forfeited its right "to remain completely present to itself in each of its representations," lies open to an arbitrary content of feeling that takes on for it the character of fixity.

Because the regression in insanity is to the feeling-life, while the subjectivity remains simultaneously in the state of waking, insanity, according to Hegel, is a contradiction "within" each of the two levels of selfhood, as well as "between" the two levels. As a "being-sunken" in a particularity of feeling, insanity is a blocking of the subject's fluid substantiality as natural being. As a clinging to the fixed idea as against the waking consciousness's "totality of mediations," insanity is in contradiction to the rational selfhood's relation to the objective world as a universal for a universal. In accordance with his notion of sickness in general, Hegel stresses that insanity is to be viewed as a sickness at once of Spirit and body. The selfhood as universality is sick inasmuch as it remains caught fast in a particularity of itself as self-feeling which it is unable to "refine" (Verarbeiten) to ideality and thereby overcome.[79] The particularity of feeling has in this way obtained the form of merely affirmative or positive Being (Seiendes) which, on the level of natural soul, means corporealization.[80] The corporealized particular feeling becomes a fixed barrier or limit (Schranke) for the soul in the universality of its selfhood.

Hegel proposes to view the main forms of mental illness according to insanity in its notion: namely, as the subject's ensnarement (Befangenheit) in a particularity of self-feeling which thereby obtains a "fixity of Being" (festes Sein) both as against the fluid organic substantiality and the mediated totality of the objective consciousness. So viewed, Hegel claims, the various mental illnesses can be classified as falling into the respective moments of the notion of "immersion within self" (In-sich-versunkensein) of the patient.[81] In the first classification fall those illnesses which manifest mental disease in its most general aspect:

---

[78] *PhM* 128.

[79] *PhM* 122-123.

[80] See above, p. 84.

[81] Although Hegel says we need to distinguish the forms of insanity "in a necessary and therefore rational manner" (*PhM* 131), there is no explicit claim to the rigor of a *Schluss*.

a "wholly indefinite" immersion within self. The second grouping
comprises those sicknesses where the immersion within self obtains
an articulated content in the form of particular delusions. The third
includes those in which the unreal content becomes evident to the
patient himself, who, comparing his subjective imaginings with his
objective consciousness, "attains to the unhappy feeling of his contradiction with himself." Here, says Hegel, we see the patient in desperate
striving to resolve the "felt split" within himself and restore his unity
with himself.[82]

In the first group, Hegel includes imbecility and related ills (cretinism,
idiocy), which in greater or lesser degree display a dull stupidity or
"shutness" (Unaufgeschlossenheit) of the soul, deriving congenitally,
accidentally, or as a consequence of excesses that induce a state of
stupefaction. Another form of the indefinite immersion within self is
manifested in what Hegel calls "distraction" (Zerstreutheit), consisting
in an unawareness of what is immediately present. Often this is a sign
of the onset of a deeper malady, says Hegel. There is a "grand oblivion,"
as in the total concentration upon some intellectual problem, where
the individual needs almost to be forced back to commonplace reality.[83]
Distraction proper, however, is an "immersion in wholly abstract self-
feeling," where the absentmindedness may be so strong that the individual
confuses his imaginings with elements of his real situation. In contrast
to these forms of inner preoccupation, there is a "rambling" (Faselei)
in which the individual seems wholly taken up with outer things. But
in fact his ceaseless flitting from one thing to another reveals his lack
of power to engage his interest long enough with any one thing to give
it its due.[84] Thus we see from this first grouping how Hegel takes maladies

---

[82] Hegel of course does not mean that the patient must pass through the three
main forms or that mental illness proceeds in this course. The classification is
logical rather than etiological. We may view the discussion of the specific types of
insanity as marginal to Hegel's main aim in the Anthropology, though it has a
certain interest in showing a Hegelian attempt to treat an admittedly empirical and
largely contingent material along the lines of the Notion. In the following summary
we shall omit many details, some of which, as in the case of the magical relation,
can hardly be regarded as acceptable.

[83] Hegel cites the case of Archimedes as an instance of grand oblivion. In Balzac's
Louis Lambert (1832) we are given an appalling picture of a man of genius who,
devoting himself entirely to inner meditation, in the end reduces (or elevates?)
himself to a kind of divine idiocy.

[84] See the discussion of the "temperaments," above, p. 68.

admittedly disparate etiologically and with seemingly opposite symptoms, but which purportedly have a common involutional tendency that justifies their inclusion in the first moment of "indefinite *In-sich-ver-sunkensein.*"

The second main grouping, according to Hegel, comprises those ills where the subject's immersion within self obtains the form of a determinate content, such as a fixed idea. In folly (*Narrheit*), such fixed ideas arise for the most part when the individual, dissatisfied with his actuality, closes himself up and spins a make-believe world to accord with his vanity, pride, envy, and other passions. The most abstract form of folly, says Hegel, sometimes appears as a disgust with life, a wavering between inclination and disinclination, a being held captive by the fixed idea of the repulsiveness of all things. In contrast to this generalized surfeit of life (*Lebensüberdruss*), there is a kind of folly where a particular content has a passionate interest for the subject. It may be related directly to the particular passion which has usurped a mastery over the man, as where he proclaims himself to be God or king; or it may display a complete arbitrariness, as where the afflicted holds himself to be a dog or to contain a wagon in his stomach. In neither case is the patient troubled by the contradiction between his fixed idea and his objective consciousness.

In this classification Hegel attempts to show the second moment of *In-sich-versunkensein* as one where the self has the power to constitute itself and its content as universal, but only in a onesidedly subjective manner. In the disgust with life the subject negates the particular by investing every particularity with disgust and holding himself abstractly for himself. The universality of the self is established, only to "evaporate" in the abstract onesidedness which renders impossible its actualization in and through the particular as concrete universal.[85] This onesidedness has its counterpart in the apparently opposite form of immersion within self: the self's investing its entire being in the particular. The patient's sunkenness in a particular passion is a reduction of himself to a particular, which is clothed with a spurious universality. His saying, I am

---

[85] Speaking of the "beautiful soul," a literary and philosophical ideal of his time, Hegel says: "The *schöne Seele* that lacks actuality, subsisting in the contradiction of its pure self and the necessity it feels to externalize itself and turn into something actual... being conscious of this contradiction in its unreconciled immediacy, is unhinged, disordered, and runs to madness...." (*Phen.* 676)

king, means in effect his saying that I, this whole, reduce myself to this passion of pride and call it my self. Thus the being caught fast (*beharren bleiben*) in the particular is no less a loss of self than the inability to actualize the self as universality of the particular.

In the third main form of insanity, which Hegel calls "madness" (*Tollheit*), the patient keenly feels his own diremption but cannot let go of his fixed idea. *Tollheit*, says Hegel, may be precipitated by a great personal misfortune, a shattering of a man's individual world, which can also come about through a violent social upheaval where the individual's ties to the old order are so strong that he cannot bring himself to accept the new. The patient's symptoms may take the form of a withdrawal and melancholy attended by phantoms of worry and despair, or a raging against the alien outer reality, where he often manifests an extreme hatred, deceptiveness, and hostility to all about him. Hegel here sees the opposition of the individual's subjectivity and universal substantial being as at a height of contradiction in his awareness of his own dividedness. His implicit universal selfhood is present to him in the pain of his own diremption. The hostile outer reality is implicitly his own being from which he feels himself cut off, and he vents his fury against it or directs his hatred inwards, tormenting himself with feelings of guilt and unworthiness that may drive him to self-destruction.[86]

---

[86] Hegel offers a brief discussion of therapy, of which we may note certain main points. Citing the rational and humane approach of the French physician Philippe Pinel (1745-1826), Hegel views the aim of therapy as aiding the patient to gain release from his immersion in a particularity of his feeling-life and to restore his fluid unity with himself in his universality. A merely physical, as well as a merely psychical treatment may sometimes suffice, says Hegel, but for the most part the two must go together. Since insanity is not utter loss of reason but contradiction within reason, the therapist should seek wherever possible to build upon the "residue" of "reason". For this the psychical treatment is of chief importance. To gain the patient's trust, the physician should approach him with respect, says Hegel, and this may mean not making a direct attack on the fixed idea. Nevertheless, the patient should be made to understand, by force if need be, that certain modes of behavior will not be tolerated. In winning the patient's confidence, the physician should also seek to become a figure of authority, one who in his own person shows that there is something worthy and important, and from whom the patient can draw strength to overcome the weakness in himself. Disciplinary measures should always have the meaning of a just punishment, for the moral sense is not dead, says Hegel, and it can be strengthened by treating the patient as far as possible as a morally responsible human being. Above all, vindictive, contemptuous, and arbitrary handling is to be avoided as evoking tendencies in the patient toward the same behavior. In resolving

The moment of self-feeling, to which insanity is a regression, is at once the feeling soul's first break with itself as abstract identity of subjectivity and substance, and its grasping itself as "subjective one" in a particular content. *Selbstgefühl* thus marks an advance from the merely passive and formal subjectivity of the feeling soul in its immediacy, and a step in the soul's taking itself in possession. At the same time, we must keep in mind, the movement is on the natural level, where the determinations of content are "incorporated," i.e., are at once determinations of the soul's natural being or corporeality. Since it is on the natural level, this stage of *Be-sunderung,* as we have seen, can mean the subjectivity's being caught fast in the particular and hence the soul's separation of itself from its organic fluid universality. Where self-feeling is not sublated as a moment of the higher consciousness, therefore, it remains as a fissure in the selfhood that can become an open break: i.e., the emergence of the psychical subjectivity in painful opposition to the rational consciousness.

However much or little can remain today of Hegel's views of particular illnesses or his attempt at classification, the general endeavor to conceive this vital realm of human experience within a philosophical doctrine of subjectivity cannot but be viewed with interest, if not admiration. The discussion of insanity under the concept of "self-feeling" forms an essential part of Hegel's effort to open up the narrow view of cognition and the artificially confined approaches to epistemology inherited in part from the Critical Philosophy. The knower, Hegel is never tired of stressing, is in the first place a selfhood, a spiritual totality. Even in its derangement the self must be seen as Spirit. The identity of self-consciousness—Kant's synthetic unity of apperception—is not to be conceived merely as a dry logical requirement that makes possible an apodictic science of physics. Self-consciousness is to be viewed as an attainment of an integrated selfhood, a victory of the finite subjectivity over the dangers of wresting itself out of its *Mitleben* with its merely natural being. *Selbstgefühl,* the second moment of the feeling soul, in the extreme of derangement is indeed a defeat for the finite selfhood; but in its general meaning of *Besonderung,* out of which Spirit regains its wholeness and attains to a new strength and depth, it is a moment of the *Befreiungskampf* of the soul in its actualization as objective consciousness.

the fixed idea, work therapy and association with good company may be effective, since these engage the patient as a person in his universal selfhood. (*PhM* 136-139)

c. Habit

In self-feeling we saw the soul immersed or absorbed in its particular feelings. This was the second moment of the feeling soul, which displayed the twofold aspect of sunderance from and particularization of the soul's relation to itself as a feeling-life. In the present third and concluding moment of the feeling soul, the psychical subjectivity comes back to itself in its wholeness through its "setting down" (Herabsetzen) of the particular in habit (Gewohnheit). The soul's regaining of its fluid universality in habit will mark an important step in the development of the psychical subjectivity's attainment of the ego of consciousness. Hegel maintains that the true meaning of habit has eluded investigators of mind and that his viewing habit as the concluding moment of the feeling soul will disclose its genuine nature and its role in the movement of the soul to ego.

Habit, like the previous stages in the soul's development, is the soul's relation of identity with and distinction from its corporeal or substantial being. Our task is to see both the continuity with and difference from those previous stages as presented by Hegel in the logical terms of the Notion. In habit, according to Hegel, the soul is united with its corporeality, but in such a manner that it is freed from its immersion in the particular.[87] In habit the soul posits itself as the ideality of its particular feelings. The necessity of the movement from self-feeling lies in the notion of the latter as a contradiction of the soul. The soul's captivity (Gebanntsein) in a particularity of itself, as in the extreme form of the idée fixe,[88] is not imposed from without. Alienation, as was shown in the notion of insanity, is a self-relation in the form of a contradiction. The soul is implicitly the self-relating universality and cannot rest in being caught fast in a particularity of itself.

Habit, says Hegel, is the soul's making itself into "abstract universal being" and its reduction of the particularity of feeling (as well as of consciousness [89]) to a "mere feature of its being" (nur seienden Bestimmung an ihr).[90] This is but one and the same movement: the soul's setting

---

[87] "The main point about habit is that by its means man gets emancipated from the feelings, even in being affected by them." (PhM 141)

[88] See above, pp. 125, 127.

[89] The content of habit can derive from consciousness as well as from the feeling-life.

[90] PhM 140.

the particular down is its setting itself up as the universal. In the soul's previous absorption in its particular feelings, passions, and their satisfactions, the soul remained implicitly the simple self-relating ideality. Habit is the soul's *positing* itself as universality in the feeling-life, so that the soul's simple ideality permeates the particular as its truth.

Inasmuch as the soul posits itself as simple ideality of the particular, the latter no longer has the status of a fixed corporeal determination. It is no longer, as in insanity, a *Seiendes* that stands as a block to the self's fluid universality.[91] Now, says Hegel, the particular on its side is formal, just "the particular being" or immediacy of the soul in relation to the soul's own formal, abstract Being-for-self.[92] The particular being of the soul is the moment of its corporeality "with which the soul breaks," in the sense that it distinguishes itself from it as its "simple being" and is as ideal *subjective* substantiality of this corporeality.

Hegel's logical characterization of habit may at first sight seem a bit puzzling. While the soul in habit has set down the particular and would therefore seem to warrant being called "concrete," it is nevertheless termed by Hegel "abstract" in the sense that the main effect in habit is that I need no longer be preoccupied with the particular, thereby leaving myself "open" for higher activity. In habit the feeling-subjectivity still has an automatic aspect. But to see the advance from the previous stages of the feeling soul we may recall the senses in which it was termed a "formal" subjectivity, "abstract," "passive," and "open."

In the magical relation of the feeling soul in its immediacy, the subjectivity was "open" to the infusing subjectivity of an other, as in the foetus-mother relation, or to its own inner genius as an "other" to it.[93] In insanity the subjectivity was open to a contingent content of the feeling-life. "Openness" in the speculative meaning indicates that something has gone before, that there has been a self-constituting of some sort, as in the openness of the blossom following its enclosedness as a bud.[94] Passivity, abstractness, openness thus have a meaning relative to the

---

[91] See above, p. 125.

[92] *PhM* 140.

[93] In the inner genius, like the Socratic *daimonion*, Being-for-self "still had the form of externality, of separation into two individualities, into a dominating and a dominated self." (*PhM* 144)

[94] In the emergence of the ego of the objective consciousness, the initially "empty" and "formal" ego will also display such an openness for a "new" content as that of an external world; see below, p. 166.

stage of development of the subjectivity.[95] In habit these characterizations of the psychical subjectivity have a more pregnant meaning than on the previous levels of the feeling soul. In habit, says Hegel, the soul "has overcome the inner contradiction of mind present in insanity, has put an end to the complete dividedness of the self." [96] Hence the soul in habit is abstract in the sense that it "makes itself" unto abstract universal being. This is a conquest, an attainment that enables the subjectivity to be receptive in a way that it has not been thus far on the two previous moments, namely, the feeling soul in its immediacy, and the feeling soul as *Selbstgefühl* in the particular feeling. Having come back to itself from its immersion in the particular, the soul now moves freely and easily in its corporeality as its own familiar element. In contrast to the dream subjectivity, the soul now has itself "in possession" by virtue of having posited the particular in self-feeling and having overcome its self-sunderance by "making" the content its own.

Habit, says Hegel, is rightly termed a second nature. What I do habitually, I do in a sense naturally. But habitual activity is not immediately natural since it is a result of the soul's own work upon itself. Habit is the soul's "self-in-forming" (*Sicheinbilden*) of its feeling-determinations in their particularity and corporeality "into the being (*Sein*) of the soul." [97] The naturalness of habit is therefore "an immediacy *posited* by the soul." Man's nature, says Hegel, is to make himself a second nature—as Spirit.[98] The soul's forming of its particular corporeal determinations into its own universal being is the soul's liberation from the particular, and forms the soil of all the mind's higher freedom, according to Hegel.

Hegel see habit in terms of the three moments of the notion: [99] a) The immediate sensation or feeling is negated, "posited as indifferent," as when the individual develops an "inurement" (*Abhartung*) toward sensations of cold, heat, weariness, or even the blows of fortune. Habituation here has the meaning that even in its particular affection the soul preserves itself abstractly for itself. b) Habit in a higher form is "indifference" to satisfaction. The inner drives and desires are

---

[95] On Hegel's rejection of the "abstract opposition" of receptivity and active capacity, see above, p. 84 n. 91.

[96] *PhM* 144.

[97] *PhM* 141.

[98] See Hegel's interpretation of the Biblical story of the Fall, *L* 54 ff.; also above, p. 99, n. 186.

[99] These are not to be regarded as stages in habit formation.

blunted through their regular fulfillment. This is the rational liberation
from these drives, according to Hegel, not the monkish asceticism in
which "the enemy creates itself in its very defeat." [100] c) In skill or
"aptitude" (*Geschicklichkeit*) habit attains its highest form. Here the
soul as ideality makes itself prevail as subjective purpose in its corporeality, permeating it and rendering it the instrument of its end. In
these moments of habit in its notion, Hegel maintains, the soul wins
release from the particular corporeal determination precisely in achieving
a higher unity with the corporeal as such.

Habit, particularly as aptitude, is a return on a higher level to the
fluid unity of the feeling soul in its immediacy. While the capability
of a particular organ, or several together, is realized in one determinate
purpose, the mechanical activity constitutes so thorough a mastery
of the particulars that the subjectivity need no longer be engaged
directly with them. Thus habit is another instance of the magical
relation.[101] It is once again a healthy living-together of the soul with its
corporeality, as in sentience, but a higher *Mitleben* than before inasmuch
as it makes possible a release from the corporeal as such.

The significance of the *Einbilden*—in the particular organ—of the
universal as subjective purpose, says Hegel, is that the implicit ideality
of the corporeality, and of the material as such, is *posited* as ideal.
Hereby the soul, in its determinate purpose, "exists" as subjective
substance in its corporeality.[102] In aptitude the corporeality is so wholly
rendered ideal that as soon as the representation is in me—e.g., a series
of musical notes—my body at once expresses its meaning in one fluid
utterance. In this "immediate *Einwirken* of mind on body," my activity
is no doubt automatic. But this automatism is not the same as in
somnambulism or the trance states, where I am as though possessed by
another subjectivity. In habit I have myself "in possession."

It is in the soul's attainment in habit to the "ideal, *subjective
substantiality*" of the corporeality that habit is seen by Hegel as the
"basis" for consciousness. In habit, says Hegel, the corporeality is

---

[100] *Phen.* 263-64.

[101] *PhM* 97; see above, p. 107.

[102] Existence, in the logic, is a higher category than Being. To say that something
"exists" is to imply that it has come forth from a "ground" and is thus part of a
context of interconnected determinations. (*L* 230) At the same time existence is not
as high a category as actuality. The difference between *Existenz* and *Wirklichkeit*
in the development of the soul will mark its advance from feeling soul to actual
soul. (See below, p. 144)

determined as "immediate external Being and limit" as against the
inner determination of the soul in its subjective purpose. The soul-body
relation is no longer that of the individual's monadic feeling-subjectivity
as inner genius of the feeling-life. As a *positedness*, habit is the soul's
own "break" as "simple Being-for-self within itself against its naturalness." [103] The naturalness is no longer in the form of "immediate"
ideality, as in the feeling-life of the dream subjectivity, but rather
"set down" to ideality as instrument of subjective purpose.

Conceived as having the inward purpose of the subjective soul thus imposed upon it,
the body is treated as an immediate externality and a barrier (*unmittelbares äusser-
liches Sein und Schranke*). Thus comes out the more decided rupture (*Bruch*)
between the soul as simple self-concentration, and its earlier naturalness and
immediacy; it has lost its original and immediate identity with the bodily nature,
and as external has first to be reduced to that position.[104]

In this relation with its own corporeality as "immediate external Being
and barrier," according to Hegel, the soul has the "intuition" of itself.
The psychical subjectivity stands on the threshold of consciousness—
upon whose crossing the soul's intuition of itself in its own corporeality
will have become the "certainty" (*Gewissheit*) of the "I" in its relation
to its content as an objective outer world.

The form of habit, Hegel points out, extends throughout all the levels
of Spirit and reveals more than anything else the "power of ideality"
which the soul exercises over the body. Even man's upright stance—
this immediate, unconscious attitude that is nevertheless so characteristically human—requires a habitual exertion of effort, however insensible. Seeing, says Hegel, is the concrete habit that, in one single act,
immediately unites determinations of sensation, intuition, understanding,
etc. Even thinking needs habitude and fluidity. Through habit, a religious
and moral content becomes for me more than a burst of enthusiasm,
a passing inspiration, or an abstract inwardness cut off from my total
actuality. For Aristotle the moral virtues are habits. In habit, Hegel,
maintains, the spiritual becomes ingrained in my being, comes into
existence in me as concrete immediacy and "psychical ideality."

But if habit exhibits these aspects of self-mastery and liberation, says
Hegel, it can also be an unfreedom. This ambivalent character of habit
derives from its notion as concluding moment of the *Schluss* of the feeling
soul. The soul's setting down of the corporeal particularity to a moment

---

[103] *PhM* 142.
[104] *Ibid.*

of its own universal being means at the same time that the corporeal is still its element. Habit is the *Existenz* of the soul in its corporeality, and for this reason can also mean the opposite of freedom. Hence Hegel says, though habit is a "posited, second nature," it is still a nature, therefore not equivalent to free Spirit but "something merely anthropological." [105] Religion can become mere ritual.[106] Habitual attitudes and modes of thought can be a bar to true thinking. The form of habit is no guarantee of content: habits can be bad as well as good. In habit, says Hegel, man is "still in the mode of natural existence, and therefore unfree." Habit is after all a mechanism, and the thorough reduction of life to habit is death.[107]

Habit develops through practice, and the in-forming of the particular corporeal determinations into the "universal being" of the soul is effected through mechanical repetition. The universal of habit, therefore, is far from the concrete universal of the Notion. The universal developed in the soul is logically akin to what Hegel terms the "universal of reflection." [108] In habit, says Hegel, the universal is but "the one and the same as an external multiplicity of sensation that is reduced to its unity, this abstract unity as *posited*." [109] To be sure, in habit the psychical subjectivity relates itself not only to a single sensation or set of contingent sensations, representations, desires, etc.; rather, through incorporating these particulars within its subjective purpose, it relates itself to itself in its "general manner of acting" (*allgemeine Weise des Tuns*). This general manner of acting is posited through the soul itself and is thus its own in which it appears free. Nevertheless the universal of repetition on the present anthropological level is in the form of an "external fastening" of the particulars, not the concrete universal from which the

---

[105] *PhM* 144-145.

[106] *L* 336-37.

[107] See above, p. 74.

[108] By *Reflexions-Allgemeinheit*, which applies more properly to the higher levels of consciousness and reason, Hegel means the universal that appears as secondary to the particulars and imposed by our subjective doing, rather than as the immanent truth of the particulars in which they are sublated as vanishing moments. Hegel also terms the universal of reflection the universal of "allness" (*Allheit*). "It is as 'all' (*Allheit*) that the universal is in the first instance generally encountered by reflection. The individuals form for reflection the foundation, and it is only our subjective action which collects and describes them as 'all'. So far the universal has the aspect of an external fastening (*äusseres Band*) that holds together a number of individuals independent of and indifferent toward it." (*L* 309)

[109] *PhM* 141.

particulars derive as necessary determinations in the self-differentiating movement of the Notion.[110]

Thus in this third and concluding moment of the feeling soul, the abstract Being-for-self of the psychical subjectivity is still a Being-for-self of the individuality in its corporeality, not yet the Being-for-self of ego in its content as an independent outer world. To be sure, the corporeality in habit is reduced to ideality. No particularity of sentience or feeling retains a subsistence on its own account as against the simpleness of the soul. But the corporeality *as such* remains "the particular being" or element in which the soul has its Being-for-self; and in this sense the corporeality is yet a "barrier" or "limit" (*Schranke*) [111] to the ideality of the soul. Though my body "is the middle term (*Mitte*) by which I come together with the external world as such," [112] I must sublate precisely that character as a *Mitte* in order to relate myself to the outer world purely as thinking ego.

But while the corporeality in habit is still a *Schranke*, it has now come into possession of the soul, which is its "simple being" and "subjective" substantiality. For this reason, says Hegel, while the feeling subjectivity is not yet ego of consciousness—not yet the universal that is for itself the universal [113]—the soul in habit is "the wholly pure unconscious intuiting (*bewusstlose Anschauen*), in the same way as empty space and empty time are only subjective forms, pure intuiting. The soul's "intuiting" of itself in its corporeality is not yet the "certainty" of self of the ego which can say "I"; this presupposes the level of pure thought. The self-intuiting of the feeling soul, says Hegel, is the "basis" (*Grundlage*) of consciousness but not yet consciousness. The soul will attain to consciousness when it has sublated its corporeality as such as its "limit"—when it has taken up into itself its natural being as this "particular being" in which it has its Being-for-self—and in this way has posited itself as pure subjectivity for itself. To this concluding movement we now turn, where we shall see the psychical subjectivity's consummation of its development as "actual soul."

---

[110] See above, p. 4 n. 6.
[111] See above, p. 49, n. 61.
[112] *PhM* 146.
[113] See below, p. 143.

CHAPTER SIX

THE ACTUAL SOUL

In habit, Hegel has told us, the feeling soul stands on the threshold of consciousness. In the present concluding section of the Anthropology, Hegel will claim to show, the psychical subjectivity "actualizes" itself and "awakens" to itself as ego of consciousness. This is the destination toward which the whole preceding movement has aimed, Hegel tells us. Hence in many ways the present chapter is the most crucial for purposes of the demonstration. Unfortunately it is also in some ways the most difficult to understand. For this reason let us begin with a brief look at the end, that is to say, the goal toward which the demonstration aims.

Hegel's Anthropology, as we have noted from the beginning, aims to demonstrate an emergence of consciousness, claims to provide a deduction of consciousness. But what is it that is "deduced" in such a deduction? How do we know if we are successful? For Hegel the deduction of consciousness consists in a demonstration of that sequence of spiritual forms wherein the pre-objective *feeling* subjectivity sublates itself to the objective *thinking* subjectivity. On both levels the subjectivity is the ideality of its manifold. Then in what, we ask, will consist the difference? The "lightning" of the "I", Hegel tells us, "pierces through the natural soul and consumes its natural being." [1] The "I", Hegel will claim to show, is "the distinguishing of itself from itself"—which self-distinguishing will constitute the condition for the possibility of the ego's distinguishing of its content as "objective."

Only when I come to apprehend myself as 'I', does the Other become objective to me, confronts me, and is at the same time converted into an ideal moment in me, and hence brought back to unity with me.[2]

---

[1] *PhM* 154.
[2] *Ibid.*

Thus as in all transcendental philosophy, the "I am I", or consciousness of self, is for Hegel the condition for the possibility of an objective world.

But was there not also a "self-distinguishing" by the monadic feeling subjectivity? We recall the importance of the notion of *Urteil* as marking every stage in the notional development of the psychical subjectivity ; and we recall how Hegel rejected Kant's formulation that self-knowledge would entail the "circularity" of the subject's making "use" of itself to judge itself.[3] The whole theme of Hegel's philosophy of Subjective Spirit is that subjectivity *is* Notion, *is* the "separating judgment" that "makes itself its own object." But the *Urteile* of the psychical subjectivity demonstrated thus far have been essentially different from the *Urteil* that will now be shown to constitute the subject-object relation of consciousness. In what precisely will consist the difference ? If we can answer this question, we will have understood the meaning of Hegel's deduction of consciousness.

On the monadic level, we recall, Hegel characterized the relation of the subjectivity to its content as follows :

At this stage, what I feel, I *am,* and what I am, I feel. I am here immediately present in the content, which only subsequently appears as a self-dependent world confronting me when I become an objective *consciousness.*[4]

As consciousness, therefore, I shall in the first place distinguish a content of mine as "other" than myself. But how do I come to do that ? In making such a distinction, according to Hegel, I must be able to think myself in the pure abstraction of "I" : I must be able to say or think, "I am." Only then can I think a content of mine as "other". The feeling-subjectivity does not grasp or make the determination "Being" (*Sein*), which is an absolute abstraction, a "pure thought." [5] It cannot do so, Hegel contends, because it cannot yet grasp itself as abstract "I". The feeling-subjectivity is not capable of saying, "I am"—and hence not capable of attributing Being to any determinate content of its feeling-life. The feeling-subjectivity cannot think its content precisely because it is "immediately present" or "immersed" in it. To think it, it has to separate itself from it, that is to say, separate itself from itself. In contrast even to the most ordinary utterance of the objective consciousness, the feeling-subjectivity—because it cannot say "I am"—cannot say of a particular content : "it is". Thus

[3] See above, p. 16.
[4] *PhM* 89-90.
[5] *L* 158.

Hegel's task in the present chapter is to show how the subjectivity comes to think itself as "I", whereby it simultaneously comes to think of its content as "objective." [6]

The actual soul is the third and concluding stage of the syllogistic *(Schluss)* movement of the soul, hence unites in itself the previous two stages : the natural soul and the feeling soul. In all of these stages we have been dealing with a self-relation, namely the relation of the soul as subject to itself as substance or predicate ; and substance on the level of natural subjectivity has meant the soul's own physical being, i.e., its corporeal determinations, which have hitherto been its "nonobjective object." This has been the meaning of the "self-enclosedness" of the monadic individuality.[7] Now on the stage of actual soul there emerges a new and higher uniting of subjectivity and substance by virtue of the soul's rendering the body the soul's own outer "sign" *(Zeichen)*. But as we saw on all previous stages, every higher uniting is at the same time a higher distinguishing : and this, as we stressed in our introductory chapters on Hegel's speculative method, is nothing other than the *Scheidung in sich* of Notion. With the actualization of the soul in its corporeality as its "sign," Hegel will seek to show, the content from its substantial being is distinguished or "let go" *(entlassen)* and invested with self-subsistence by the very subjectivity that has "let it go." In this way, that in which the psychical subjectivity has thus far been *versenkt* will henceforward be regarded by the subjectivity as "object." Hereby we see that the meaning of "objectivity" in Hegel's demonstration arises out of the *Urteil* of the soul-body unity. It will help us to see the meaning of this *Urteil* by comparison with certain main features of the previous stage of habit.

The significance of habit, we recall, is that the soul breaks with its corporeality as its "particular Being" *(besonderes Sein)* in which the soul has been immersed as self-feeling. But the "break" is also a uniting, inasmuch as it is the soul's distinguishing itself from its corporeality as the latter's "simple Being." But in this way the soul is not yet "for itself" as subjectivity, not yet the "Being-for-self of the simple in the simple, the relation of the universal to the universal." [8] The corporeality in habit is still a "limit". Its idealization by the soul in its subjective "purpose" affords the psychical subjectivity only an "unconscious in-

[6] See *JR* 179 ff.

[7] See above, p. 105.

[8] *PhM* 152.

tuiting" of itself as universal.[9] In habit, I act mechanically, I am borne along—albeit by a momentum I myself have created. For this reason, as we saw, the soul has only its "abstract" Being-for-self in its corporeality. But from this unconscious self-intuiting through rendering the body an "instrument," the soul now advances to a "knowing" or "certainty" (Ge-wissheit) of itself through rendering the body its very "sign." Having thoroughly informed (durchgebildet) its corporeality and made it unto its own, the soul actualizes itself for itself as single subject, and the corporeality is the externality (Ausserlichkeit) as predicate wherein the subject relates itself purely to itself.[10] This externality does not stand for itself but for the soul, and is its "sign." As this identity of the inner with the outer, the latter subordinate to the former, the soul, says Hegel, is "actual" (wirklich).[11]

To understand how this "actualization" of the soul is connected with the advance from the unconscious self-intuiting to the conscious self-certainty of the "I am," we must see the advance in idealization of the "externality"—meaning here the body—from "instrument" to "sign." "Externality" in habit, we recall, included two opposed but connected meanings : indifference (Gleichgültigkeit) and limit (Schranke). In habit as "inurement," the affection is reduced to "an externality and immediacy," so that I am no longer "involved with it," not disturbed. In habit as "aptitude," I attain something more concrete. Taking for granted my inurement and indifference to outer and inner affections, I no longer have to do with them directly but with my corporeality insofar as I develop it to an instrument of my subjective purpose. As against the inwardness of purpose, says Hegel, "the corporeality is determined as immediate external Being and limit." [12]

Thus the corporeality as "instrument" retains the aspect of an "externality" in the sense of an "other" that is not directly one with the soul's inner purpose. To be sure, the soul in habit has reduced the particular (in which it was formerly versenkt) to but a moment in the universal fluid element in which it now moves freely. But an element in

---

* See above, p. 138.
[10] PhM 147.
[11] In the logic, "actuality (Wirklichkeit) is the unity, become immediate, of essence with existence, or of inner and outer. The expression (Ausserung) of the actual is the actual itself... Its externality is its energizing (Energie) ; in it it is reflection within self ; its determinate Being (Dasein) is but the manifestation of itself, not of an other." (L 257-58)
[12] PhM 142.

which I move freely is still not yet the medium in which I give myself "expression," is not yet that in which, in relating myself to it as an outer, I am directly reflected back into myself. An instrument points outside itself toward the goal for which it is a "means." Hence in habit the corporeality is externality qua outer *Existenz* of inner purpose and therefore not yet one with the inner. The *identity* of inner and outer—the meaning of "actuality"—is first achieved, according to Hegel, where the externality no longer stands for itself but is the very "sign" of the inner, the "free form" in which the soul *"feels itself* and makes *itself felt."* [13]

The "externality" of the body as "sign" of the soul thus marks an ascension in ideality. The subject-substance relation is characterized by a higher logical category or form of the Notion than that in which the body plays its role in habit as "instrument" of the soul's inner purpose.[14] Its total configuration informed by the soul, the body becomes the soul's "work of art." The body in its *Gestalt* is invested with the peculiarly human physiognomic expression—this "note of spirituality diffused over the whole, which at once announces the body as an externality of a higher nature."[15] The corporeality as the soul's sign, says Hegel, expresses an inner spirit that distinguishes man from the animals in a way that he is not distinguished merely anatomically. As far as the body as such is concerned, man is not very different from the higher apes.

According to Hegel, man in the first place expresses his humanness in the upright stance, this "absolute gesture of mankind." [16] The charac-

---

[13] *In der sie sich fühlt und sich zu fühlen gibt.* (See *PhM* 147)

[14] I have stressed perhaps more than the text itself the distinction between sign and instrument in order to bring out as sharply as possible the more ideal meaning of "externality" (of the body) in the actual soul, as compared with the feeling soul in habit. A sign, to be sure, may also be said to be a kind of instrument. One could say, perhaps, one employs the hand as an instrument to convey meanings. Yet there is a difference between using the hand for writing, for example (see *PhM* 146) where it is strictly an instrument, and for gesturing—and of course both may be said to be habitual. In gesture, the hand as the "outer" is directly one with the inner meaning, and this is its higher ideality. "An instrument does not yet itself possess activity. It is an inactive thing, does not return to itself. I must still work with it." (*JR* 198 ; see also *Phen.* 352)

[15] *PhM* 147.

[16] According to Socrates (as reported by Xenophon), man is "the only living creature" whom the gods "have caused to stand upright." This position affords man "a wider range of vision in front and a better view of things above, and exposes

teristically human inwardness also shines forth in the shape of the mouth and the mobile play of facial features, in the formation and use of the hand. Man's body comes from nature, but its *geistige Ton* is man's own doing as Spirit, the soul's mastery of its corporeality through learning and habit. In rendering his body the *Äusserlichkeit* of his *geistige Innere,* man is for himself in his corporeality differently from animals. The animal's claws, mouth, teeth, etc., Hegel points out, are mainly limited to the nature-given functions of grasping, tearing, biting, and for these purposes they are far more efficient than man's equivalent organs. As having been made by the soul unto its own, however, the particular human organ obtains a release from the immediate natural functions and takes on a universal character deriving from the subjectivity as such. The hands, the features of the face, the whole upper body freed by the upright posture, become the *Dasein* of the inner subjectivity in its universal being. They express meanings, i.e., universals, in the language of gesture, attitude, play of features.

The corporeality as sign exhibits not only the *geistige Ton* of man in his human being but also the individual in his particularity. The body as sign is not only for others but confirms the individual in his own feeling and image of himself. Gesture, gait, and carriage reveal something of the inner spirit of an ethnic group, serve as signs by which the members recognize each other, feel themselves and make themselves felt. Temperament, character, even to some extent occupational role become etched into the lines of the face, build themselves into posture, gait, and musculature.[17]

Thus in contrast to its treatment in the Philosophy of Nature, the body now comes into consideration not merely as the "existence" of the organic individuality in its physical *Gestalt*,[18] but as an externality "posited" in its very *Dasein* as ideal. The body is "externality" so made by the soul unto its own that in it the soul has the sense of its own oneness and

him less to injury." But Socrates goes beyond utilitarian purposes. Although he does not explicitly term the upright position a "gesture" of man's inwardness, he connects it with man's possession of "the noblest type of soul" and his worship of the gods. (*Memorabilia*, I. iv. 11-14) Cf. Herder's treatment of the upright stance in *Ideen zur Philosophie der Geschichte der Menschheit* (1784-1791), books iii and iv (extensively quoted by Kant in a review of Part I: see *Kant on History*, ed. L. W. Beck, Bobbs-Merrill, New York, 1963, pp. 31-32)

[17] See *Phen.* 339 ff.

[18] *PhN* 357.

self-identity.[19] In my upright stance, which requires an effort of will
however insensible, I do not merely have a sensation in the soles of
my feet or arch of my back but—however dimly—a certain sense of
myself in my physical totality. In gestures, mannerisms, facial expressions,
however unconsciously carried out, I have the implicit feeling of myself
as universal in the particular. My turning up my nose to express disdain,
for example, does not mean that I have at this moment a particular
unpleasant olfactory sensation but that I turn away from what is "odious"
to me because, in an abstract or ideal way, it is contemptible or repugnant.
In its corporeality as its sign, says Hegel, the soul is Being-for-self
universality; the *body is "externality"* as *Dasein* of the soul in its
universality.[20] The externality as sign is a universal; and the soul, as
geistige Innere that is "for itself" in its body as its sign, is for itself as
universal, whilst at the same time it is in its corporeality this individuality.
This, according to Hegel, constitutes the actualization of the soul in its
notion.

In noting the advance from the feeling soul, however, we must not
overstress or exaggerate the soul's actualization in the body as identity
of inner and outer. As materiality, Hegel points out, the body can never
be the adequate expression of the inner spirit.[21] Gesture at its best is but
limited. Words and speech, moral deeds and actions are more genuine
expressions of the individual than the body, which remains but the *Dasein*
of the inner selfhood. Hence for Hegel, physiognomy, phrenology, hand-
writing analysis, palmistry, etc., are but quackery when they pretend
to the status of sciences.[22] In the body as sign, the identity of inner and
outer remains in many ways contingent, because "to the content expressed

[19] Kant too notes that man in a sense creates himself physically in order to render
his body capable of carrying out his rational purposes. In his discussion of the body,
gestures, etc., however, Kant does not, like Hegel, seek to show a return to self of
subjectivity as ideal unity of its corporeality. (See *APH* 321 ff.)

[20] The soul-body relation also plays a role in Hegel's notion of right. "As a person,
I am myself an *immediate* individual; if we give further precision to this expression,
it means in the first instance that I am alive in this bodily organism which is my
outer *Dasein*, universal in content and undivided, the real possibility of every further
determined *Dasein*." Hence when my body is maltreated by others, I, as personality,
am maltreated. "...So far as others are concerned, I am in my body. To be free from
the point of view of others is identical with being free in my *Dasein*." (*PhR* 43-4; see
also *PhM* 145, 171)

[21] *PhM* 151-152.

[22] *PhM* 147; see also *Phen.* 348 *passim*.

the peculiar nature of that by which it is expressed is completely indifferent." [23]

In having rendered its corporeality into its own "free shape," the soul has completed its development as Spirit on the natural level and is now "as single subject for itself." Hitherto the soul has only been implicitly an individuality in its body. As monadic subjectivity whose predicate was its own universal substantial being, the soul was at once singular and universal, but only abstractly or "formally" so. The dream subjectivity was "immediately" identical with its substantiality, but this its Being-for-self was not properly its own doing but rather its being borne along in the current of its own natural feeling-life. The sunderance of this immediate identity took place as self-feeling in the soul's being for itself in the particularity of feeling. In habit the soul reduced the corporeal particularity of feeling to an abstract *seiende* determination of its own abstract universal *Sein*. Now, as "actual," the soul has so permeated its corporeality with its ideality that the body is but the soul's "predicate, in which the soul relates itself only to itself." The soul's singularity is now "concrete" and at once identical with its Being-for-self as universality. In this identity consists the subjectivity's being able to say "I".[24]

But if the soul's actualization as Being-for-self in its corporeality is emergence of the subjectivity as ego, how does this mean too the emergence of the content of the inner feeling-life as "objective"?

Implicitly, says Hegel, materiality (*die Materie*) has no truth in the soul.[25] In its Being-for-self as actual soul, the soul separates (*scheidet*) itself from its immediate being, sets itself opposite (*gegenüberstellen*) its being as its corporeality that can offer no resistance to the soul's informing (*Einbilden*). As having thus opposed (*entgegengesetzt*) to itself its being, sublated it and determined it to its own, the soul has lost the immediacy of spirit signified by the term "soul." In the habit of sentience and concrete self-feeling, the actual soul is implicitly the Being-for-self ideality of its determinations—in its very externality

---

[23] *Phen.* 345. On Hegel's distinction between "sign," which can be made to stand for any arbitrary content, and "symbol," which remains linked to sensuous intuition, see *PhM* 212.

[24] "The self-related universal exists nowhere save in the 'I'". (*PhM* 152)

[25] Because of the key importance of the present paragraph (*PhM* 151) for Hegel's deduction of consciousness and objectivity, I have presented it in virtually literal translation.

inwardized (*erinnert*) within itself and infinite self-relation. This Being-for-self of the free universality is the higher awakening of the soul to ego : to the "abstract universality insofar as it is for the abstract universality." As such, it is now "thinking" (*Denken*) and subject "for itself." More specifically, it is subject of the judgment (*Urteil*) in which the ego excludes the natural totality of its determinations as an "object," [26] a world external to itself, and to which at the same time it relates itself in such a wise that in the externality it is immediately "reflected within itself," is *consciousness*.

The meaning of this decisive transition—the climax of the movement in the Anthropology—may be seen from various points of view in Hegel's notion of Spirit. From the most general point of view, the oppositing act of the subjectivity here derives from Spirit's eternal necessity to be "for itself" what it is "in itself." [27] This is the most general meaning of the lightning-flash of ego that pierces through the natural soul and "consumes its natural being." The subject's act of oppositing is the original self-sunderance (*Ur-teil*) and negative self-relation within which is contained all objectivity as having been "posited" as such, i.e., "set opposite" the subject. But to say this does not yet show specifically how the oppositing here is different from habit, where the soul posits itself as abstract Being-for-self *in its corporeality* and "sets down" the particularity of feeling to a moment in its own universal *Sein*. The *Gegen-überstellen* by the subjectivity that generates the "object" must be seen as the kind of advance that always features the movement of the Notion: the higher distinguishing that is also a higher uniting, the more intensive inwardization that is also a higher externalization.[28]

Hegel has already indicated to us, in the discussion of the unhealthy magical relation and the various forms of mental illness, how "objectivity" required a certain stance or posture on the part of the selfhood, a moral resolve wherein it is strong enough not to remain immersed in its passive feeling-life but is able to "let go" its content, view it detachedly, so that in it it can remain the universal for itself as universal. Objectivity is

---

[26] In showing the necessity for this *Urteil*, we may say, Hegel has shown in terms of a genesis of consciousness as Spirit the necessity for the Kantian dictum that in an objective judgment the meaning of the copula "is" is "nothing but the manner in which given modes of knowledge are brought to the objective unity of apperception." (See above, p. 105 n. 7)

[27] See above, p. 51.

[28] See above, p. 37.

thus a higher form of the subject's healthy *Mitleben* with itself in its substantial being. In the objective attitude the subjectivity sets off the content from itself in the sense that it restrains its own subjective prejudices and interferences (*Einmischungen*) and lets the content "come to power" in itself as an objective connectedness (*Zusammenhang*) structured according to objective categories. But these categories and connections of objective reality are in fact the subject's own very laws as a rational consciousness.[29] Hence the *Gegenüberstellen* means not only the subject's letting the content come to power in itself as a rational *Zusammenhang* but also the subject's coming to power in itself as rational subjectivity. The subject's setting the content opposite itself is in fact its bringing it closer to itself ; the content is grasped within a necessary connectedness, hence grasped more firmly and truly. And since the subject's own being lies within this total connectedness and the content is its own, the oppositing also means the subjectivity's grasping itself more firmly and truly.[30] Hereby we see the *Gegenüberstellen* or *Entgegensetzen* more specfically in terms of the teleology of the Being-for-self of Spirit. But we must also view it in other ways to see it more concretely as a movement on the present level of subjectivity.

According to Hegel, the initial thought-determination of the conscious subjectivity—which expresses at once its certainty of self as this "I" and its content as this objective entity—is "Being." The "immediate" consciousness, Hegel shows in the science of Phenomenology, initially says. "I," as this singularity, "am"; "this" object I now mean, "is." [31] Let us see more closely how the *Denkbestimmung* "Being" emerges in the "lightning flash" of ego, how the former subjectivity of "feeling" raises itself to a subjectivity of "thinking" by the attainment to this initial category of pure abstract thought.

"Objectivity," even in its nonphilosophical or ordinary usage, carries a certain meaning of distinterestedness, a separateness of the subject from the "thing" as *Sache selbst*. In talking about something as an "object," does not the ordinary man mean it as implacably "there"— apart from his or anyone's seeing it or thinking about it ? The natural consciousness, says Hegel in the *Phenomenology*, maintains that the object

---

[29] This will only become evident in the sciences of Phenomenology and Psychology.

[30] For example, in my giving due care to my body according to its own laws and needs. (*PhM* 145)

[31] See below, p. 168.

"*is,* quite indifferent (*gleichgültig*) to whether it is known or not."[32] This "indifference" on the part of the object is an essential component or "moment," as Hegel would say, in its status for us as an "object." But whence does this determination of "indifference" allegedly belonging to the object arise *in us* ?—for the object is not "for itself" indifferent. No doubt the indifference with which I invest the object is part of my determining of a content as a "not-I" that "is" on its own account. But just how does this determining come about on my part ? For Hegel, this is not a question that can be answered in terms of the "facts of consciousness" (*Tatsachen des Bewusstseins*), an approach which Hegel everywhere eschews as an uncritical empiricism.[33] If it is a "fact" that consciousness takes an object as an indifferent "other," philosophy must account for this fact.

In habit, we recall, Hegel developed the moments of its notion in terms of "indifference" and "limit." These moments were essential in constituting habit as the higher break that is at the same time a higher union of the soul in its corporeality. The determination "indifference" arises originally in the soul's relationship to its corporeal and feeling-determinations. It consists in that the soul in habit has reduced the particular corporeal and feeling-determinations to its own "pure Being" (*blossen Sein*) ; the soul is "no longer in difference" as against them and thereby no longer in a relation of "interest, preoccupation, and dependency" toward them.[34]

The determination "limit," we recall, consists in the relation of the soul in habit to its body as the materiality which the soul must inform with its subjective purpose. Here too we can refer for witness to the natural consciousness. Dr. Johnson supposedly refutes the idealist philosopher by stubbing his toe against the rock. Here the natural consciousness imputes more than "indifference" to the object ; it also invests the object with the determination of "limit" or barrier to the subject. The object offers "resistance." But Dr. Johnson does not see that he renders the object's determination as "resistant" something for himself. Even Dr. Johnson would not claim that the rock is a limit for itself. This determination of *Schranke* as a moment in the natural consciousness's constitution of the object as a "not-I," Hegel has shown, originally arises

---

[32] *Phen.* 151.

[33] *PhM* 5 ; *L* 134 ; *PhR* 29.

[34] *PhM* 140. In habit, we see that "our self just as much *appropriates* the *Sache* as, on the contrary, it draws away from it." (*PhM* 147)

in the soul's relation to itself in its corporeality as its "particular being." The body is thus the original "externality" which the soul informs with its subjective purpose but whose resistance as materiality is not completely overcome.[35]

We have now accounted for the object as an "other" in the senses of "indifference" and "limit" for the natural consciousness. That the determination "Being" is for the natural consciousness also a necessary moment of the "objectivity" of the object will hardly be disputed. Whatever else Dr. Johnson may say of the object, he will surely say with most conviction that "it is." Yet no object that Dr. Johnson ever kicked, or Plato's "terrible fellows" ever held in their hands, carried the label that it "is." Dr. Johnson does not kick Being. Where then, if we do not see it, squeeze it, stub our toe on it, do we get this most abstract of all determinations : Being ?

Both Leibniz and Kant pointed out that our apprehending of anything as an "object" contains the determination of its Being ; and both these thinkers said that this determination derives from my apperception of self, my being able to say, "I am." But neither showed how I come to be able to say this. For Kant the possibility that something can be an object for me lies in my being able to accompany my representation of it by my saying, "I think" it. But for Kant this was a logical requirement, not a living condition. As we have seen, no philosophical demonstration, according to Kant, can show how I come to be able to say "I am" or "I think" by virtue of some deeper necessity or principle of mind. Hegel's doctrine of Subjective Spirit takes up the Leibnizian theme of the monad's inner development, which Kant had passed by, and at the same time shows how Fichte's "oppositing" has an immanent necessity as an original self-dividing of the soul which has its directly preceding condition in habit. The feeling soul in habit has raised itself to "abstract universal being" and reduced the corporeal and feeling-particularity to a "merely *seienden* determination in it." The immediate and abstractly positive character

---

[*] "The soul's pervasion of its bodily nature... is not absolute, does not completely set aside the difference of soul and body. On the contrary, the nature of the logical Idea which develops everything from itself demands that this difference still remain in being. One side of corporeity remains, therefore, purely organic and consequently withdrawn from the power of the soul, so that the soul's pervasion of its body is only one side of the latter. The soul, when it feels this limitation of its power, reflects itself into itself and expels the corporeity from itself as something extraneous to it. By this reflection-into-self, the mind consummates its liberation from the form of mere being, gives itself the form of essence and becomes 'I'." (*PhM* 151-152)

of the particular consists in the fact that the soul "has the particulars in itself and insensibly and without consciousness moves in them." It is for this reason that the soul's Being-for-self in habit is still abstract and formal, the content remaining *an ihr* and not yet *gegenübergestellt*. The soul in its subjective purpose comes back to itself as "simple being" in its corporeality as its "particular being," and this, as we saw, is the "intuition" of self but not yet consciousness.

In the soul's rendering of its corporeality as but the soul's own "sign," the externality is directly one with the spiritual inner. The soul has hereby "posited" itself as subject "for itself." In rendering the corporeality the very sign of its inwardness, the soul is for itself as universal for a universal, no longer, as in habit, merely for itself in its corporeality as its "particular being." The corporeality now stands not for itself but for the soul and is "as predicate, in which the subject relates itself only to itself." This higher distinguishing and uniting—of a universal for a universal [36] —constitutes the oppositing (*Entgegensetzung*) wherein the subjectivity is no longer in immediate feeling-unity with itself but in a "mediated" unity. In the corporeality as its sign, the subjectivity has attained to a "certainty" (*Gewissheit*) of itself. The soul has actualized itself in its corporeality as its *Dasein* and in so doing has posited the *Sein* within itself. In this its actualization as soul, the subjectivity distinguishes itself from itself and remains directly one with itself in its distinguishing.[37] The subjectivity hereby has itself as *Gegenstand*. For the first time it distinguishes itself from itself in such a way that it can say : "I am." This *Ur-teil* makes possible that, in its very content distinguished, the subjectivity is "immediately reflected in self." In this self-reflectedness, according to Hegel, the soul has "lost the immediacy of Spirit, the signification of soul."

In its actualization as soul, Hegel thus claims to show, the subjectivity has "awakened" to the ego of consciousness. The former inner content of feeling has become the world of conscious life. In this *Ur-teil* of the formerly natural and immediate identity of subjectivity and substance, there has emerged the reflected identity of consciousness in the subject-object relation. It was with this relation that most thinkers from Descartes to Kant began and which Hegel has now demonstrated to be a pre-supposition that should properly be known as a "result." Before we proceed in our Appendix to develop some implications of this demon-

[36] *PhM* 152.
[37] See above, p. 36.

stration, let us briefly go back, not to call up again details but to gain a sense of the spirit and general note that is struck by Hegel in his account of the soul as Spirit.

The Anthropology, the first of the sciences of Subjective Spirit, has purportedly shown Spirit as psychical subjectivity arising out of universal nature through its active permeating of its individual substantial being as its ideality and rendering the body an outer sign of its spiritual inwardness. To view the Anthropology briefly in historical perspective, we may see it as an endeavor to grasp man in his kinship with divinity. Hegel's notion of Spirit is in many important ways a return to the Aristotelian notion of *Nous* [38] but a return that seeks to rethink *Nous* in terms of the Kantian notion of subjectivity. Hegel's indebtedness to the Aristotelian concept of *psyche* as entelechy of the body is evident everywhere in Hegel's treatment of the soul. Nevertheless *Nous*, according to Hegel, receives its truer expression in the modern notion of Spirit,[39] and the Hegelian speculative development of soul is to be understood above all as Spirit's struggle in coming to power in nature as its own otherness. Unlike the Aristotelian entelechy, therefore, the soul as Spirit only attains its actualization as Being-for-self through ascending stages of its relation of identity with and opposition to its own natural being. For this notion of Spirit as Being-for-self in its substantial being, Hegel is most indebted to the Kantian identity of the subjectivity in its manifold. Yet the whole thrust of the Anthropology, as we have seen, is to demonstrate, as against Kant, the existence of such an identity on a natural level not yet structured by the unifying *Aktus* of consciousness and its objective categories of understanding. In the modes of the Being-for-self of the soul in its natural being, Hegel has claimed to show, there are implicitly universal forms of apprehension, such as sentience, mood, feeling and presentiment, general modes of unreflective acting. Thus Hegel has sought to demonstrate ways of the subjectivity's Being-for-itself in its manifold that are not yet the ways of the self-reflecting ego of consciousness but rather the very preconditions out of which the ego itself emerges.

In the speculative development of the soul as Spirit, the subjectivity on the succeeding levels becomes ever more "truly" a subjectivity, ever more a subjectivity that has itself "in possession." In this movement of the soul toward consciousness, we are afforded the notion of a possible

---

[38] See Hegel's quotation of *Metaphysics* xi, 7, at the conclusion of the *Enzyklopädie*.

[39] See above, p. 83 n. 88.

"regression" of the finite spirit, where the higher selfhood can fall back
to the very feeling-subjectivity which it normally contains within itself
as but a moment. In the discussion of the feeling-life, forms of the
magical relation and gazing-knowing, the *Seeleneinheit* of the hypnotic
relation, and the Being-with-self in the negative of oneself that marks
the self-alienation of insanity, Hegel's speculative approach claims to
show that the self's struggle to gain moral strength—to "bear itself," to
hold itself "erect"—is inseparable from its development to the level of
objectivity.

For Hegel, the problem of epistemology cannot be approached in a
narrow and formal fashion that abstracts the knowing subject from his
total living selfhood.[40] To view the individual subject in his concrete
totality as Spirit, Hegel requires that we push into that area where,
for Kant, the two stems of human knowledge, sensibility and understanding, "perhaps spring from a common, but to us unknown, root."
Hegel claims to have uncovered this root in the identity of the soul
as subjectivity in its substantiality as its natural being. The soul's knowing
of its feeling-manifold, according to Hegel, is a form of Spirit's being
for itself in its determinations as natural subjectivity. The soul in its
very being is a pre-objective knowing that implicitly contains the universal
and is therefore a moment of the truth.

In Hegel's demonstration of the soul's making itself for itself in the
body, we see a return to the ancient doctrine that the body is the
instrument of the soul.[41] But one of the ancients who expressed that
concept also said: "He whose knowledge extends only to the body knows
the things of man, not the man himself." [42] The Kantian Critical
Philosophy, as we saw, tells us we can know the body as we know
external nature but not the soul itself.[43] In showing how the soul makes
itself the permeating ideality of the body, Hegel claims to demonstrate
a deeper notion of subjectivity as Spirit which overcomes the Critical
Philosophy's limitation of our theoretical knowledge to "the things of
man, not the man himself."

The soul's development in the Anthropology is presented by Hegel
above all as a struggle toward freedom, a striving by the psychical

[40] See Otto Pöggeler, "Die Komposition des Phänomenologie des Geistes," *Hegel-
Studien*, Beiheft 3, 1964, p. 66.

[41] *Phaedo* 98C ff.; *De Anima* 415b19.

[42] *Alcibiades I*, 131.

[43] See above, pp. 14 ff.

selfhood to actualize its telos as Spirit by rising above its immersion in its feeling-life to genuine self-determination. The struggle requires a sunderance of the self from its natural being. It involves effort and pain, and for the particular finite subjectivity it is not without dangers of wreck. Objectivity—though we take it for granted like our standing erect—requires that the subjectivity hold itself firm, so that in the particular it remain the universal that is for itself the universal. Thus Hegel sees the objective consciousness as a freedom which the human spirit must win for itself as an attainment.

APPENDIX ON THE NOTION OF CONSCIOUSNESS

CHAPTER SEVEN

CONSCIOUSNESS AND ITS SCIENCE

Consciousness, according to Hegel, is the truth of the soul, the destination and goal of the soul's development.[1] In our preceding chapter we saw how this destination was purportedly attained. In order that we may gain as clear an understanding as possible of the import of Hegel's demonstration of consciousness as an "emergence," let us note certain main features of Hegel's notion of consciousness and briefly look again at some principal problems of knowledge and self-knowledge. In this way, in good Hegelian fashion, we shall be circling back to those issues discussed in our introductory chapters. In so doing we shall focus on three main points: a) the notion of consciousness as Spirit in its "appearance" ; b) ego as both transcendental and empirical; and c) the deduction of objective categories in a "genuinely synthetic progress." In all three instances we shall note again Hegel's differences from Kant and try to see the role of the Anthropology in Hegel's notion of Subjective Spirit, which is meant to liberate philosophic science from the subject-object antithesis and supplant the Kantian doctrine of cognition.

a. Consciousness as Spirit in its Appearance

In the Anthropology we observed Spirit in its darkness and sleep, Spirit wrapped up within itself. The emergence of ego was said to be the soul's awakening to the light. But now the light, which is indeed consciousness's very own, seems rather to come from outside itself, namely, from the object, which provides consciousness with its knowledge. The development of the soul to consciousness was supposed to have signified the subjectivity's taking itself in possession. But the subjectivity's attainment of

---

[1] *PhM* 152.

self-possession as ego meant its relating itself to its content as an "other," i.e. something not at all in the subjectivity's possession. These ambivalences of consciousness : of identity in opposition of subject and object, of relation to self in and through relation to other, are comprehended logically by Hegel through the notion of "essence" as demonstrated in the science of logic. But the determinations wherein consciousness will be viewed in the science of Phenomenology—namely, the determinations attributed by consciousness to its object—will be seen to derive from the subjectivity's own act of oppositing.

Consciousness, says Hegel, constitutes the stage of Spirit as "reflection" or "relationship," the stage of Spirit as "appearance" (Erscheinung).[2] The subjectivity that has attained to abstract freedom for itself as ego has "let go" its content as likewise free and standing for its self. It is this self-subsistent externality that the ego now knows as "object" and it is just by this knowing that the subjectivity is consciousness. As having sublated the manifold of its feeling-life in its own ideal identity, ego is "absolute negativity" and implicitly "identity in otherness."

The ego is itself that other and stretches over the object (as if that object were implicitly sublated)—it is one side of the relationship and the whole relationship— the light, which manifests itself and something else too.[3]

Hegel's terms "reflection," "relation," and "appearance," which characterize the subject-object opposition of consciousness, are basic for Hegel's attempt to supplant the Kantian doctrine of knowledge. Fichte and Schelling, as well as Hegel, sought a concept of the pure ego as self-reflectedness that would overcome the difficulties of the thing-in-itself and other difficulties arising from the Kantian dualisms. In Kant, the pure self-consciousness, while making possible synthetic knowledge a priori, was itself a merely formal identity expressible only in an analytic or identical proposition.[4] Fichte and Schelling were the first to seek a concept of the pure self-consciousness that would not be merely analytic [5] —or rather would render the very distinction between analytic and synthetic a distinction deriving from the ego's own original act of self-

---

[2] PhM 153.

[3] PhM 153 ; see also Phen. 219

[4] See above, p. 32.

[5] In his System des transzendentalen Idealismus (1800), Schelling says "The principle of all knowledge must be expressed in the proposition I = I, for this proposition is the only possible one that is at once identical and synthetic." (Werke III, p. 372)

positing. The act itself would be at once a self-*distinguishing* by the ego that constituted the ego the very self-*identity* that it is. In this way the ego could be conceived as a free spiritual life, and not merely a formal logical principle. But the question for post-Kantian idealism was how to show this self-positing. Hegel, as we saw in the Anthropology, demonstrates the act as the subjectivity's own *Urteil* consequent upon the soul's actualization as ideality of the body.

Thus Hegel was not the first to say that "object" only emerges through an act of the subject, that the empirical consciousness must look to a transcendental principle as its ground. This was the heritage from Kant, for whom the manifold of intuition is first constituted an object in the unifying *Aktus* that is the identical self-consciousness itself. But since intuition for Kant is the faculty of receptivity, the appearance to intuition must derive from the thing-in-itself.[6] Hence when Hegel says that the object is constituted through an activity of the subject, he means something quite different from Kant. For Hegel, the content emerges as objective simultaneously with the subject's emergence as ego. This means that in Hegel's notion of object (*Gegenstand*), the objectivity (*Gegenständlichkeit*) derives in no sense from a thing-in-itself: rather the "in-itself-ness" of the object derives from the subject's act of *Gegenüberstellen*.[7] For this reason the meaning of "appearance" for Hegel is essentially different from that in Kant. Kant, according to Hegel, considers ego in its relation to a "something out in the beyond" (*Jenseitsliegendes*). But

---

[6] *CPR* B xxvii, A 252.

[7] In Kant's notion of the constitution of the object, there is nothing of such an oppositing. The object as appearance must be "given" to consciousness: this otherness is primordial and irreducible. Apart from the givenness of appearances, there would be no need for a "special act" of synthesis of the manifold. (*CPR* 139) But the question for the Kantian position must be: how does the object acquire its character of otherness for me, an otherness which I need even for the very thought of myself? For according to Kant, since I have no intellectual intuition of my existence, I cannot connect the thought "I am" with my empirical consciousness without the consciousness of a relation to "something outside me." (*CPR* B xl) Hence says Kant, we need an intuition of "the permanent" in space in order "to make comprehensible to ourselves the successive existence of ourselves in different states." (*CPR* B 292) But such an intuition of "something outside me" presupposes the thing-in-itself. Here we see how Hegel's demonstration of the "I am" as an *Urteil* is connected with his endeavor to overcome the Kantian thing-in-itself. The "I am," for Hegel, may be said to entail a consciousness of "something outside me" not in the Kantian sense of presupposing a thing-in-itself but as deriving from my act of oppositing, which is one with my coming to be able to say "I am."

such an approach already derives out of an external reflection on the part of the philosopher: it is not the role of the philosopher to posit such a *Jenseitsliegendes,* according to Hegel, but to view critically and to explain how consciousness comes to posit it. That each side is not absolute in its separation from the other, Hegel claims to have proved in the demonstration of their emergence as opposites in the *Urteil* of the soul. That their opposition is destined to be overcome in the very movement of consciousness as "appearing" Spirit, will purportedly be shown in the science of Phenomenology. Let us briefly note the logical meaning of "appearance" and the general nature of the categories of "essence," since these will be important in the exposition of the subject-object relation of consciousness.

By the soul's reflection-into-self in its actualization, as we saw, Spirit frees itself from the form of mere Being and "gives itself the form of essence."[8] In contrast to the soul's determination in the Anthropology mainly in the categories of Being,[9] consciousness and its objective content will be determined in the Phenomenology according to the categories of essence.[10] Essence, as demonstrated in the Hegelian science of logic, is Being "inwardized." [11] Being is no longer present in its immediacy but as referring to its own inner truth. This referring to its "inner" constitutes it as "appearance." [12] Throughout the logical doctrine of essence, the categories have this form of Being-in-self as reference to other (*Beziehung-auf-anderes*), or Being-in-self as mediateness.[13] Consequently essence "has the unessential as its own proper show (*Schein*) within itself." [14]

[8] *PhM* 152.

[9] For example, in the "natural qualities" (see above, p. 63 n. 14)

[10] "Essence—which is Being coming into mediation with itself through the negativity of itself—is self-relatedness only in so far as it is relation to other—which other, however, is not immediately as *Seiendes* but as something posited and mediated." (*L* 207)

[11] "...That reflectedness constituting its distinction from immediate Being, its showing (*Scheinen*) within itself, and is the characteristic determination of essence itself." (*L* 208)

[12] See above, p. 49 n. 60.

[13] In essence, "determinateness is not a simple immediacy but is present only as posited by essence itself." (*SL* 391) In consciousness, which came to be in the subjectivity's self-positing, all necessary determinations of both subject and object likewise prove to be such a positedness.

[14] "The sphere of essence therefore turns out to be a still imperfect combination of immediacy and mediation. In it every term is expressly posited as related to self

By virtue of this "Being-in-self as reference to other," the categories of essence are "doubled," e.g., positive and negative, inner and outer, substance and accident. Similarly each of the two sides of the subject-object relation on the ascending levels of consciousness reflects into itself only as reflection out of self into other; each side "shows" into the other. Spirit as soul was the immediate unity of subjectivity and substantiality. In consciousness the subjectivity now knows this substantiality as the negative of itself, the "not-I." Hence Hegel says, consciousness, "like relation in general" (*wie das Verhältnis überhaupt*), is the "contradiction" of the independence of both sides and their implicit identity.[15] On the one hand, the object of my knowing is "in" me as my knowledge, hence contained within my certainty of self; on the other hand it has an independent outer existence. Since the object that I know on the level of consciousness remains an "in itself," my own certainty as self-identity is rendered "only a show."[16] Or, stated in terms of the categories of the logic, since reality in the sphere of essence is posited as immediately *seiend* and at the same time as ideal, Spirit as consciousness is only the "appearing" of Spirit.[17]

The science of Spirit in its "appearing" is entitled by Hegel the Phenomenology of Spirit.[18] Phenomenology here comprises the second of the three sciences of Subjective Spirit, as consciousness is the second moment of Subjective Spirit in its notion. Just as essence, in the logic, stands midway between Being and Notion, the science of Phenomenology, Hegel

and as forced to go out beyond itself; it has a Being of reflection, a Being in which an other shows, and which shows in an other. It is thus the sphere of posited contradiction, which in the sphere of Being is but implicit." (*L* 211-12)

[15] *PhM* 155.

[16] *SL* 781.

[17] Appearance, for Hegel, is not the Kantian phenomenality, which, in Hegel's view, "has a subjective meaning only" and is separated in principle from the thing-in-itself. Still less is it merely error or a dross to be stripped away in order to yield essence by itself. *Erscheinung*, for Hegel, is the "showing" (*Scheinen*) of essence. It is essence in its existence, or as "immediate unity of reflection in self and reflection in other." Hence, says Hegel, essence does not hide itself "behind or beyond" appearance but "shines forth" or "appears." But as "immediate" unity of reflection in self and reflection in other, appearance is positedness as "external immediacy" and also positedness as "self-identity." In the first of those two moments the content of appearance is "contingent and unessential, subject in its immediacy to transition, arising, and passing away"; in the second, however, it is "simple content-determination exempt from this change; it is the enduring part of it." In this latter aspect, appearance is law. (*L* 239 ff.; *SL* 500 ff.; see also, above, pp. 31 ff.)

[18] *SL* 781.

tells us, "stands midway between the science of natural Spirit and Spirit as such." [19] While the Anthropology considered the self-enclosed psychical subjectivity as Spirit "in itself," the Phenomenology considers Spirit as "*for itself*, but at the same time in its *relation to its other*, an other which... is determined by that relation as both *implicitly* an object and also as negated." Hence the science of Phenomenology deals with Spirit "in its manifestation (*als erscheinend*), as exhibiting itself in its own opposite." [20] This opposition within Spirit as consciousness will be overcome by consciousness itself. The succeeding stages of consciousness, which develop the opposition simultaneously with the movement of its sublation, constitute the subject matter of the science of consciousness.

b. Ego, Transcendental and Empirical

We have now seen how the demonstration in the Anthropology makes possible the notion of consciousness as "reflectedness," whose logical categories underlie the demonstration of the movement of consciousness in the science of Phenomenology. We cannot follow this movement itself, whereby Hegel will claim to resolve the subject-object opposition and lift the Critical Philosophy's limitation of knowledge to appearances. Our aim can only be to show the link between the respective demonstrations in the Anthropology and the Phenomenology.

Another issue where Hegel rests his case in large part on the demonstration in the Anthropology is that concerning the Kantian distinction between the transcendental and empirical ego, and the alleged impossibility of a knowledge of the former as the ego "in itself." [21] On this score, we recall, Hegel said that Kant was wrong to hold that the ego must "make use" of itself in all its judging. Rather the ego *is* judging, and precisely in its acts of judgment it will reveal itself in its concrete nature and not remain for us an unknown x.[22] That the ego is judgment has purportedly been revealed to us in the *Urteil* of the soul that marked the emergence of subjectivity as ego. Thus from the demonstration in the Anthropology we know the nature of ego as that which distinguishes

[19] *Ibid.*
[20] *SL* 781-782.
[21] See above, pp. 13 ff.
[22] See above, p. 16.

itself from itself and at the same time returns to itself from its "other" as individually determined and, in its determinations, purely self-relating universality.[23] The meaning of ego as "negative self-relation" or "absolute negativity," as it is characterized by Hegel, consists in that the ego is at once ideality of its manifold, or pure universality, and also abstract simple singularity.

This essential determination of ego as "abstract universal singularity," says Hegel, constitutes ego in its very being.[24] Hence I and my being—or better, my egohood and my being—are inseparable. The distinction of my being from myself as ego is a distinction that is none, or rather vanishes straightway on its being made.[25] Being, which is the absolutely immediate, the purely indeterminate, the undistinguished, is on the one hand to be distinguished from ego, since the latter is thought (*Denken*) or the self-distinguishing that is mediated with itself through sublation of distinction. On the other hand, Being is also identical with thought, since the thinking subjectivity returns to transparent unity with itself in its distinguishing. For this reason, says Hegel, ego is Being—or has Being as a moment within it. Insofar as I am able to say, "I am," I posit this my being opposite me, and in the very act of oppositing I remain at the same time identical with myself. In this way I am "knowing" (*Wissen*) and have the "certainty" (*Gewissheit*) of my being. This my certainty of self is no mere property or quality that can perchance belong to me, says Hegel, but my very essence as ego. Ego would not be ego without this self-distinguishing and identity with self in its distinguishing, without this "knowing" of self and being just this "certainty" of self.

Thus we see here Hegel's rejection not only of Kant's barring of a knowledge of the transcendental ego, but also of Kant's contention that, since I have no "intellectual intuition" of my existence in the representation "I am," I need a spatial intuition of "the permanent" even in order to think myself as a one in the flux of empirical representations of inner sense.[26] In Hegel's presentation, the thought "I am" is not an "intellectual intuition"; but neither is it an empirical representation. As the as yet abstract self-distinguishing of the self from itself, it is but a *Gewissheit* or subjective certainty that needs concrete filling and veri-

[23] *PhM* 153.
[24] *Ibid.*
[25] See above, p. 32.
[26] See above, p. 161 n. 7.

fication to become *Wahrheit*.[27] The movement from *Gewissheit* to *Wahrheit*, from the abstract self-certainty of the singular "I" to the concrete truth of the universal self-consciousness,[28] does not proceed through "experience" understood in any a posteriori fashion but as the necessary concretization of both subject and object in their mutual "showing" of the one side in the other that characterizes the relation of the categories of essence.[29]

The self-reflectedness of opposing means not only the emergence of the subject as ego but also, as we saw, the emergence of the object as something that "is" on its own account. The certainty "I am" is the condition for the possibility that any content of mine be "objective." An "objective" perceiving entails an implicit negative reference to myself : that original judgment (*Urteil*) of self-dividing that meant the "birth" of the ego. A chair, a book apprehended as an "object" is implicitly judged as a "not-I".[30] Any *Wissen* of an object is implicitly also a *Gewissheit* of myself as singular subject "for myself" in any content that I can be conscious of as "objective." It is in this way that Hegel demonstrates that any consciousness of a content as objective must contain thought-determinations, logical categories. For any content to be objective, the subject must have risen from "feeling-subjectivity" to "thinking-sub-jectivity" which can say "I am" and can endow its content at the very least with the category of Being.

But not only is the ego's opposing of itself to itself a necessary condition for its knowing of a content as objective. Its knowing of a content as objective is also a condition for its knowing of itself as more than the abstract "I am." The mere *Gewissheit* "I am" is but the abstract ego, ego in its implicit being or pure notion. It is the ego as but indeterminate ideality, the sublation of all determinations formerly contained in the soul. In the subject's opposing of its being in the thought "I am," the opposing is yet tenuous, the distinguishing but formal and not yet actual distinction. To achieve actuality the abstract

---

[27] *Gewissheit* or certainty at the stage of mere consciousness "is something as yet untrue and self-contradictory, since here, along with the abstract certainty of being at home with itself, mind has the directly opposite certainty of being related to something essentially other to it." (*PhM* 157) We see here how Hegel's notion of the "I am" is not, like Kant's, dependent on a specifically spatial intuition, but rather entails "other" in a general sense as opposite to the ego.

[28] *PhM* 178.

[29] See above, pp. 162 ff.

[30] See above, p. 141.

ego must allow its being to take on concrete determination. Only in this way can the ego maintain its self-possession, develop its certainty of self and not lapse back to the "impotent natural soul," [31] whose content is not genuinely opposited to the subjectivity.

Here Hegel indicates to us why the science of Phenomenology can be developed within a problematic of "experience" (as was the *Phenomenology of 1807*),[32] though "experience" would have to be understood in the *Enzyklopädie* in the general sense of the whole doctrine of Spirit : namely, as Spirit's becoming aware of itself—and not in any sense of "experience" as in Kant or the empiricists.[33] Since the ego in the first instance is but formal, indeterminate self-distinguishing—the mere "repelling itself from itself"—distinction appears to come wholly from the side of the object. To consciousness itself the succeeding forms of the object as singular "this," as "thing of many properties," as "force" and "law," seem to come not through any doing on its part. Yet, since ego is implicitly identity of self and other—as the demonstration in the Anthropology showed—the subject is necessarily "referred" to the distinctions within the object, and in such reference is immediately reflected within self. The necessary course of development of the object from the sense singularity to the universal of perception to the supersensuous "law" will therefore at the same time be the necessary course of development of the subject from the sense consciousness to the perceiving consciousness to the understanding. In this way the ego is shown to be the light that can manifest itself only in lighting up the dark.[34] Spirit, whose manifestation is ever a revealing of itself to itself,[35] can only become manifest to itself in manifesting its other. It is in this notion of consciousness as implicitly revealing itself in its object, that Hegel claims to overcome the Kantian notion of a pure ego that is both inaccessible and unknowable.

c. The Genuinely Synthetic Progress

Having seen the role of the Anthropology in Hegel's purported overcoming of the inaccessible transcendental *x* both within and without us,

---

[31] *PhM* 155.

[32] See above, pp. 25 ff.

[33] See *PhM* 161-162. As far as I can discover, this is the only mention of the term "experience" in the Phenomenology of the *Enzyklopädie*.

[34] *PhM* 154.

[35] See above, p. 47.

we may turn finally to another Hegelian claim as against the Critical Philosophy. While in Hegel's view the identity of self-consciousness was one of the most profound of Kant's insights,[36] the pure forms of self-consciousness, namely, the categories, were merely taken over by Kant from the logic textbooks, according to Hegel, instead of being truly demonstrated in a "genuinely synthetic progress" from the notion of the identical self-consciousness itself.[37] Hegel's charge concerns not only the adequacy of Kant's demonstration as such but also the alleged "formalism" of the Critical Philosophy's whole approach to the problem of knowledge. It remains for us to see briefly what role the "emergence" of consciousness plays in Hegel's claim to show the objective categories in a genuinely synthetic progress, "the self-producing Notion."

The emergence of consciousness as the truth of the soul yields at least one direct consequence for the problem of a deduction of the categories. For Kant a "transcendental" deduction was necessary because the source of our knowledge consisted in two separate "stems": while all appearances must be "given" to sensibility, a deduction is required to establish that the pure concepts are a priori necessary for objects to be thought.[38] For Hegel the problem of a deduction is not formulable in this fashion. As we have seen in the preceding chapters, Hegel's notion of the soul rejects the two-stems doctrine and shows the emergence of a thinking ego as sublation of the feeling subjectivity. What the psychical subjectivity "contained" is for the self-reflecting ego "set forth as an object." [39] The ego emerges as a totality, a selfhood on the level of objective consciousness. There can be no question as to whether its categories are "applicable" to objects : that ego is "thinking" and that its content is "objective" are one and the same thing. Hence there can be no objects without categories. Thought-determinations are present even in the "immediate" consciousness—the sense consciousness which takes its object "as an existent, a something, an existing thing, a singular, and so on." [40] Thus a different principle of "deduction" is contained in the fact that ego has been shown to have emerged as "subject of the judgment" in which it relates itself to itself in relating itself to the outer world. By virtue of the simultaneous

[36] See above, p. 13.

[37] SL 789.

[38] CPR B 122.

[39] PhM 153.

[40] PhM 159. "These are logical terms introduced by the thinking principle, i.e. in this case by the ego, to describe the sensible."

emergence of the "I am" and the "outer world" through the *Urteil* of the soul, the necessary forms of consciousness must be *eo ipso* the forms of an external world, and conversely.

But the whole problem of a deduction of categories takes on a different cast in the Hegelian notion of Phenomenology as showing Spirit in its "appearance," from the transcendental deduction of Kant. The deduction of categories is not, to be sure, incidental to the task of the Phenomenology but it is subsumed under—or encompassed within—the deeper task of showing the movement of consciousness according to its notion.

The goal of Spirit as consciousness, says Hegel, is to make its "appearance" identical with its "essence," to raise its "certainty" to objective "truth." Consciousness itself is spurred toward this goal by its own contradictory nature which, "like reciprocal dependence in general, is the contradiction between the independence of the two sides and their identity in which they are merged into one." [41] The contradiction is at once the demand for and possibility of its resolution. [42]

In the development of consciousness, the object is raised from the transient singularity and self-externality of sense consciousness's "this," to the abiding universality that inwardly distinguishes itself and preserves itself in its distinctions: understanding's object as "law." In this progressive determination (*Fortbilden, Fortbestimmung*) of the object, those "objective" categories emerge such as : the "thing" of many "properties" or "matters"; cause and effect; force "inner" and "outer"; and the "law of force." In the object as "life," the "objective" categories sublate themselves to the "subjective" categories of the free self-determination of Notion, where subject and object have become one. Simultaneously with this "inwardization" of the object, the subject as singular consciousness has likewise developed and become inwardized, although its development seems to have come about through alteration of its object. Only when the object has been inwardized to the inner self-distinguishing of Notion, which is identical with ego itself, does Spirit as consciousness come to know its own inwardness as effectual in the object. [43] At this point, consciousness of the "object" has become consciousness of self, self-consciousness. As self-consciousness, subjectivity opposes to itself an "object" that is at once identical with it and an independent Being-for-self. In the struggle for "recognition" and in the subsequent social forms

[41] *PhM* 155.
[42] *PhM* 157.
[43] See above, p. 32.

of mastery and subjection—the emergence of polity—the singular self-consciousness comes to know its other, like itself, to be permeated by the subjectivity of the Notion. Knowing its other as itself and itself in its other, self-consciousness has emerged as "universal" self-consciousness, or the absolutely free reason that explicitly knows itself as objective in the world.

With this emergence of Spirit as reason or "Spirit as such," the science of Spirit in its "appearing" concludes.[44] In showing the forms of consciousness as the forms of "world," and by demonstrating the categories through consciousness's relation with the natural and social world in which it dwells as implicitly a relation of the subjectivity with its own substantial being,[45] Hegel has claimed to show the forms of thought through "a genuinely synthetic progress—the self-producing Notion." Like the doctrine of the soul, the doctrine of consciousness shows consciousness not merely in its logical forms but as a spiritual life. Defined in terms of the subject-object opposition emerging from the *Urteil* of the soul, the movement of consciousness displays Spirit's liberation from this opposition. Hereby the Phenomenology is a continuation on a higher level of the *Befreiungskampf* theme of the Anthropology and one that remains central throughout the Hegelian doctrine of finite Spirit.

---

[44] *PhM* 178.
[45] See Ernst Bloch, *Subjekt-Objekt : Erläuterungen zu Hegel*, 2nd ed., (Suhrkamp, Frankfurt am Main, 1962), pp. 188-189.